MANIFESTO FOR A DREAM

MANIFESTO FOR A DREAM

INEQUALITY, CONSTRAINT, AND RADICAL REFORM

MICHELLE JACKSON

STANFORD UNIVERSITY PRESS
STANFORD, CALIFORNIA

STANFORD UNIVERSITY PRESS
Stanford, California

Printed in the United States of America on acid-free, archival-quality paper.

Library of Congress Control Number: 2020939904

Cover design: David Drummond

Cover image: *Arm of Liberty,* Shutterstock; flame from the Peace Garden, Nathan Phillips Square, Toronto. David Whelan.

Typeset by Newgen in 10/14 Minion

For William H. Jackson
Always the radical

CONTENTS

PREFACE

From the dawn of sociological time, academic sociologists have described a world in crisis. We have diagnosed crisis from the ashes of the French Revolution, from the alienation wrought by industrialization, from the disintegration provoked by war and conflict. We have seen the end of society in the mass migrations and population growth of the nineteenth century, and then again in the anomie and individualism of the twentieth. We are attuned to the relentless threats to social structure.

Whatever comfort may be found in diagnosing the crises of modernity, diagnosis alone only rarely produces social change. Our willingness to diagnose crisis has not been matched by a similar enthusiasm for developing sociologically informed policy. As a result, the country's social policy agenda is defined and dominated by other social science disciplines, disciplines with their own interests, visions, and assumptions.

The absence of sociologists from the policy world is unfortunate, because we truly do seem to be living in a time of crisis. Income inequality is at unprecedented levels, and many types of social and economic mobility are stalling and even declining. Disease and economic hardship have wreaked havoc, and will continue to wreak havoc for years to come. The racial wealth gap is a persistent feature of the American economic landscape, while police violence and mass incarceration continue to tear at the fabric of poor and minority communities. As the forces of climate change play out, these and other inequalities are likely to intensify and stretch the social contract to the breaking point.

In the context of such monumental challenges, the policy community has—with a few prominent exceptions—maintained a strikingly timid approach to reform. We have developed a precisely focused and ostensibly science-based approach that offers specific, narrow-gauge, and evidence-informed "interventions." We have pushed toward a set of policy recommendations that are ever more incremental. This approach assumes that the best we can do is to contain the problem. It is largely taken for granted that we will never solve it.

Outside of the policy community, the larger public sees the world burning. Even politicians have stopped trying to pretend that the United States is a land of opportunity. Senator Elizabeth Warren channeled sociologists when she proclaimed in a speech to the Democratic National Committee, "This is a time of crisis . . . not the time for small ideas."[1] And Alexandria Ocasio-Cortez struck a similar note when she introduced her Green New Deal legislation, stating that "small, incremental policy solutions are not enough. They can be part of a solution, but they are not the solution unto itself."[2]

In 1999, Alvin Roth delivered a lecture to the Econometric Society in which he made a case for the economist as engineer. His purpose was to encourage economists to develop a science of design economics, a science that would use data and economic theory to design well-functioning economic systems.[3] This science would allow economists to engineer markets that operated efficiently and effectively, thus improving the outcomes of those markets for both participants and society.

By 2017, Esther Duflo was ready to argue that economists should be not engineers but plumbers. As plumbers, economists would be required not simply to provide blueprints for the economy but to ensure that those blueprints were well implemented. This meant focusing on the details and technicalities that must be addressed when any policy is rolled out. Duflo described the key difference in approach, claiming that "engineers will start from the outcome they are seeking to attain and engineer the machine to reach it. Plumbers, on the other hand, will have to adopt a more tentative approach, starting from the machine's characteristics and identifying their effect."[4] Although Duflo's vision was of an economics with a healthy representation of both engineers and plumbers, plumbing was the aspect of the discipline that she felt had been historically undervalued.

A relatively esoteric debate about the nature and purpose of applied economics turns out to provide a useful illustration of how our social scientific landscape has changed over time. Economists have moved from engineering systems to focusing on the operations of individual system components, and they have taken social science and policy with them on this journey. Incrementalism may be a useful model for policy during ordinary times, but in moments of crisis we have an obligation to move beyond incrementalism and its mechanistic understanding of the social world.

Our narrowed social science provides the normalizing basis for an incremental policy agenda. We have discovered beauty in the details and lost interest in the integrity of structures. For academics with an eye to having impact, narrow-gauge proposals for reform offer a seductive appeal. Such proposals can be robustly defended because they tackle established inequality-producing mechanisms, and their efficacy can be demonstrated in a straightforward fashion. Politicians, foundations, and research institutions have enthusiastically embraced small-scale reforms, for they provide the opportunity to have an impact even when resources and political will are in short supply. All of the actors involved in the process of policy design have incentives to highlight the promise of incremental policy, and to work on the assumption that enough incremental changes might bring forth profound social transformation.

We should celebrate all that is gained through incremental science and policy. But it is important that we do not dismiss what has been lost. When we focus on precise mechanisms, quasi-experiments, and nudges, we lose an overarching appreciation of where inequality comes from, and we thereby lose an opportunity for authentically radical reform.

In this book, I describe an inequality-generating process. At the heart of this process is a set of deeply flawed and poorly integrated social institutions, with which parents must engage to raise a child to full flourishing. Instilling necessary human, social, and cultural capital in a child requires navigating this sprawling and complicated constellation of institutions. We have developed highly specialized human development institutions, each configured to solve a very narrow problem, but we have not developed the integrative capacities that help children and families to successfully negotiate the resulting highly specialized and disconnected institutions.

It is up to parents to ensure that hospitals and health care institutions are doing their job at the prenatal moment, that a low-stress and high-engagement postnatal period is available, that the nutritional needs of the child are met, that high-quality child care is delivered, that an environment conducive to cognitive stimulation and language acquisition is present, that the transition to preschool is well negotiated, that properly stimulating extracurricular activities are available, that a college preparatory curriculum is set in motion by the time the child reaches adolescence, that any potentially perilous interactions with drugs, gangs, or the criminal justice system are nipped in the bud, that internships are set up and volunteering activities organized, that SAT prep courses are attended and taken seriously, that high-quality teacher recommendations are cultivated, that the risk of college dropout is deterred via active mentoring and other interventions, that the initial integration into the labor market is well facilitated, and so much more.

Raising a child has not always looked like this. It used to be that even poor children could follow a simple and well-lit path; there was no complicated array of institutions that had to be successfully negotiated to get into the middle class. But over the past half century we have developed a highly specialized and poorly coordinated array of such institutions that only richer parents are able to make work. In effect, privileged parents have knitted together a pathway from one human-development institution to the next that serves as a virtual cocoon for their children, so that from the child's point of view it is a single, coordinated institutional structure. By contrast, when underprivileged parents face this complex of social institutions, they find that they do not have access to the same road map, and so they lack ways to coordinate their engagement with institutions so as to ensure their child's opportunity. To them, each institution presents a new set of constraints, a new set of challenges, a new and foreign world. It is this hybrid institutional structure—interlocking and coordinated for the privileged and disconnected for the underprivileged—that is overlooked in a small-scale, mechanistic, and incremental approach to policy.

In a time of crisis, there is a hunger for change. But when an entire policy infrastructure has been built on a foundation of incremental reform, endogenous change is hard to come by.

Meaningful social change will require radical reform, which means that we must attack the institutional roots of inequality of opportunity. The aim of radical policy is to discern the larger institutional whole and then reconstruct it for everyone. While privileged children experience a well-integrated and coordinated cocoon of institutions, which protects and promotes their opportunities, the underprivileged are caught in a fractured institutional web. We must reconstruct our institutions so that everyone, not just the well-off, has a route to success. There are many ways to achieve a positive outcome. This book is not a tract for a single proposal for reform. Instead, its aim is to outline a process by which we can begin to see—and test—a variety of radical options that provide the same well-orchestrated pathways for underprivileged children as are currently available to privileged children.

To illustrate the promise of radical policy, I draw upon models from other countries that have taken seriously the task of building webs of institutions, webs that are available to all rather than purchased by the few. I outline how radical policy can be undergirded by a new type of radical science, and indeed, I stress that an emboldened social science has an obligation to develop and test the radical policies that would be necessary for equality to be assured to all. I show that when we adopt this new approach, we suddenly discover many available paths to full equality of opportunity in this country.

A central theme of this book is that sociology as a discipline is indispensable to the task of developing radical reform. The flaws in social institutions are clearly evident, as is the potential for change. Or as Emile Durkheim put it, "The purpose of sociology is to enable us to understand present-day social institutions so that we may have some perception of what they are destined to become and what we should want them to become."[5]

Although as sociologists we have no doubt been influenced by the incremental tendencies of modern-day social science, we continue to hold institutions close in understanding society and social inequality. The development of radical policy does not require of sociologists that they embrace engineering or plumbing, for sociologists have always understood that societies are complex and responsive systems. Radical policy simply requires that sociologists think like sociologists.

In writing a book, one is frequently reminded of one's good fortune in being part of an academic community that offers criticism, encouragement, and friendship. All of these elements are important in seeing a book through to completion, and I have benefited from all three.

I thank the administrative staff, faculty, and students of the Stanford University sociology department for providing a supportive and stimulating intellectual environment. So many of the conversations that I have enjoyed within the department have shaped the arguments and evidence in this book. I have been particularly touched by the enthusiasm that my students have expressed for the project. My friends and colleagues at Nuffield College, Oxford, continue to guide and encourage me even when my time in the dreaming spires is limited. In the 2018–19 academic year, I was based in Stanford's Center for

Advanced Study in the Behavioral Sciences (CASBS). Although much of the book had been completed in advance of my CASBS year, the manuscript still benefited greatly from my discussions with the community of interdisciplinary scholars brought together under Margaret Levi's leadership.

I was fortunate to receive detailed comments on the manuscript from David Cox, Matthew Desmond, Kathryn Edin, Michael Rosenfeld, Martín Sánchez-Jankowski, Kim Weeden, and Cristobal Young. Each has contributed to shaping the manuscript and has pushed me to develop the argument to its full fruition. I had stimulating conversations on topics related to the book with Corey Fields, Jeremy Freese, Sihla Koop, David Pedulla, Deborah Rhode, Aliya Saperstein, Florencia Torche, and Robb Willer. My sister Alexandra Wall provided both provocative commentary on the book's argument and the wonderful drawings included in Chapter 3. I am grateful to Jan McInroy for her sociologically nimble edit of the final manuscript. I also thank Marcela Maxfield and the reviewers for Stanford University Press for helpful comments. Stanford University Press provides a vital outlet for research on the sociology of inequality, and I appreciate the work of SUP staff in helping to develop the project.

Throughout the years spent working on this book, I have been blessed with a supportive and thoughtful partner. David Grusky provided comments on the manuscript and was always generous with his time. He and Rover, our beautiful dog, were a constant source of comfort and encouragement.

I had expected to conclude this preface with acknowledgments to my family for their unwavering support. My mother and father, Susan and William Jackson; my sisters, Catherine Rose and Alexandra Wall; and my grandmother Eva Jackson have always provided warmth and genial encouragement. As I completed revisions to the manuscript, my father was diagnosed with a glioblastoma, a brain tumor with a devastating prognosis. Of everything that I have written, this book is the piece of work that most shows his influence. He was saddened by injustice, and throughout his career as a teacher he worked to help those who would otherwise be left behind. His loss will always be felt, and I dedicate this book to him.

Stanford, California
April 2020

MANIFESTO FOR A DREAM

CHAPTER 1

THE PHANTOM DREAM

There has been much talk recently that the American Dream has died. If it ever lived, it is by now certainly dead. But few appear to have noticed that it has died twice.

The original Dream was born in the Founders' hopes for a new country, unencumbered by the institutions and political systems of the Old World. All good students of American history know that this country, from its very inception, promised to its citizens the unalienable rights to life, liberty, and the pursuit of happiness, rights that had been denied to subjects of the English Crown. As Tocqueville, among others, observed, new Americans had witnessed the destruction of the social barriers that defined the societies in which they originated, and now embraced the idea of freedom from the constraints of feudalism.[1] This city on a hill offered prosperity and hope to those who surrendered to the ideal, and the country drew its strength from the bonds that knitted together diverse peoples and talents in pursuit of a common purpose. The shackles of a social structure defined by aristocracy and nobility were thrown off, and a new society was established.

It was from these roots that the Dream grew, pulling together themes of freedom, self-determination, and democracy, alongside the Puritan values of hard work and self-discipline, and a culture of self-reliance born on the frontier. In the book that popularized the term "American Dream," James Truslow Adams wrote:

> The American dream that has lured tens of millions of all nations to our shores
> in the past century has not been a dream of merely material plenty. . . . It has
> been much more than that. It has been a dream of being able to grow to full-
> est development as man and woman, unhampered by the barriers which had
> slowly been erected in older civilizations, unrepressed by social orders which
> had developed for the benefit of classes rather than for the simple human be-
> ing of any and every class.[2]

Writing in the midst of the Great Depression, Adams identified the American Dream as a unifying principle that tied together generations of Americans, from the founding of the country right through to the present day. But
the Dream that Adams described—a vision of a society that freed individuals from the institutional barriers that might limit their opportunities for self-
advancement—was not long for this world, and it slowly slipped away.

In its place was established a phantom. The phantom retained elements
of its old form, but there was a subtle shift in emphasis: this Dream focused
squarely on individual talent and motivations. Although individual responsibility had always been a key element of the Dream, the ideological power
of the original lay in the contrast between the Old World and the New,
between a society with fixed social structures and barriers to opportunity and
a free society in which only hard work and talent would be recognized and
rewarded. The new Dream shifted the focus away from the structural barriers
to success and toward the individual actions that were necessary to achieve
success.[3] President Obama summarized the current incarnation of the Dream
in his remarks to the College Opportunity Summit:

> Now, as a nation, we don't promise equal outcomes, but we were founded on
> the idea everybody should have an equal opportunity to succeed. No matter
> who you are, what you look like, where you come from, you can make it. That's
> an essential promise of America. Where you start should not determine where
> you end up.[4]

The Dream of the twenty-first century is distinctively individualistic, emphasizing the importance of individual qualities and the goal of success, while alto-
gether silent on the constraints to individual ambition. It is this Dream that has
been pronounced dead time and time again in recent years.[5]

The original Dream was profoundly sociological. It recognized the power
of institutions to constrain individuals and to erect barriers that restrict indi-

vidual opportunities for success. That Dream concerned a property of the society, and could never be realized through any single individual's actions. It simply took for granted that the social structure conditioned the lives of individuals and families. To be sure, it also took for granted that Dreamers would be exclusively white and male, and that the great promise of these United States was an exclusive promise with well-defined limits.[6] But within these dismal limits, the Dream drew a contrast between two models of society, highlighting a truth that is self-evident to sociologists: that regardless of talent or capacity, an individual's life course will differ across societies with different institutional configurations.

In contrast, the phantom Dream is aggressively non-sociological. It focuses attention on atomized individuals, ignoring the fact that individuals are embedded within networks, families, and communities.[7] It focuses attention on cognitive and non-cognitive capacities, when we know that equally capable individuals have unequal chances of achieving economic success.[8] It focuses attention on economic outcomes, emphasizing the importance of accumulating capital and downplaying the significance of alternative status hierarchies and sources of meaning.[9] The Dream of the Founders might have originated long before the advent of a professionalized social science, but it displayed a more sophisticated understanding of where inequality comes from than does its modern-day incarnation.

In considering how best to reduce inequality, our policy agenda reflects the phantom Dream more strongly than it does the sociologically aware original. Favored policy solutions to poverty and inequality tend to take a narrow-gauge, atomistic view, focusing on individuals and families rather than addressing significant institutional reform: incrementalism reigns supreme. In part, this narrow-gauge agenda reflects the concerns of the public, and in part it reflects the interests and concerns of political elites, but it also reflects trends in quantitative social science. In this book I will contrast the different policy approaches to poverty and socioeconomic inequality in the United States, and argue that social scientists need to engage in two conversations. The first is the conversation that currently dominates the policy agenda, in which narrow, evidence-informed policies aim to target with pinpoint accuracy a particular aspect or symptom of inequality and nudge it away. The second, in contrast, is a broader conversation that requires us to take on the question of where inequality comes from and to consider more seriously the arguments for radical societal reform.

Embracing the Phantom

James Truslow Adams used the term "American Dream" to describe what he viewed as one of the fundamental ideological foundations of American society, and the term was quickly adopted by academics and the public alike. Academics embraced it partly because it provided a useful benchmark against which current levels of inequality could be measured. Social scientists, trained to be value-neutral in their research, are reluctant to describe inequality as "bad," or "wrong," or "undesirable," even when it is clear that inequality in the contemporary United States is damaging, unfair, and has broad societal consequences. The language of the Dream allowed social scientists to compare their empirical results against an undefined "ideal" level of inequality, and to emphasize the injurious consequences of an unequal society.

The Dream that all social scientists—even sociologists—have embraced, however, is the phantom Dream. This interpretation is widely understood to capture the distinction in political philosophy between equality of outcome and equality of opportunity, a distinction that carries with it normative implications. "Inequality of outcome" describes the unequal distribution of goods among individuals, families, and households. When adults experience inequality of outcome, it translates directly into inequality of condition for children, since the resources available in a household (or the lack thereof) influence the conditions into which a child of that household is born. "Inequality of opportunity," then, describes the extent to which inequality of condition results in unequal opportunities for success: is a child born into the most deprived household conditions just as likely to achieve success as a child born into the most advantaged conditions? The concept of equality of opportunity—the idea that where you start should not determine where you end up—has been adopted by social scientists as an operationalization of the standard contemporary reading of the Dream.[10]

The stream of research flowing from this interpretation has produced an impressive body of evidence documenting the extent to which social origins are associated with a wide range of outcomes. This work has established, for example, that Black men raised in families at the very top of the income distribution have rates of incarceration similar to those of white men born to families making $36,000 per year;[11] that poor children are half as likely as non-poor children to be proficient in reading by fourth grade; and that the neighborhood environment in which a child is raised will have effects throughout the child's life, shaping her future chances of upward mobility, her earnings, and her prospects of marriage.[12] For any given socioeconomic group, a host of statistics can be marshaled to express the extent to which conditions of birth influence life outcomes.

An operationalization of the original Dream would look a little different. Recall that the original envisioned a country in which individuals were liberated from the institutional barriers of the Old World. Whether or not this Dream is satisfied is a matter of whether or not there are institutional constraints that generate unequal outcomes. To be sure, standard measures of inequality of opportunity speak to this question, but only in a roundabout way: we measure the constraints by asking to what extent individuals are able to overcome the constraints, the equivalent of examining light by measuring the shadows that it casts. An analysis of the light itself entails identifying whether the social structure throws up barriers to success, barriers that are likely to disproportionately affect disadvantaged individuals and groups. An analysis of the light insists that we focus on the institutional barriers, and the extent to which individuals experience inequality of *constraints*.

There are benefits to looking beyond the shadows. First, there is value in having a term that explicitly identifies the institutional roots of inequality of opportunity. Language shapes our understandings of social processes, and if our key interest lies in understanding the societal barriers that limit the opportunities of some groups while promoting the opportunities of others, it is important to state this clearly. If racism is at the root of the disadvantages that people of color experience, racism is the societal barrier that must be in focus when we describe the transmission of inequality across generations. If children of poor households are locked out of high-quality schooling, unequal access to schools is the barrier that must be overcome. The term "inequality of constraints" may occupy the other side of the same conceptual coin as "inequality of opportunity," but the societal constraints determine the individual opportunities and should be recognized at every step in our scientific language.

Second, a term that emphasizes societal constraints has the potential to push social science in productive directions. An approach that focuses exclusively on individuals is likely to yield ambiguous conclusions regarding the role of institutional constraints, largely because of the difficulty of ensuring that individual differences are attributable to any particular institutional constraint. Emphasizing the constraints, in contrast, underscores that our scientific task is to document the institutional differences between socioeconomically advantaged and socioeconomically disadvantaged children. Social scientists may not always know what the societal barriers are, or how much of the total inequality between socioeconomic groups can be attributed to each of the barriers, but the language of unequal constraints recognizes that our task is to examine the inequality-generating process, not just the outcome of this process. Once institutional differences are carefully described, we have a clear path toward reducing and eliminating those differences.

From My Clay

If the concept of inequality of constraints is to be scientifically productive, it must be operationalized. What does it mean to understand the world as a set of institutional constraints? What are the barriers that an individual faces when negotiating the social world? How can a social institution have inequality-producing consequences for the individuals encountering it?

To address these questions, we must refocus our gaze. Institutions have come to play such a minor role in contemporary discussions of inequality of opportunity that it has become all too easy to forget the power and ubiquity of institutional constraints. And yet social institutions are the building blocks of society; they structure, organize, and constrain individual lives. For a simple definition, we may turn to Geoffrey Hodgson, who defines institutions as "systems of established and prevalent social rules that structure social interactions. . . . Generally, institutions enable ordered thought, expectation, and action by imposing form and consistency on human activities. They depend upon the thoughts and activities of individuals but are not reducible to them."[13]

Social institutions include families, schools, the labor market, and government. The sociological meaning of "institution" thus differs from the colloquial use of the word, which most frequently refers to "total" institutions such as mental hospitals, prisons, or boarding schools, where individuals are set apart from the wider society and are subject to the rules of the institution.[14] Although sociologists may reject the colloquial use, it is on the mark insofar as it highlights the extent to which individuals are subordinated to the structures that surround them. From the beginning, children are embedded in social institutions, institutions that will shape their paths to adulthood and in the shadow of which they will live their adult lives. The "self" that comes into the world is modified forever through its contact with social institutions.

Discussions that focus on the relative importance of structural versus individual factors in determining the trajectory of a life course are often derailed by the intellectual convenience of treating the "self" and "external structures" as easily separable at any given moment. We appear to be enormously willing to build into our self-concept all of those changes to the self that have already happened, while classifying as "structural" all of those external forces that now confront the self and hold influence over our decisions. The dynamic process, whereby at almost every moment institutions produce changes in individuals, is lost.

There are two broad mechanisms through which the self is continually modified by social institutions. First, institutions straightforwardly change individuals; they shape and structure each individual who encounters them. Second, institutions alter the decision calculus that individuals confront whenever they must make an explicit decision in everyday life: the same person may make very different decisions when he or she is placed in different social contexts. Both mechanisms will be consequential for the individual's future trajectory.

To understand how contact with institutions might change individuals, consider a hypothetical newborn, who at conception holds a given set of genetic and biological endowments. These endowments place lower and upper limits on what that child might achieve in the world. But between those limits the child's future is undefined. It is through contact with social institutions that the specific life trajectory of our hypothetical child is largely determined.[15] Let us assume, for example, that a child holds at conception a given level of cognitive capacity, which later in life will be described as "intelligence" and measured as "IQ." This cognitive capacity can be damaged by social institutions, just as it can be nurtured and enhanced by social institutions. Even if we limit ourselves to considering the effects of the institution of the family on a young child, we can already see multiple paths through which cognitive capacity might be manipulated. Take diet, for example. An important function of the family, particularly where young children are concerned, is to provide practical support for its members, support that includes food, shelter, and safety. Diet can damage cognitive capacity: deficiency in certain vitamins and minerals, such as iodine or iron, has been shown to lead to reductions in measured intelligence.[16] The social institution that is responsible for providing food to young children—the family—thus has the potential to change the cognitive capacity of the individual who encounters it.

The effect of diet on cognitive capacity is just one example of a path through which social institutions have biological effects. And biology is just one example of a path through which social institutions change individuals. In subsequent chapters, I discuss many other examples of individuals being changed by social institutions, although no single book could document them all.

Social institutions also set the boundaries within which any individual decision is made. The features of a social institution shape the costs and the benefits associated with a particular decision, and they determine the probability that a given decision will pay off. A simple example can be drawn from education. The education system is a social institution that touches the vast majority of children across the world. But the structure of education systems varies substantially from one country to the next: in some countries, such as Germany, education systems are highly stratified, with distinct tracks that determine progression through the system, while in others, such as the Netherlands, movement through the system is relatively straightforward, so that earlier educational decisions do not tightly constrain later decisions. The costs, benefits, and probabilities of success associated with educational decisions will differ across these various educational systems, so that the same person might make decisions that lead to a degree qualification in one country, but that lead to a qualification below degree level in the other. A cautious individual, for example, might be unwilling to make an ambitious choice in the German system, because of the risk of outright failure, but more willing to make an ambitious choice in the Dutch system, where mistakes can be corrected relatively easily. Once again, this describes only one instance of an individual's decision (or set of decisions) being influenced by institutional context. The social world is replete with examples of institutions imposing constraints on individual decisions, from childhood onward.

To state that social institutions modify individuals through two distinct processes is not to claim that these processes always operate independently. Individuals might be changed through contact with institutions in ways that also change the payoffs associated with any given decision. A person who has experienced cognitive damage through contact with social institutions faces a very different set of costs, benefits, and risks at a given educational decision point than a person who has not suffered damage. Similarly, an early change may make individuals more susceptible to being changed again, and an early decision will change the costs, benefits, and risks of a later decision. Adverse childhood experiences (ACEs), for example, have been shown to be associated with behaviors such as drug use, smoking, and overeating during adolescence.[17] These behaviors may then lead to problems with law enforcement, to problems with peer groups and schools, and to employer discrimination during the recruitment process. Processes of cumulative advantage and disadvantage thus have the potential to "bake in" the effects of social institutions early in life, such that these effects are amplified throughout the rest of the life course.[18]

The structure of social institutions would have little effect on inequality if individuals born into different parts of the socioeconomic status distribution were still embedded in similar institutions. For example, if children from different socioeconomic backgrounds were compared to one another at the moment of birth and then again at some point thereafter, the results would likely show that they were more similar at birth than they were at any point in the future. The observed differences would arise partly from socioeconomically induced differences in the type of prenatal environment that the children experienced.[19]

Environmental variation with respect to socioeconomic origin increases substantially after birth. Members of our society have come to expect, and even to view as natural, the idea that socioeconomic position is consequential for the type of social institutions with which an individual will come into contact. We may describe some areas as "poor neighborhoods," but what we mean when we use that term is not that people who are poor happen to live in the same place, but that the neighborhoods in which poor people live can be easily identified. We implicitly acknowledge that there is little variation in the structure and characteristics of such neighborhoods relative to the variation among all neighborhoods. Research in which subjects are asked to estimate the social class of neighborhoods by examining photographs from Google Street View shows that people are remarkably good at identifying which neighborhoods are socioeconomically advantaged and which ones are disadvantaged.[20] It is easy to identify the "class" of a neighborhood precisely because we know the characteristics of rich and poor neighborhoods. The identification of neighborhoods as rich or poor may also generate further disadvantage. Discrimination against individuals is well documented, but social psychologists have demonstrated that actual physical spaces can also be the subject of negative stereotypes, and that people are more tolerant of harm to physical spaces when those spaces are associated with disadvantaged social groups. It has been shown, for example, that people are more willing to condone environmental pollution in Black neighborhoods than in white ones.[21]

The linguistic simplicity of talking about poor neighborhoods—or poor schools, or poor families—obscures the extent to which institutions are conditioned by socioeconomic factors. It also disguises the multidimensional nature of socioeconomic advantage and disadvantage: our labels of "rich" and "poor" bundle together beliefs about income, class, race, exploitation, and power. To emphasize that our everyday terms of "rich" and "poor" are but a shorthand for groups that may be advantaged or disadvantaged on a whole range of socioeconomic dimensions, I will use the terms "privileged" and "underprivileged" throughout this book to refer to the most socioeconomically advantaged and most socioeconomically disadvantaged groups respectively.[22]

Why do neighborhoods, schools, or families have different characteristics depending on the socioeconomic position of those who are embedded within them? It is not, after all, a necessary feature of the world that those neighborhoods that we label as "poor neighborhoods" should contain disproportionate numbers of poor people. We could surely imagine a world in which the distribution of neighborhoods with respect to quality did not overlap with the distribution of people with respect to socioeconomic position.

There are two reasons why this world remains only an imaginary one. First, neighborhood quality must be purchased, so people who wish to live in a high-quality neighborhood will have to pay for that benefit.[23] Underprivileged people lack the resources to access high-quality neighborhoods—money, power, connections—and are therefore forced to choose from the available set of lower-quality neighborhoods. Second, neighborhoods are shaped by those who live in them. The resources, interests, and priorities of residents will have implications for neighborhood investments, spending on public goods, and the types of businesses and services that are located in the neighborhood.[24] Many (but not all) of the characteristics that we associate with high-quality neighborhoods are less likely to be present if a neighborhood is composed of poor people: the public park that requires tax revenues for upkeep, the bank that seeks consumers with high credit ratings, the children's theater that relies on parental donations, or the artisan bakery that charges eight dollars for a loaf of bread cannot be sustained in a neighborhood with a poor population.

As with neighborhoods, so with other social institutions. "Poor schools" look different from "rich schools," just as "poor families" look different from "rich families." Moreover, social institutions cluster together: poor families and poor schools are found in poor neighborhoods. Institutions structured in different ways will have different effects on individuals, and children who grow up embedded in "poor" social institutions are likely to look different than they would have had they grown up embedded in "rich" institutions. When people identify "inequality" in the world, they are most often referring to the effect of resources on these social institutions, or the effect of the social institutions on individuals.

And yet when we discuss the raw facts of inequality, the institutions disappear. When we note that children born to poorly educated Black mothers are three times more likely to die in infancy than are children born to highly educated white mothers, the institutions disappear.[25] They disappear when we note that children born into the top quintile of family income are three times more likely to end up in the top quintile than children born into the bottom quintile of family income.[26] And they disappear again when we note that the richest American men live fifteen years longer than the poorest American men.[27] We continue to accumulate statistics that describe inequality in the contemporary United States, and all the while the institutional landscape falls further out of view.

Inequality of Constraints

The original Dream spoke of barriers, of institutional constraints that had the power to deny individual success. When social scientists use the term "equality of opportunity," we do a poor job of capturing the intentions bound up in that Dream. There are two areas in particular in which standard invocations of equality of opportunity fall short. First, by embracing so enthusiastically the conceptual distinction between equality of condition and equality of opportunity, social scientists give credence to the idea that equality of condition and equality of opportunity are easily separable in practice. And second, the "equality of opportunity" term encourages a focus on individuals, not on institutional constraints.

It is common to hear a commitment to equality of opportunity expressed alongside an acceptance of inequality of outcome. Although there is no question that inequality of outcome has cruel effects for those on the wrong side of it, it is quite possible to mount a compassionate defense for inequality of out-come. Many claim, for example, that it is the incentives generated by inequal-ity of outcome that partly account for why the contemporary United States is such a powerful economic force.[28] As Milton and Rose Friedman memorably argued, "Life is not fair. . . . But it is also important to recognize how much we benefit from the very unfairness we deplore."[29] From this perspective, the short-term suffering inherent in inequality of outcome is far outweighed by the long-term benefits of economic security and continuing economic growth. The critical issue here, and perhaps the only issue left unresolved, is that of precisely *how much* inequality and *what types* of inequality are needed to deliver the necessary incentives.

The commitments to equality of opportunity and outcome come into con-flict when we consider the empirical relationship between them. First, there is growing evidence that inequality of outcome, in and of itself, undermines equality of opportunity. Research by Miles Corak, for example, shows a nega-tive association between income inequality and intergenerational income mobility, a finding labeled the "Great Gatsby Curve."[30] Corak shows that countries with high levels of income inequality have low levels of intergenera-tional mobility, suggesting that income inequality raises barriers that inhibit equality of opportunity.[31] And second, inequality of opportunity has conse-quences for life chances only insofar as there is inequality of outcome. If the same socioeconomic status, prestige, income, and working conditions were dispensed to every person, whether that person was a lawyer or a checkout clerk, it would matter little whether or not every child had an equal chance of becoming a lawyer. People might have a preference to work in one or the other of these occupations, but the consequences of being blocked from a law career would be modest in an equal society relative to the consequences in, say, the contemporary United States.

The focus on individuals that is encouraged by invoking the "equality of opportunity" term is also problematic in evaluating the extent to which the United States lives up to the ideals embodied in the original Dream.[32] Or, to put it in scientific terms, "equality of opportunity" as we interpret it today is a weak operationalization of the concepts in the original Dream, and arguably a weak operationalization of what social scientists mainly care about when they study social stratification and inequality.

To be sure, social scientists are often rather vague in defining and opera-tionalizing equality of opportunity. For example, they diagnose inequality of opportunity from evidence of unequal chances of social mobility for those of different socioeconomic backgrounds, for those of different socioeconomic backgrounds but similar levels of education, and for those of different socioeconomic backgrounds but similar levels of education, IQ, and effort.[33] Each of these approaches to estimating the degree of social mobility reflects different underlying assumptions about what would constitute evidence of inequality of opportunity. Similar lack of agreement is evident across the field of inequality and mobility research. When we estimate the gender gap in pay, should we account for the fact that men and women tend to enter different occupations? When we estimate the racial wealth gap, should we take family structure into account? When we estimate class inequalities in educational attainment, should we control for test scores? Even a cursory examination of scientific writing on these subjects would lead one to conclude that there is little precision in our standard treatments of "equality of opportunity." But something that all of these measures have in common is that the institutional barriers to individual success identified by the original Dream are captured only indirectly. Indeed, our main concern is to establish which individual-level characteristics must be controlled in order for inequality of opportunity to be diagnosed.

A further problem is that if ever our standard analytic tools were to suggest that opportunities are equally available to all, we would simply distrust those results. We would distrust them precisely because we *know* that there is profound inequality of constraint. For example, if we found that students from underprivileged households were just as likely to attend college as those from privileged households, despite the fact that the privileged students had special access to high-quality schools, private tutoring, extracurricular activities, and a whole range of other educationally relevant amenities, we would assume that the underprivileged students must have peculiarly high aspirations, or that they are peculiarly smart, or that they have other characteristics that account for their achievements.[34] Social scientists would be forced to search for these alternative characteristics precisely because we know that it is implausible that equality of opportunity could be achieved given the numerous barriers that are in place with regard to underprivileged students.

If "equality of opportunity" is an indirect operationalization of the original Dream, how should we go about measuring barriers to success? The key point here is that our objective should be to identify the institutional constraints, and subsequently the extent to which those constraints are responsible for producing inequalities of opportunity among individuals. It is for this reason that I use the term "inequality of constraints" throughout this book. The focus on inequality of constraints rather than inequality of opportunity signals a move away from misleading rhetoric on the sources of inequality, but the contrast between the two terms is more than symbolic. The term "inequality of constraints" pinpoints the source of inequality in a way that "inequality of opportunity" does not: individuals face unequal opportunities primarily *because* society offers unequal constraints. Only after we have examined institutional constraints can we ask whether or not there may exist compensating or amplifying forces that would alter our understanding of the effects of institutional constraints on an individual's outcomes. "Inequality of constraints" forces us to consider the question of whether the contemporary United States offers equality of institutional context to all of those who live in this country.

I consider here three possible approaches to measuring inequality of constraints. First, and most preferably, is an approach that directly measures institutional barriers. Second is an approach that measures the extent to which inequalities can be attributed to non-institutional sources. And third is an approach that assesses the extent to which individuals are held back by institutional constraints. The third approach comes closest to existing analyses within the "inequality of opportunity" tradition, but, as I shall argue below, it is less desirable than the first and second approaches.

The Search for Smoking Guns

The ideal methodological approach is to measure inequality of constraints by carefully examining inequality-generating social institutions and cataloging their features. This is the most direct approach to operationalizing the original Dream, in that it straightforwardly captures the extent to which there are institutional barriers to individual success.

We can use a small part of a single social institution, namely application to a four-year college, to demonstrate how this strategy might work. The process through which an individual applies for college consumes only a brief part of that person's life—perhaps no more than six months to a year—but it involves many decisions and actions that are likely to be conditioned by socioeconomic background. By this time of life, the individual's aspirations and ambitions have already been shaped, grade point averages for previous years of schooling are in place, and both cognitive and non-cognitive traits are relatively firmly established.[35] And yet a whole array of new obstacles arises and must be addressed. One of those is the SAT, which plays an important role in channeling students into different kinds of four-year colleges.[36] To take the SAT, students must register online and pay a fee, although those from low-income households can apply for a fee waiver. Achieving a high score on the SAT is essential for entry into almost all of the highest-status colleges, and students from privileged families will use books, additional study materials, and private tutors to improve their scores, resources to which students from lower-income households will not have as ready access.[37] Students then apply to colleges, and although some institutions use the Common Application, many of the most prestigious universities require completion of individually tailored application packages. Once again, fees are generally required for submitting the applications, although in this situation as well, students from low-income households may apply for a waiver. In privileged households, students can again marshal books and private tutors, along with parental advice, for assistance in completing applications, while students from underprivileged households will have to work alone. A final key piece of the application process is the financial aid application, known as FAFSA, which determines eligibility for federal grants and loans. The application form is longer and more complicated than a standard tax return, and it represents a hurdle that ultimately reduces the rate of college attendance for students from low-income families.[38] At every step of the college application process, students from underprivileged households must put in more effort, spend more time, and show more personal initiative if they are to overcome their lack of cultural, economic, and social resources. Given these institutional barriers, it would be rather surprising if students from underprivileged families applied to college at the same rate as those from privileged backgrounds.

Institutional barriers like these are not invisible. If we were to consider the key transitions in our own lives, we could likewise identify a whole range of constraints that resulted in some options being out of bounds and others being preferred.

It is no simple task to catalog all of the relevant constraints. For any process that we might evaluate, the barriers to success will be a function of both the extent to which an individual has already been "changed" (e.g., poor academic preparation throughout the school career will reduce the chances of performing well on the SAT regardless of current access to books, study materials, and private tutors) and the extent to which the current process throws up barriers that disproportionately affect particular groups (e.g., college application fees). Identifying these barriers requires careful and cumulative social science. The holistic accounts of ethnographers must be merged with the experimentalists' accounts of mechanisms, with the policy evaluators' randomized controlled trials, and with the descriptive and causal accounts of quantitative researchers. Identifying these barriers also requires an understanding of how different features of the institutional landscape might influence individual decision making, whether that understanding comes from theory, empathy, or observation. Cross-national and longitudinal comparisons can be helpful in identifying barriers, helpful in assessing whether or not features that exist in one place and time would necessarily have the same effects on outcomes as features that exist in another place and time would. After the barriers are identified, it becomes possible to judge whether or not there is inequality of constraints.

This approach has been successfully applied in other areas of social science, including areas in which it might otherwise be difficult to identify the contribution of individual differences to larger empirical trends. A classic example is the work on executive compensation, which assesses the extent to which the large financial rewards reaped by an elite set of executives can be attributed to the special talents and characteristics of the individuals who occupy these positions. Given the difficulty of evaluating the productivity of executives and their value to the company, an alternative approach has investigated the processes through which executive compensation is determined. This research shows that information about peer groups is brought to bear on decisions about compensation, so that a larger-than-normal level of compensation for one executive may generate larger-than-normal salaries for other executives, who are able to argue that their compensation should be benchmarked to that of their better-paid peers.[39] Although there is disagreement in the literature about whether or not executive compensation reflects true market worth or market worth plus rent, the institutional literature on executive compensation has made it incumbent upon those arguing in favor of true market worth to explain why executive compensation is not upwardly biased by processes such as benchmarking.

The ultimate aim of this methodological approach is to document all of the differences in institutional context that individuals from different socioeconomic groups experience: the differences in health care provision for chil-

dren of different socioeconomic backgrounds, the differences in educational
provision for children of different socioeconomic backgrounds, the differences in every institutional function provided by every institution that children interact with every day. It is of course important to remember that not all
differences will have consequences for an individual's life course: what at first
appears to be a barrier might turn out not to be.

An approach that holds some promise in identifying the consequences of
institutional barriers is the quasi-experimental approach, which applies a set
of statistical techniques to identify the causal effects of institutional barriers. Such techniques have been used to great effect in examining the extent to
which a social institution like the law changes individual behavior. For example, how significant are changes in financial aid restrictions in altering the
college-going behavior of disadvantaged youth?[40] Do changes in immigration
law alter the outcomes of individuals subject to those laws?[41] Will millionaires
flee to distant lands if their income is taxed at a higher rate?[42] Although these
techniques neatly speak to the question of whether any particular barrier does
indeed shape individual behavior, they are at present limited to understanding
how changes in a relatively small set of barriers might change the constraints
that individuals face. This approach carries the danger of encouraging a focus
on small snippets of social institutions, rather than on the institutional structure as a whole, which in turn is likely to promote narrow-gauge reform at
the cost of thoroughgoing institutional change. But there is no reason why, in
principle, quasi-experimental methods should not be used to measure a more
substantial range of institutional effects.

The true test of the original Dream lies in a full investigation of the barriers to individual success. If individuals from different backgrounds do not
face similar barriers to success, they experience inequality of constraints, and
inequality of outcome is likely to result.

Measuring Non-institutional Sources of Inequality of Outcome

Inequality of opportunity, as conventionally measured, assesses the extent to
which two equally talented individuals from different social backgrounds have
equal chances of success. It is the end result of the interaction between the
individual and all of the social institutions that he or she comes into contact
with. A true measure of the equal opportunity concept would involve comparing equally talented individuals who, *at conception*, had equal chances of
success. After conception, social institutions will already have begun to shape

the individual in ways that will be consequential for inequality of opportunity. Assuming that such a comparison is not feasible, a reasonable approach to identifying the institutional barriers to success might be to attempt to rule out all of the non-institutional sources of inequality of opportunity.

If our aim is to identify non-institutional sources of inequality of opportunity, a good place to start is to measure the contribution of genetic factors to outcomes of interest. A prominent paper published in *Nature* in 2016 on genetics and educational attainment illustrates this approach.[43] In the paper, researchers identify a set of genes that are significantly associated with educational attainment, and further state that the genes identified in this study explain a maximum of around 3.2 percent of the variation in educational attainment among individuals.[44] Can we use this estimate, or the others that will inevitably arise in this research stream, to derive an estimate of inequality of constraints?

Unfortunately, state-of-the-art research on genetic influences will not provide this estimate, largely because there are limits on the extent to which we can measure a "pure" genetic effect. The extent to which genes can explain, say, differences in educational attainment depends both on individual genetic differences and on the extent to which environmental factors have made such differences salient for individual outcomes. Further, those in the sociogenomics field have identified a large number of mechanisms through which an interplay between genetics and environment might occur.[45] For example, as Jeremy Freese has argued, "When social environments encourage individuals to develop their strengths and these strengths are genetically influenced, then the main consequence of effective environmental causes may be to make the consequences of genetic differences larger."[46]

The interplay between genetic and environmental factors raises serious questions about whether it is sensible (or indeed possible) to measure "purely genetic" effects. In the study of educational attainment described above, researchers demonstrated this point by comparing the predictive power of genetic influences on educational attainment across cohorts in Sweden: genes were found to be less predictive of educational attainment for younger cohorts than for older cohorts. The researchers argued that the educational reforms that Sweden introduced for younger cohorts likely reduced the power of genes to determine educational success, and thus that an interaction between genes and the institutional environment explained overall educational attainment.[47]

As this brief overview demonstrates, there is less potential to identify inequality of constraints through an analysis of genetic influences alone than might be assumed on the basis of everyday understandings of sociogenomics. But this approach might have substantial promise when it is paired with one that outlines the various features of social institutions and describes how these features might inhibit or encourage the development of inequalities derived from individual genetic differences.

Measuring the Extent to Which Individuals Are Constrained

A final approach to capturing the original Dream is to leave as "unexplained" the individual-level differences that determine outcomes, and instead examine to what extent the total effects of socioeconomic background can be explained by characteristics that might reflect the influence of social barriers. This is arguably a business-as-usual approach for those who work on equality of opportunity, who will begin with an association between socioeconomic background and an outcome and then use statistical controls to evaluate the extent to which differences among social groups can be attributed to institutional characteristics. For example, we might start with a gross association between socioeconomic background and educational attainment, and then decompose that association into parts attributable to differences in cultural capital (e.g., knowledge of classical music or the arts), social capital (e.g., access to educationally relevant social networks), economic capital (e.g., access to learning materials), and so on. Such an analysis might demonstrate that, say, 15 percent of the total estimated inequality could be accounted for by measures of cultural capital, thus implying that if the level of cultural capital could be equalized across socioeconomic groups, inequalities in educational attainment would become 15 percent smaller than they are at present.

One difficulty in using such an approach to measure equality of constraints is that it is hard to identify where the barriers come from, because the variables that are measured are one step removed from the social institutions that might produce them. For example, we may find that educational inequalities can be partially "explained" by the number of extracurricular activities that children of different socioeconomic background engage in, but this finding in and of itself provides few clues as to which institutional constraints produced the difference in extracurricular participation. It would be equally plausible to argue that these differences were caused by differences in neighborhood characteristics, differences in economic resources, differences in family culture, or differences in individual preferences. We do not measure the constraints per se; we simply observe the outcome after individuals have been constrained. This approach, then, is quite unsatisfactory for assessing the institutional constraints in play.

Dreaming, Big and Small

In 1936, Herbert Agar made a heartfelt appeal to a country then suffering the lingering pain of the Great Depression. He argued that economic recovery could come only through the country recommitting to its national ideals, embracing neither "monopoly capitalism" nor communism. As many others have done before and since, he invoked the American Dream as an unadulterated expression of these national ideals. The Dream that he described was not our modern-day phantom, but the original, in which "the large majority . . . should be able to count on living in an atmosphere of equality, in a world which puts relatively few barriers between man and man."[48]

What Agar and his contemporaries identified as barriers were the social institutions that organize everyday life. In the context of extreme inequality, the shape of social institutions differs fundamentally for the privileged and the underprivileged. The social institutions that ease the path of privileged children into socioeconomically advantaged positions simultaneously block the paths of the underprivileged.

If the original Dream is to be realized in the contemporary United States, we must address the barriers that are generated through the interaction between socioeconomic inequality and social institutions. One approach would be to tackle the problem at its source, to fully eliminate the socioeconomic inequality that turns institutions into barriers. Although this is in principle possible, even the original Dream allows for socioeconomic inequality and differential rewards insofar as they do not generate societal barriers. An alternative, therefore, is to pay no heed to current levels of inequality and instead work to reshape the social institutions in order that they no longer operate as barriers to success. The degree of intervention necessary to accomplish either of these goals would be radical.

The point at which a social intervention could be labeled as "radical" is the point at which practically minded social scientists begin to look for alternative solutions. And yet if the country wishes to recommit to its founding values, there is little question that radical change is what will be required.

The radical policy agenda that I outline attacks the roots of inequality of constraints. In contrast to the incremental policies that have dominated the social scientific agenda in recent decades, radical policies do not take the current structure of social institutions as a given. Instead, the goal is to fundamentally change social institutions, and to attack the effects of socioeconomic resources on institutions. Radical policies create webs of high-quality institutions around underprivileged children, cocooning them on their path to adulthood and beyond. The radical policy agenda targets the institutional barriers that stand in the path of the underprivileged, and builds a social infrastructure that supports all children. If the current institutions cannot provide equality of constraints, we must consider new institutional forms, and new interpretations of existing institutions.

Why do most of the social scientists engaged in policy recoil from recommending radical change? First, and most obviously, applied social scientists hope to change the social world. They are likely to view incremental change as feasible and radical change as unattainable. Second, social scientists proceed by testing specific hypotheses against available data; concrete policy proposals must therefore be piloted before they are implemented in the wider world. It is difficult to pilot radical changes to social institutions in advance, and difficult to implement them without pilot programs, although, as we shall see, radical changes to social institutions have sometimes been implemented in the name of reducing inequality of opportunity, even if the changes were not initially represented as radical. And third, the association of radical proposals for change with political movements (of both the left and the right) contaminates the social science discussion, because calls for radical change immediately bring to mind these strongly held ideological positions.

In this book, I make the case that science requires us to be honest and up front about the extent of reform that would be required to eliminate unequal barriers to success. Proposals for radical change are fully consistent with the fundamental principles of social science, and social scientists should not shy away from making the case that the original Dream—and, indeed, even the phantom Dream—can be satisfied only if social institutions are radically reshaped. It is important for social scientists to straightforwardly lay out the scale of the changes that would be required to guarantee that all individuals face the same societal constraints. Judgments about feasibility and ideological palatability are often value judgments, and to pull back from outlining the extent of the problem because of worries about feasibility or ideology is to pull back from our responsibility as scientists. Discussions about the over-whelming and far-reaching effects of inequality on social institutions are only undermined by the suggestion that small, or even moderate, changes to policy might be able to substantially counter its effects. Profound inequality cannot be nudged into oblivion.

Manifesto for a Dream

In the coming chapters, I will argue in favor of a radical policy agenda that has the potential to deliver on the promises of the original Dream. I begin in Chapter 2 by laying out the current policy agenda, one that emerged from standard narratives about inequality of opportunity. I highlight the relatively narrow ambitions at the heart of the contemporary policy agenda and provide examples of programs that are consistent with those ambitions. Finally, I ask why so many social scientists are attracted by small-scale policies when almost all would agree that only large-scale reforms would eliminate inequality of opportunity. I argue that the pressures imposed by both society and social science are what accounts for the tendency to embrace relatively narrow reforms.

In Chapter 3, I describe the full scale of the problems that policymakers must address if the aim is to equalize opportunity. I further develop the concept of "inequality of constraints" to describe the barriers to success for those born into underprivileged families. I encourage social scientists to focus not just on the constraints on opportunity experienced within any single social institution, but rather to consider the entire network of institutions with which individuals must interact on the path to adulthood. I draw a contrast between the "cocoon" of institutions experienced by privileged children and the fractured web experienced by the underprivileged, with an emphasis on the negative consequences for future opportunities of a lack of institutional coherence. The web of institutions must be the primary focus of any radical policy agenda.

In Chapter 4, I offer examples of policies that might have a place in a radical policy agenda. I draw upon models from other countries that have taken on the task of building webs of institutions that are not influenced by socio-economic position (even if the task has not been expressed in such terms). Later in the chapter I move from existing models in other countries to models drawn from the imagination. The aim of this discussion is to encourage the design of ambitious and wide-ranging policy, even where there is little hope of putting that policy into practice.

In Chapter 5, I conclude with a discussion of how a radical policy agenda might gain ground in the United States. I argue that there are paths to realizing greater equality of constraints in this country, and that an emboldened social science has an obligation to outline the radical policies that would be necessary for equality of constraints to be assured to all. This book rejects the position that the scale of current policy is sufficient to deliver on the promises of the original Dream. Instead, it emphasizes the substantial barriers that are produced when inequality interacts with institutions. It outlines the type of radical policy that would be required to bring down these barriers. Instead of mourning a Dream that was long ago replaced by a phantom, this book focuses on a strategy for revival.

CHAPTER 2

THE INTERVENTION

in·ter·ven·tion
Origin: late Middle English: from Latin interventio(n-), from the
verb intervenire, from inter- "between" and venire "come."

As we travel through life, we engage with a set of social institutions that shape
and constrain us. All of these institutions are human-made, even if no individual can be identified as a creator.

In Chapter 1 I discussed how institutions unequally constrain us, by shaping us as individuals and by changing the decision calculus at those points
where individual choices come into play. In this chapter, I will argue that
many policy interventions are predicated on the belief that existing social
institutions are to be preserved and that the role of policy is to layer on top of
these institutions some inequality-reducing remediation. These interventions,
then, aim to reduce inequalities of opportunity with respect to socioeconomic
background without explicitly tackling the institutional constraints.[1] I here
consider the reasons why social scientists typically shy away from proposing large-scale reforms, instead favoring the smaller-scale intervention in the
fight to reduce inequality.

"Intervention" is the byword of social policy. Policymakers, often hand in hand
with social scientists, aspire to design interventions that will disrupt the processes generating inequality of opportunity. In general, these interventions
operate by offering aid to underprivileged families and children, with the aim
of improving their outcomes. Interventions do not usually hamper the opportunities of the privileged. A standard explanation for this imbalance is that

holding back privileged children in the name of equality would be damaging to overall economic productivity, because many of the institutional contexts that privileged children enjoy promote positive biological and sociobehavioral development. In contrast, underprivileged children are damaged through their contact with institutions, suffering both absolute harm (i.e., where children are diminished through their contact with institutions and institutional failure—for example, physical illness caused by stress) and relative harm (i.e., where all children are improved through their contact with institutions, but underprivileged children are improved less than privileged children).[2] There are, then, good economic reasons for allowing privileged children to flourish to the fullest extent possible, even if this flourishing comes at the expense of equality. Regardless, the political explosion that would occur should those of privilege be systematically held back means that we are unlikely to see the economic productivity assumption tested in the near future.

Policy interventions are usually tailored to operate in one of three ways. First, an intervention may remediate disadvantage, by compensating for experiences and resources that were absent in the past. This type of intervention does not aim to eliminate the sources of disadvantage: by definition, remediation interventions are implemented only after social institutions have produced damage in individuals. Second, an intervention may replace a function or process that is usually controlled by an institution. This replacement occurs concurrently, or close to concurrently: the intervention stops institutions from producing damage by stepping in to provide the missing function, with positive consequences for equality of opportunity. And third, an intervention may recalibrate the decision calculus that an individual faces, after that individual has already been changed by an institution or set of institutions. It is possible for interventions to operate in all three of these domains, but in most cases the intervention can be fairly characterized as specializing in just one domain. I will briefly describe how each type of intervention operates to reduce inequalities related to socioeconomic background.

Remediate

Interventions that remediate for past disadvantage are common. In fact, many of the interventions that are targeted at improving the lives and opportunities of adults can be understood in terms of remediation. Remediation policies do not attempt to alter any of the institutional structures that generate inequality; rather, they compensate after the fact for the unequal outcomes that have been produced by these structures.

One type of policy intervention that falls under the heading of remediation is adult employment and training programs. These programs provide general and vocational education, alongside apprenticeships, work experience, and job training.[3] The recipients are often young people from underprivileged backgrounds who have fallen out of the education system before the end of secondary schooling, but some programs also target older adults (e.g., job search assistance and retraining for the long-term unemployed). Such programs are not typically well integrated into the educational training that individuals have previously experienced on the path to adulthood—they stand as an alternative to the "standard" educational pathway of a two- or four-year college degree. Many job training programs, for example, are administered by the Department of Labor (Employment and Training Administration) or by specialized offices within the Department of Education (Office of Career, Technical, and Adult Education), rather than by the offices that are responsible for initial education and training (i.e., Office of Elementary and Secondary Education, and Office of Postsecondary Education). There are good reasons why administration of specialized adult training programs might need to be different from that of elementary, secondary, and even postsecondary schooling, but the bureaucratic separation of training functions emphasizes the extent to which these programs operate as remediation for past institutional failures rather than as an integrated part of business-as-usual educational provision: training programs develop skills and capacities that childhood training institutions failed to provide.

Another form of remediation simply involves providing direct compensation to improve the lives of those who have been left behind. The most obvious example of this type of remediation policy is the transfer of money, and in fact, a great deal of our inequality-reducing policy does just that. The Earned Income Tax Credit (EITC), a key component of this nation's anti-poverty policy, involves a simple transfer of money in the form of tax credits to working families (and to a lesser extent, to individuals without children). In addition to improving the economic position of the poor, the EITC results in increased labor market participation, improved maternal health, and decreased rates of smoking among EITC recipients.[4]

Policies that focus on remediation for adults will also have consequences for the children of those adults. Research shows, for example, that children of EITC recipients have better health, higher test scores, and improved labor market outcomes in adulthood than children born into non-EITC households.[5] The EITC is therefore opportunity-generating for the children of the target generation, but importantly, these effects of the policy are unlikely to operate through the remediation mechanism. Instead, a policy that remediates in the parental generation is transformed into a policy that "replaces" in the child's generation.

Replace

Replacement interventions reduce inequality of opportunity by changing the child through the social institutions that he or she is currently in contact with. Such interventions will replace existing institutional functions and processes, often because existing institutions are failing to provide the requisite functions and processes. The desired outcome is for an institution to operate effectively and to provide the function or process that would otherwise be absent. Replacement interventions may operate in one of two ways.

Some replacement interventions introduce a function or process into an existing institution: activities that ideally would be carried out by the existing institution are instead provided through the policy intervention. For example, if a family or school is failing to provide essential functions, such as emotional support or socialization, the intervention will provide that function instead. This first type of replacement is relatively uncommon in our current policy landscape, but there are some prominent examples of the approach, such as foster care and intensive emotional and cognitive development programs during early childhood. Indeed, many of the interventions carried out under the "early intervention" rubric provide child care, socialization, and early training that might under different circumstances be provided in the context of a family, community, or school.

Other types of replacement interventions may introduce information or resources intended to encourage and support an institution in providing a certain function, thereby ensuring that the change takes place. In this case, the intervention itself will not provide the missing function, but the family or school will be induced to provide it. Food stamps, for example, do not directly deliver food to recipients, but they make it easier for families to afford and provide food to their members.[6] This intervention is expected to reduce inequality of opportunity for members of the recipient families, particularly the children. Money transfers to the poor (such as Temporary Assistance for Needy Families) similarly make it possible for poor families to execute their social functions effectively. Some other replacement interventions, such as those developed by researchers in the early education field, focus on different aspects of family life. One intervention involves sending frequent text messages to parents to encourage them to support the educational development of their young children.[7] This intervention is designed to replace the socialization and training function usually provided by the family, not by offering a straight replacement but by encouraging members of the family to change their behavior and provide the function themselves.

Recalibrate

A final type of policy intervention aims to recalibrate the decision calculus of those from underprivileged households in directions that will lead to increased equality of opportunity. This type of intervention aims not to change the social institutions that an individual comes into contact with, but rather to change the decisions that an individual might make in the future. Many so-called "information interventions" in education work in this way, on the understanding that children from underprivileged households are often wary of making ambitious educational decisions because they are not aware of the benefits of further study, or they simply don't know that grants and loans may be available to offset the immediate costs. Interventions often target high school students and provide basic information at crucial decision points in order to alter a decision in an inequality-reducing direction.[8] "Nudge" interventions that do not replace an institutional function frequently work by pushing individuals to pursue a path that they would otherwise not have chosen.

Recalibration interventions are increasingly used to encourage eligible claimants to access welfare benefits. In surveying the landscape of American welfare policy, one could be forgiven for imagining that the system had been designed with the aim of discouraging some individuals from accessing benefits to which they are entitled: administrative hurdles and poor dissemination of information about eligibility create barriers to access. Indeed, there is evidence that such barriers have been deliberately introduced in some states to limit the numbers of those claiming welfare benefits, and further evidence that people of color are particularly likely to face administrative hurdles when navigating the welfare system.[9] Recalibration interventions provide information to eligible claimants about available programs and streamline the application process to smooth the path to proving eligibility to state and federal agencies. These interventions frequently rely upon recent technological advances; smartphone applications, text messages, and administrative data linkage have all been exploited to simplify access to the welfare system by the underprivileged.

The Limits of "Intervention"

This brief survey of the policy landscape illustrates the diversity of approaches to reducing inequality of opportunity. But it is diversity of a very limited form: most of these policy interventions have in common a focus on narrow-gauge reform—that is, reform that largely preserves the existing institutional structure. To be sure, they have many positive effects, but the majority of interventions remediate and recalibrate, helping individuals who have already been changed by social institutions, while interventions that replace the functions of institutions are few and far between. Our current policy provision is clearly limited in both size and scope.

The "size" problem is striking when we compare the limited extent of government assistance to the gulf in economic resources available to privileged and underprivileged families. If we compare households with children at the bottom of the income distribution to those at the top, we find a difference in pre-tax income of around $230,000. Taxes reduce the income of the rich families, and transfers increase the income of the poor ones, but even after federal taxes and transfers are accounted for, the difference in income between rich and poor families still stands at more than $162,000. State taxes and transfers will reduce the gap by another $9,000 on average, but even in the most progressive states the difference in the post-tax-and-transfer incomes of rich and poor families is likely to be around $150,000. While the child of a poor family is living in a household that even after taxes and transfers has less than half of the median household income at its disposal, the child of a rich family has access to a substantial sum that can be invested in opportunity-enhancing goods and services.[10] Government safety net programs are cost-effective, inequality-reducing, and opportunity-promoting, but they do not come close to removing the financial constraints that poor children face.

The magnitude of the problem means that our existing interventions will fall short. To further demonstrate the limits of existing policy, we may take as an example one particular institutional domain: food provision. The key policy intervention in the food provision domain is food stamps (the Supplemental Food Assistance Program, or SNAP), a policy that is widely regarded as one of our most effective antipoverty programs. Yet hunger and malnourishment are still common among the poor. According to a recent study, half of the households that receive food stamps continue to experience food insecurity.[11] Other programs designed to improve the food provision for poor families (such as free school lunch and WIC, the Special Supplemental Nutrition Assistance Program for Women, Infants, and Children), similarly fail to lift recipients out of food insecurity, with around 40 percent of the families who benefit from these programs still experiencing the problem.[12] In the richest country on earth, poor families are going hungry. To be sure, these food-provision programs improve the lives of the recipients, but they do not provide sufficient resources to ensure that all poor Americans are well nourished.[13]

And what of the "scope" of current policy? The general public and political leaders have shown little enthusiasm for ensuring that no American goes hungry. All policy decisions with respect to particular interventions are made in the full knowledge that there will be well-prescribed limits to the type of policy on offer. Many Americans are willing to tolerate hunger among able-bodied adults who are not working, for example, or among families who lack the requisite legal permissions to live in the United States.

But limits are also imposed because certain types of policy would challenge the integrity of existing institutions. For a moment, let us assume that we could implement a policy that would directly replace the food-provisioning function of the family for children that required it. We are familiar with the idea of free school lunches, but what if all meals were prepared and provided by an entity external to the family? The combination of these meals could be planned to ensure that children would receive a balanced diet with an appropriate number of daily calories. This is a policy that would—with an absolute guarantee—ensure that poor children and rich children were equivalently nourished. It is also a policy that would change an existing institution (i.e., the family) by wholly taking over the food-providing function that the family is currently responsible for. We decide as a society that we do not wish to equalize diet and nutrition by replacing the family's function in this way. But we must recognize that the gap between the current situation and the equal-provision situation is a gap that will create barriers for poor children, leading to unequal opportunity. It also represents an active decision to limit the scope of policy intervention.

If the scope of current policy is limited by the type of interventions that are considered within the food domain, it is also limited by the fact that food provision in and of itself could never be enough to ensure equal opportunity. Even the best-nourished children will flounder if all of the other institutions in which they are embedded cause damage. A child who grows up in a violent community, for example, will perform worse on achievement tests than a child who is not exposed to violence.[14] The gains of proper nutrition can be easily undone by the stress, anxiety, and fear engendered by living amid violence. A policy success in one institution can thus be directly undermined by a policy failure in another.

Lack of food and exposure to violence are but two examples of institutional failure that underprivileged children face. A chronicle of institutional failure would add to this list scores of other examples, among them exposure to environmental contaminants, family instability, erratic access to child care, poor-quality education, lack of access to dental services and health care, and housing insecurity. Any (or all) of these failures may undermine the intent of our current inequality policies. Research on food stamps, for example, reveals an underground market that allows individuals to sell food stamps, albeit at around 60 percent of their face value.[15] The poor sell food stamps to afford other items, including basic expenses such as rent.[16] Thus the power of intervention with respect to food is undermined by failures in the provision of other basic necessities.

The limits of current policy aimed at reducing poverty and increasing equality of opportunity are obvious. In this context, what must be appreciated is the striking failure of social scientists to emphasize that while contemporary "opportunity policy" may have positive effects, it will simply never provide equal opportunity for all children. No one who is familiar with our current policy architecture could imagine that current interventions are sufficient to guarantee that children from privileged and underprivileged families face equal constraints in achieving educational and occupational success.

A Radical Distance

We have built an intervention apparatus that will not succeed. But if our standard policy interventions cannot guarantee equality of constraints, why do most of the social scientists engaged in policy work fail to push for the alternative of more-radical reform? All of the researchers who work on poverty and inequality could have worked on alternative social science questions. All of those involved in policymaking and implementation could have worked in different fields. Indeed, the majority of academic social scientists who spend their careers diagnosing the problems of inequality and poverty will never try to engage with policy addressing these problems; disciplinary specialization and disinterest pull many researchers away from applied research. It would therefore be sensible to assume that all of those who do work to attack inequality through policy intervention are firmly committed to the project. And yet this firm commitment exists alongside an acceptance that policy intervention will never eliminate unequal constraints.

Poverty and inequality researchers themselves face a complicated set of incentives and constraints when determining how best to intervene in policy. Not all researchers will respond to these concerns in the same way, and some factors may weigh more heavily than others. Here I will focus on four possible reasons why we do not see social scientists who are engaged in policy work clamoring for sweeping institutional reform: pragmatic, scientific, ideological, and self-interested.

Pragmatic

Most social scientists working on inequality, particularly those involved in proposing policy interventions, are pragmatists at heart. They understand the extent of inequality, the barriers to opportunity, and many of the mechanisms that are likely responsible for generating empirically observed patterns. They understand the immense gap between the size of the inequality problem and the policy interventions that are marshaled to address it. But they also have back-of-the-envelope estimates of the probability that any given policy reform will be supported by the public, politicians, and institutional actors, and of the probability that the policy will be funded and ultimately implemented. If social scientists expect that each step from invention to implementation will meet with resistance, the overall estimated probability that such a policy will ever be implemented on a large scale must clearly be low. There are two important consequences of this pragmatism that shape the policies that are proposed and implemented.

First, the policies proposed tend to be small, have limited scope, and focus on a particular domain (e.g., food insecurity) rather than a more comprehensive set of institutions. They are tolerable to a budget-conscious public and political class. And they have a good chance of being implemented, thereby allowing us to chip away at poverty and inequality. The promise of being able to improve the lives of the underprivileged, and of being able to achieve some leveling of the playing field for privileged and underprivileged children, is powerful. Pragmatic researchers and policymakers are doubtless responsible for much of our current policy landscape, and they deserve to be congratulated for the successes of current anti-inequality program provision.

An extreme example of the small-scale pragmatism at the heart of inequality policy is the "nudge" philosophy derived from behavioral economics. Thaler and Sunstein describe a nudge as "any aspect of the choice architecture that alters people's behavior in a predictable way without forbidding any options or significantly changing their economic incentives. To count as a mere nudge, the intervention must be easy and cheap to avoid. Nudges are not mandates. Putting the fruit at eye level counts as a nudge. Banning junk food does not."[17]

Nudges were first proposed as a general approach to social policy around the turn of the twenty-first century, and the idea spread rapidly across the policy arena. Governments, seeing the potential for social change at low economic and political cost, introduced "nudge units" to identify social problems that could be solved with a nudge approach.[18] In the poverty and inequality field, nudge solutions include (a) summer text message prompts to the low-income high school students who registered for college in the spring but are at high risk of never enrolling in the fall,[19] (b) text messages that inform eligible individuals of available tax credits and benefits,[20] and (c) letter mailings to those who are known to be eligible for the EITC but have not claimed this benefit.[21]

Nudges are the very opposite of sweeping institutional reform. If a nudge were to straightforwardly replace the function of an institution, it would—by definition—no longer be a nudge. The possibility of nudges directly replacing institutional functions is therefore ruled out by design. Nudges are also unlikely to remediate for past harm. On the whole, nudges operate to recalibrate the decision calculus of individuals while preserving the current social structure. Note that insofar as nudges do have any "replacement" effect, as I label it, they operate through the intergenerational effects on children of a nudge aimed at parents. For example, in the text message intervention described above that prompts parents to read to children, the replacement function of the nudge operates for the children, and not for the parents who are the subject of the nudge. The principle that a nudge maintains the "choice architecture" (i.e., institutions and their functions) for a given individual is maintained.

The nudge is an especially extreme rendition of the more general tendency to prefer incremental reform. But it is indicative of our very circumscribed discourse and our preference for tailored interventions. And it is born of the pragmatism of social scientists and policymakers, who push to reduce inequality of opportunity even in the face of substantial economic and political constraints.

If one of the consequences of pragmatism is to generate a bias toward small-scale policy, another is that policies that are more expansive in size and scope tend not to be framed as such. The Earned Income Tax Credit (EITC) provides a sum of money to poor families that exceeds the sums recommended in some of the proposals for basic income, and yet the EITC is represented as straightforward "tax policy" rather than as an audacious rethinking of U.S. inequality policy. Similarly, early childhood intervention is, in its most encompassing form, a radical institutional intervention, as it involves replacing many of the functions that were previously viewed as belonging to the domain of the family and community. But early childhood intervention is rarely described as a radical reform. Indeed, the recent popularity of the term "intervention" as a label is striking in itself: the word derives from *intervenire*, a compound of the Latin words for "between" and "come." The implication is that the aim of an intervention is to "come between" a process and its outcome, rather than replace the process entirely. The term "intervention" defuses the radical content and intent of the policy. That we present radical interventions as non-radical is both pragmatic and understandable, but it is likely to further undermine claims that radical intervention is necessary.[22]

Scientific

Social scientists may be committed to pragmatism, but for most researchers the highest commitment is to science. The standard scientific study progresses by deriving hypotheses from theory, testing those hypotheses against empirical evidence, and drawing conclusions from the results of those tests that might be used to predict future outcomes or behavior.[23] In the inequality field, the empirical evidence brought to bear on scientific questions usually comes from randomized control trials, laboratory or field experiments, existing survey or administrative data sets, and ethnographic or interview data. Work on policy evaluation looks much like a standard scientific study, but there is rather more emphasis in this field on experimentation than on the analysis of existing data sets and the collection of qualitative data. The invention of policy is most frequently a three-stage process: first, a specific hypothesis is developed and tested in the course of normal scientific work; second, this research leads to policy proposals, which are then refined as specific interventions; and third, the interventions are tested on small and then large populations, to ensure that they have the desired effects and that they will "scale" (i.e., the effects will remain in place even when the policy is extended to a large population and when the implementation is not carried out under the watchful eye of a researcher).

A small-scale policy intervention is easily tested. A radical institutional change is not. No social scientist could state with a high level of certainty that a radical change would work as predicted, let alone convince policymakers to take the risk. To the extent that we have evidence on the power of radical initiatives, it has been gathered by unusually visionary politicians, scientists, and foundations that have been willing to undertake reform and experimentation that, although informed by evidence, lack the evidentiary foundation that is generally required in the contemporary policymaking environment.[24] Although there have been periods in U.S. history when government appeared to support the principle of radical reform—the New Deal and Johnson's Great Society, for example—the contemporary period is one in which incremental, scientifically established reforms are generally preferred. Ironically, contemporary radical initiatives often draw on research that originated in the Great Society period: an example of this phenomenon is the discussion of universal basic income (see Chapter 4). Although a similar policy was tested in several U.S. states in the 1960s and supported by the federal government under the auspices of the "negative income tax," almost all contemporary basic income initiatives in the United States are foundation-driven.[25]

A further potential "scientific" barrier to radical, institution-changing reform is trends not in policy but in professional social science. An increasing scientism and specialization within social science disciplines have generated pressure to catalog precise mechanisms that address small parts of the puzzle of inequality, without considering the web of policies and institutions that affect inequality of constraints. This is perhaps most obvious in contemporary quantitative social science, particularly in the experimental and quasi-experimental literature.[26] These methods make it possible to design exact tests of hypotheses, to nail down causes (given certain assumptions), and to establish the conditions under which those causes will lead to observed effects. But given that the aim of an experiment is to identify effects by holding all other variables constant, there is a necessary focus on well-defined and narrow questions.

Specialization within science is commonly understood to work to the benefit of human knowledge; a hallmark of science is that it relies upon the accumulation of knowledge across a great many individual scientists and research projects. But specialization also reduces the incentives to study certain types of effects that would be observable across multiple domains, and methods that involve the manipulation of a small number of factors necessarily exclude any possibility of amplifying or offsetting effects. This, in turn, increases the likelihood that policymakers will satisfice, because while it is easy to identify small interventions within a narrow domain that will produce better outcomes than the status quo, it is much harder to identify what would be needed to produce the optimal outcome across domains.[27] By focusing only on the fragmented impact of inequality across many small domains, the larger story is lost.

Ideological

Alongside the pragmatic and scientific explanations for why social scientists demur from proposing radical change is a class of explanations that relate to ideology. By "ideology," I mean those occasions when social scientists will choose to recommend small-scale rather than larger-scale change even when they are committed to reducing inequality of opportunity because they are also committed to another value or outcome. Three different dimensions of ideology are particularly important: (a) competing economic values, (b) a commitment to the integrity of existing institutions, and (c) the association of particular types of policy initiatives with strongly held political positions.[28]

Competing Economic Values

The most obvious alternative value that would reduce the chances of a social scientist pushing for radical change is a commitment to economic growth. Economic growth refers to the increase in the economic productivity of a society: societies produce goods and services that have market value, and the extent to which this market value increases over time describes the extent to which those societies have experienced economic growth. The dramatic rate of growth experienced in the United States during the nineteenth and twentieth centuries raised the standard of living of all Americans, with downstream effects for health and welfare.[29] Healthy economic growth is an outcome that many social scientists and policymakers are strongly committed to; the economist Kenneth Rogoff describes growth as the "be all and end all" of modern macroeconomic policy.[30] The depth of a scientist's ideological commitment to economic growth tends to vary by discipline: sociologists rarely express any commitment to growth, whereas economists typically privilege it.

For a person committed to economic growth, the existence of inequality of outcome is not necessarily problematic. There are two important reasons for this. First, the policies that might best encourage growth might also increase inequality, but at the same time they might increase the welfare of all, including that of the worst off. The loss in relative financial status may be outweighed, therefore, by an increase in absolute financial status. Second, inequality of outcome is thought to be important in order to encourage economic growth, for why should individuals work hard, innovate, and invest without the incentives introduced by inequality? The precise level of inequality needed to induce this incentive effect is not well defined, but the highest rates of growth during the twentieth century were observed when the United States was far from full equality. Thus not only is inequality of outcome unproblematic for those who are primarily committed to economic growth, but it might even be necessary to achieve that growth.

The commitment to economic growth is a powerful ideological alternative to a commitment to inequality reduction. If high growth can improve the welfare of the bottom of the income distribution to a greater extent than inequality reduction in the context of low growth can, perhaps growth should be the goal.[31] And if small-scale policies can produce reductions in inequality alongside economic growth, it would be reasonable to prefer such policies over more-radical, growth-threatening change.

While the positive effects of economic growth should not be ignored, there is good reason to question whether the trade-off between economic growth and inequality reduction is real. A person fully committed to economic growth must also be concerned about inequality of outcome: too much inequality appears to be detrimental to growth.[32] There is also reason to question why inequality of *opportunity* is an acceptable by-product of growth. As I discussed in Chapter 1, inequality of outcome for the parental generation turns into inequality of opportunity for the child generation, and even if we accept the view that inequality of outcome provides necessary incentives for adults to work hard and thereby promote economic growth, it is not obvious why any child should be motivated to work hard on the basis that his or her parent is privileged. Furthermore, for the child who grows up underprivileged, the constraints imposed by these "incentives" on the parental generation are likely to inhibit both the development of human capital and human flourishing. Given that a loss of talent of this magnitude will clearly be damaging to economic growth, the relationship between inequality of outcome and inequality of opportunity cannot be ignored, even by those who would, all else being equal, favor growth policy over inequality policy.

Commitment to the Integrity of Existing Institutions

We have seen that ideological conflict on the economic dimension might lead social scientists to favor small-scale policy over radical change. Another form of ideological conflict occurs with respect to normative views on existing social institutions. An example of this situation is the extent to which societies allow parents to make decisions on behalf of their children, even when those decisions have consequences for equality of opportunity. The commitment to the sanctity of the family is so widely shared that we rule out a range of state policy on this issue without even being conscious of doing so.

It is obvious that parents make investments in their own children that they do not make in the children of others. Because levels of resources that can be used for social reproduction vary among families, parental investments are likely to be higher for children from privileged backgrounds than for those from underprivileged backgrounds. This becomes clear when we consider the direct transfer of money from parents to children, but it is also evident in the case of non-pecuniary transfers that are potentially consequential for future educational and occupational success.[33] This distinctive bond between parents and children is deeply damaging to equality of opportunity.[34] If we were to take a group of ten children at birth, and suggest that two of those children should be chosen at random to grow up in poverty and two should be chosen at random to grow up with all of the riches that they might desire, we might immediately see that the underprivileged children and the privileged children face strikingly different sets of constraints on opportunity.[35] We might also conclude that this is unfair, and that it is self-evident that policy should eliminate the effects of such a birth lottery on life outcomes. But when we add in familial bonds (the algorithm that links those children to the socioeconomic context within which they will grow up), the policy solution is less clear. This is because the family bond is regarded as sacrosanct.[36]

Our commitments to familial autonomy and to the special bond between parents and child are in sharp conflict with our commitment to equality of opportunity. And the family is just one social institution with ideological underpinnings. A similar valuation of autonomy might be found with respect to communities, religious institutions, or schools, to name but a few other social institutions. Indeed, many of the beliefs that Americans hold about what is "right" or "reasonable" or "fair" in the policy domain may rest upon their understandings of the appropriate functions of social institutions and the conditions under which the sanctity of those institutions might be violated. The ideological conflict between the aim of equality of opportunity and the aim of preserving social institutions may well explain why some social scientists would advocate small-scale adjustments rather than radical change: these scientists may simply believe that there is little public or political appetite for undermining institutional bonds and institutional autonomy. In this sense, small-scale policy changes represent an ideological compromise, allowing some reductions in inequality of opportunity while largely preserving the sanctity of existing institutions.

The commitment to familial autonomy is not unwavering, and the public and politicians alike appear to have a great deal of tolerance for violating the institutions of the underprivileged. In fact, where institutions are perceived to be "failing," intervention is not just tolerated, it is expected. The promotion of marriage, for example, is such a conventional policy that it is included in major party platforms in many countries, even though it is undoubtedly a substantial intrusion into familial autonomy for the state to insist on the precise form of any partnership. And one could list any number of other policies that aim to recalibrate the decisions of less-privileged families and communities in order to bring them in line with ideological principles drawn from political or religious doctrine. These proposals have in common the goal of remaking institutions in keeping with an idealized model of what social institutions should look like. Rarely is the main goal to increase equality of opportunity.

Politics and Partisanship

The final type of ideological conflict is the association of particular types of policy initiatives with strongly held political positions. It is well known that partisanship can become a lens through which we understand the world.[37] Social scientists engaged in policy might be influenced by their own partisanship, but they might also be influenced by the fear that others will perceive them as partisan: most social scientists do not wish to have their work "tarnished" by the suggestion that they advocate partisan interests. In either case, the result will be to bias policy recommendations toward small-scale solutions and away from radical change.

Most social science professors have well-developed political views, and research shows that these views are probably further to the left than those of most Americans.[38] No doubt diversity across disciplines does occur within the social sciences, but the group of researchers proposing policy solutions is likely drawn disproportionately from those with left-leaning, liberal viewpoints.[39] It is quite possible that these political positions have little effect on the types of policy solutions that are proposed to address the equality of opportunity problem. After all, social scientists are trained in the Weberian tradition that "statements of fact are one thing, statements of value another, and any confusing of the two is impermissible."[40] But it seems likely that political views do impinge on the types of solutions that are proposed for the equality-of-opportunity problem, particularly the extent to which one ideological aim is favored over another (e.g., growth vs. equality, sanctity of the family vs. equality of opportunity).[41] The tendency for some social scientists to embrace left-wing ideologies probably generates a bias toward rather than away from the world of radical policy initiatives, but to the extent to which existing political ideologies are unsympathetic to radical policies, social scientists committed to those ideologies might choose to advocate smaller-scale policies that are consistent with the aims of a mainstream party platform.

The type of ideological consideration just described leads to social scientists' shying away from recommending change that conflicts with their own political values. But another type of ideological consideration may come into play as well: a concern that the association of radical policy initiatives with non-mainstream political organizations will lead to a loss of scientific status or power for those who propose such initiatives. To propose radical change is to align oneself with voices that are generally discredited in mainstream public discourse. If proposals for radical change come only from, say, Marxist or anarchist political voices, academic researchers might reasonably be concerned that similar proposals will lead to accusations of naïveté, ideological bias, or lack of competence.[42] This creates a vicious circle: if scientists pull back from engaging with and advocating radical views, those views become discredited. Withholding the legitimacy of science from proposals for radical change makes it ever more difficult for academic researchers to push for radical policy solutions.

This is not to say that stereotypically "radical" voices currently dominate those pushing for radical policy solutions with regard to inequality: Marxists, anarchists, and other radical thinkers are in fact rarely found on the front lines of policy development and implementation. Within academia, radicalism is too frequently expressed through regression into disciplinary disagreements and emphatic rejection of the practical considerations and compromises that are part of day-to-day policy work. Accompanying this tendency is a rejection of the markers that usually accompany competence and legitimacy, such as adherence to standard scientific protocols or engagement with empirical evidence.[43] The distance between self-identified radical thinkers and those who drive policy is therefore significant.

Under what conditions have we seen radical policies gaining ground in scientific discourse? The rapid spread of early childhood interventions in recent years provides a useful example. As I argue in Chapter 4, early childhood intervention is a radical policy initiative, in that the aim is to reduce inequality of opportunity by replacing a set of existing institutional functions. In addition to research evidence that shows the effectiveness of early childhood policy, two factors have been particularly important in the transition of such policy to being now regarded as "business as usual."

First, although early childhood intervention has a long history, this type of policy initiative found a powerful advocate in the economist James Heckman, a Nobel Prize winner who alongside many other social scientists pushed for reform. His backing of early childhood intervention—and in particular, his support for the most extensive form of the policy—was referenced by the Obama administration, and it helped to move this radical reform into the policy mainstream.[44] Prominent economist advocates have had some success in increasing the visibility of other non-incremental policies; William Darity Jr. and Darrick Hamilton, for example, have proposed a suite of policies designed to remediate racial and economic inequality, and Emmanuel Saez and Gabriel Zucman have developed new tax plans to address income and wealth inequality. These policy proposals have received much public attention, and some elements have been taken up by politicians with an interest in radical reform.[45]

Second, advocates for reform have primarily used the language of "return on investment" to make their case.[46] There has been little emphasis on a moral imperative that societies should foster the development of the young, presumably because over the course of the twentieth century moralistic arguments in favor of policy initiatives were discredited in favor of arguments based on cost-benefit analysis. Thus the argument in favor of early childhood intervention has been that this policy encourages economic growth (largely through its effects on the development of human capital) and that any amount spent on intervention in early childhood will be significantly offset by personal and societal returns in adulthood. This strategy illustrates the importance of framing radical policy intervention in language that appeals to the widest possible audience.[47]

Self-interest

I include the final category, "self-interest," for reasons of completeness, although it is unlikely that this is the primary motivation for most of the social scientists working in the inequality field. Full professors earn an average of more than $130,000, a figure that is substantially higher than the median American income.[48] Professors also have high rates of intergenerational reproduction of socioeconomic status: the child of a professor has a good chance of also becoming a professor.[49] Although many professors wholeheartedly support increasing equality of opportunity, a radical change in social institutions would improve the chances of children from the bottom of the socioeconomic hierarchy at the cost of the children of these professors. Small-scale changes, on the other hand, would protect the individual interests of social scientists and their families.

Although the economic self-interest explanation is logically possible, it is surely very far down the list of reasons why social scientists would advocate small-scale policies rather than radical reform, not least because few scientists would ever imagine that their research could have such impact that it would jeopardize their own interests. It is more plausible that self-interest operates with respect to career incentives. Those social scientists who value attention from policymakers and politicians know that small-scale interventions are more likely to be embraced than radical reforms; a "pragmatic" position with respect to policy may therefore be a self-interested position in disguise. Further, personal motivations are likely to be primarily unconscious, originating in the comfort and familiarity of the status quo.

The reasons why social scientists focus on small-scale policy changes are many and wide-ranging. Any one of them might be sufficient to persuade a researcher to choose to push for incremental change rather than large-scale reform. Taken together, the set is overwhelming. So why even consider proposing radical change? Why dream?

CHAPTER 3

BRICK BY BRICK

If there is a unifying commitment among advocates of targeted interventions, it is that substantial and persistent reductions in inequality of opportunity would be possible, if only we could discover the right interventions. The assumption is that with the appropriate bundle of interventions we could reduce inequality of opportunity to acceptable levels. Hidden from view in this approach, however, are the institutional roots of inequality of opportunity. As I described in Chapter 2, an incremental and small-scale policy agenda pushes forward hand in hand with a mechanistic understanding of the social world, where social processes are pulled out of their institutional context and individually examined. Individual social mechanisms are matched to individual policies, with the implicit understanding that adding an intervention to the policy landscape is comparable to adding a mechanism to the body of social scientific knowledge.

Science progresses because of the accumulation of small pieces of knowledge, collected and contributed by a very large number of researchers. The eventual aim, although we rarely state it directly, is to understand how every feature of our world came to exist and persist, and how each feature interacts with all of the others. It is far from obvious that this is an optimal model for policy. It is surely not practical that a discrete new intervention be developed to address each small mechanism that produces inequality. A further difficulty is that unlike science, in which new facts and understandings can be added one by one to the body of knowledge, if interventions are added one at a time there is every possibility that the desired end result may be under-mined by the privileged before the body of policy is complete. An incremental approach means that the optimal policy mix will remain unknown until far into the future, at which point some of those policies might have already fallen to subversion.[1] Given these risks, it is not sensible to base policy infrastructure on simple accumulation.

The principle of accumulation may be central to scientific progress, but there is another (related) principle at the heart of most scientific endeavors: scientists search for a set of basic and fundamental laws that can account for a range of observable facts. How much effort we should devote to discovering laws relative to discovering facts is the subject of much debate in the philoso-phy of science, but it is perhaps not too controversial to state that if a pattern of empirical regularities can be understood as the outcome of a general pro-cess, we are likely to improve the quality of our predictions when faced with a new or previously undocumented phenomenon.[2] Whether or not the search for laws should guide scientific discovery, a strong argument exists for bas-ing policy architecture and institutional design on knowledge of both general processes and particular empirical findings. While it is undoubtedly true that any individual policy should be brought to scale only after there is evidence that it works, in designing comprehensive policy programs it is important to keep a clear view of the fundamental processes that produce inequality of constraints, not just the individual instances of those processes.

In this chapter, I propose an outline of some of these fundamental pro-cesses. I will describe a world structured by social institutions, a world in which every barrier to opportunity can be traced back to the function of a social institution. If our aim is to reduce inequality of constraints, and thereby inequality of opportunity, these institutional barriers must be addressed.

The Building Blocks

At the core of the general inequality-producing process that I will describe is a set of social institutions. These institutions serve as the building blocks of inequality, and they must therefore lie at the center of any scientific under-standing of inequality and any large-scale policy solution.

Social institutions are fundamental because they provide the framework within which our individual lives are constructed; through their effects on individuals, they produce "relatively stable patterns of human activity with

respect to fundamental problems" that all societies must confront.[3] The common solutions that societies have developed in response to such problems may
be thought of as the "functions" of social institutions. For example, the social
institutions of marriage and the family allow societies to create and rear children successfully; the family, community, and parts of the welfare state provide food, safety, and shelter, while medical institutions (alongside families
and communities) provide health-related support. Functions of the family
thus include the creation and rearing of children; sub-functions may also be
identified to delineate precise tasks such as language training, the development of social skills, or the development of a moral code. Of particular importance in the structure of social institutions is what I label the "core" social
institutions for child development, such as the family, the economic system,
the health care system, education, and the state.[4]

We grow and develop through our contact with social institutions. Individuals enter the world as biological objects—albeit objects already shaped by
their relationship to the social world as mediated through the mother—and
are reshaped by the social institutions that they encounter throughout the life
course. Individuals are changed by social institutions both because the institutions actively modify and restructure the individual and because the institutions alter the contexts within which any individual will make decisions.[5]

With regard to the changes that social institutions produce by modifying
individuals, we may distinguish between changes that are "biological" and
changes in the "social self."[6]

Biological changes refer to changes in the structures of the body, perhaps
particularly those that take place in the brain. Neuroscience research shows
that brain structure develops through interaction and experience, especially
throughout early childhood and adolescence, when brain plasticity is highest.[7]
A child's exposure to language, to interaction, to stress, and to other experiences will therefore have consequences for that child's physical form. The
effects of the lead poisoning in Flint, Michigan, for example, will be long-
lasting for the children who were exposed, since lead causes irreversible damage to the brain and other organs.[8]

In addition to inducing biological modifications, social institutions may
also induce changes in the "social self," including changes in aspirations,
motivations, personality characteristics, cultural understandings, and social
or technical skills. Some institutions are even specifically designed to produce
these changes: if our education system did not encourage skill development or

the development of certain personality characteristics, it would be viewed as having failed in its central mission.

Changes to both the biological self and the social self have the potential to be consequential, particularly if they occur in childhood. This is not simply because children are biologically and socially more pliable than adults, but also because human life courses are deeply path-dependent, and any change has the potential to alter the entire life course from that point forward. Changes that occur early in life therefore have the most time during which to exert their effects, although many later-life changes may also have substantial effects.

Even when social institutions do not generate changes in the individuals who encounter them, they may potentially have substantial influence by demarcating the boundaries surrounding decisions. We make many decisions over our lifetimes, not only in relation to the particular scenes and situations that we confront on a day-to-day basis, but also with respect to our investments in physical, social, or human capital. The chances that an individual will choose to go to college may increase during a recession, for example, because the labor market exerts less of a pull for recent high school graduates when jobs are more difficult to find. Although it is natural to focus on how social institutions change our fundamental natures, our decisions can sometimes have longer-lasting and more consequential effects.

We are, then, the product of our interactions with social institutions. It is inevitable that the roots of inequality are also to be found here.

The Golden Key

Social institutions would have no relevance to the production of inequality of opportunity unless they themselves were changed by socioeconomic resources. Social scientists have spent much time documenting how the functions of institutions are altered by the presence or absence of resources, and the constraints that these alterations place on the individuals interacting with institutions. We know that well-resourced families can make substantial investments in child development activities, which will pay off in higher test scores and better educational opportunities.[9] We know that well-resourced neighborhoods can make substantial investments in public goods such as libraries and parks, which will pay off in reduced crime rates and increased well-being.[10] We know that well-resourced schools can make substantial investments in student support and instruction, which will pay off in higher graduation rates and labor market success.[11]

But individuals from different backgrounds face different constraints on opportunity not simply because they interact with institutions that differ with respect to resources. In fact, they face an entire network of interlocking institutions, each of which creates constraints related to resources. It is the interconnected nature of the institutional structure that offers such a high degree of protection for the opportunities of privileged children.[12] And it is the interconnected nature of the institutional structure that is overlooked in a small-scale, mechanistic, and incremental approach to policy.

To demonstrate the importance of interconnections, we may contrast the lives of a privileged child, Chloe, and an underprivileged child, Kaylah, as they embark on their journeys to adulthood through their interactions with social institutions.[13] From the moment of birth, these children are enmeshed in social institutions no less encompassing or consequential for future life chances than the wombs from which they emerged. At birth, both children become members of a family, and simultaneously begin to interact directly with other social institutions: the hospital staff involved in a safe delivery, the community of which the family is a part, and perhaps also a religion, should the family be so inclined. Importantly, Chloe is advantaged even at the moment of birth. Prenatal conditions are likely to be more favorable for a privileged baby than for a less-privileged one, given the differences in health, nutrition, and stress between privileged and underprivileged mothers.[14] And from this moment onward, the children will always be embedded in a set of institutions that are influenced by socioeconomic resources.

Chloe was born to a privileged family, in a university hospital with state-of-the-art facilities. Her birth went according to plan, but her parents could feel reassured that had anything unexpected happened, the hospital would have been able to deal with it quickly. Her parents had comprehensive health insurance, which covered all of the costs of the birth, and the medical staff were oriented to providing holistic care. During her few days in the hospital, Chloe was carefully monitored in case any problems developed, and her parents were able to focus on mother-child bonding, effective feeding, and other practices that are encouraged in the field of preventive medicine.[15] Because the socioeconomic status of the doctors and other medical staff was similar to that of Chloe's parents, there was a strong "cultural match" between her parents and the medical institution, reducing the anxiety and stress induced by being in the hospital, increasing her parents' perceived control over important decisions, and allowing all ambiguities about care and medical advice to be resolved.[16] Once she was released from the hospital, Chloe went to live with her family in a home that was safe and secure, in a neighborhood that was safe and secure. She was not even a week old, and she already had an entire network of institutions working on her behalf.

Kaylah's parents were poor, with a family income in the bottom 10 percent of all family incomes in the United States. Although some poor families might be lucky enough to receive high-quality medical care, Kaylah's was not, and so her birth experience differed substantially from Chloe's. Her parents did not have access to private health insurance; the costs of the pregnancy and birth were instead covered by Medicaid.[17] Medical treatment was guaranteed, but many hospitals do not accept Medicaid payments because of the low reimbursement rate, and so Kaylah's mother gave birth a considerable distance from home in an overburdened hospital.[18] Her mother was in a poor state of general health coming into the pregnancy. She had lost a previous child after a long and painful labor that the doctors handled badly, and Kaylah's birth was also a difficult one.[19] Medical adversities are known to be damaging to the health of both mother and child, and they also create substantial disruption in the child's crucial first days. When Kaylah was released from the hospital, she went home to a rented house that had been poorly maintained, in a neighborhood with high rates of crime and disorder.[20] Kaylah's parents were together at the time of the birth, although the relationship was rocky, and this had consequences for the availability of financial and emotional support.[21] Before the birth, Kaylah's mother had been the primary breadwinner, but she received no maternity leave benefits and the birth therefore generated further financial anxiety and stress. In contrast to her more-privileged counterpart, Kaylah, within her first days of life, encountered flaws in the institutions that surrounded her. Each of those flaws had potential consequences for her opportunities later in life.

One approach to improving Kaylah's life and the lives of other underprivileged children like her would be to address each of the individual institutional failures. Medicaid programs could be improved, giving the family access to high-quality health care. Housing programs could provide underprivileged families with additional resources to secure their homes. Parental leave programs could be implemented, allowing mothers and fathers some breathing room after the birth of a new child. Each of the problems identified could, in principle, be corrected by policy. We might likewise anticipate correcting each of the new problems that will arise as Kaylah moves through childhood, adolescence, and early adulthood. If it were possible to address each and every difference between Chloe's and Kaylah's institutional surroundings with a comprehensive set of interventions, it might be possible to move toward equalizing the opportunities available to the two children. However, there are three important themes that can be identified in our young children's lives, themes that will recur time and again.

First, socioeconomic resources touch all institutions. Most obviously, the quality of health care is influenced by money, since health care has been marketized in the United States.[22] Childbirth, an event that for thousands of years was managed by the family and the local community, is now managed by the medical system for a charge. Other institutions are also shaped by resources. For example, the safety and security of the child's home depend upon whether the family has access to enough money and socioeconomic privilege to make it possible for them to buy or rent a well-maintained home in a safe neighborhood. Access to adequate resources provides a safety net for parents, so that during the period surrounding the birth it is not necessary for either parent to work, and even in the absence of parental leave the period will be free of financial stress. Resources also exert their effects on the child indirectly: because marriage is increasingly linked to socioeconomic status, those with resources find it easier to marry than those without. The family structures of our privileged and underprivileged children—from which the child's financial and emotional support is ultimately derived—are not bought and paid for directly, but are certainly influenced by resources. Each institution with which the child comes into contact from birth onward is shaped by socioeconomic resources.

Second, not all of the differences that we observe when comparing institutions serving the underprivileged to those serving the privileged are flaws. To be sure, when privileged parents purchase their spaces in exclusive maternity wards, they are likely buying a better quality of health care for the mother and her newborn child. Accommodations for the privileged are often safer, more spacious, more conveniently located, and more attractive than accommodations for the underprivileged. A clear hierarchy of value is evident in these institutional functions: money buys better quality. Other differences between the typical privileged and underprivileged institutions come to be seen as flaws only in the context of current configurations of the labor market and society.

One example pertains to the cultural differences between privileged and underprivileged families. Privileged families raise children who develop different patterns of speech, different forms of self-presentation, and different styles of social interaction than those observed among underprivileged children.[23] It would be hard to argue that any expression of these cultural characteristics is inherently better or worse than another, and yet in the context of our current labor market there is a payoff to having cultural characteristics that "fit."[24] Many jobs, including those that pay well, value the types of cultural and social characteristics that are associated with being born into a privileged family. Thus cultural differences across families have labor market effects only because society is shaped by the dominant culture.

Third, social institutions offer a coherent and complementary external set of functions for the privileged, all operating to improve opportunities for their children. Socioeconomic resources have shaped the provision of each of the functions integral to child development, both within the institution of the family and in all of the institutions external to the family. This produces a neat alignment across institutions—and particularly across the core institutions of the family, the health care system, education, and the state—such that the privileged parents can trust that all of those functions, which lie outside of their direct control, will nevertheless work for the benefit of their child. For all of the focus on the "helicopter parenting" of the anxious rich, one of the immense but unspoken privileges that these parents enjoy is that their resources usually make it possible for them to freely choose the form of the social institutions that their child comes in contact with, and to assume that those institutions can be trusted.

In contrast, underprivileged parents face a dual problem. They do have a set of functions under their direct control—the provision of accommodations, for example—but they are constrained in providing these functions because of a lack of resources. In addition, they cannot trust that external institutions will always work for their children. Their children encounter a fractured web of institutions, some functioning well and others functioning poorly. The consequences of this are threefold. First, there is likely an interactive effect of having access to a coherent web of institutions, such that the benefits of the full set far outweigh the benefits of a partial set. Second, even if it were possible for underprivileged parents to construct an equivalent coherent institutional web, it would require substantial time, thought, and effort to do so. These resources are all in short supply when the more proximate aim of financial solvency is foremost in the parents' minds. And third, unlike the children of the privileged, underprivileged children must confront the fact that social institutions do not work in cooperation to improve their opportunities, a realization that presumably has profound consequences for levels of stress, anxiety, and externalized trust.[25]

These themes have important implications for the inequality policy agenda. Given that we have not yet reached the point at which interventions can be matched to each of the mechanisms that produce inequality—particularly because many additional mechanisms are presumably still waiting to be discovered—all interventions are operating in an unfriendly institutional environment. No intervention could correct all of the identified institutional failures, and any positive effects of a single intervention therefore exist in an unfriendly context. It is clear that we must dispense with the idea that any single targeted intervention could be the "magic bullet" that all policymakers hope to find. A magic bullet would need to overcome not only the precise institutional failure that it was designed to address but also the myriad failures in the entire institutional network surrounding the underprivileged child. There is, of course, immense temptation to describe new interventions as if they were magic bullets, given the standard career incentives and the necessity to publicize and fund new initiatives. Nevertheless, magic bullet interventions simply cannot exist when the underprivileged do not have access to the same coherent web of institutions that the privileged enjoy.

These themes recur throughout the child's life course. If we were to visit Chloe and Kaylah on the eve of their first birthday, we would find two children who have already been molded by the institutions within which they are embedded, and who are being further molded with each new experience. In the early years of life, profound biological and neurological changes occur in response to environmental stimuli, and the way the children are shaped at this point may be particularly consequential for the educational and occupational opportunities that will arise later in their lives.[26]

Importantly, the differences between Chloe's privileged household and Kaylah's underprivileged one have continued to play out since birth in much the way one might have expected. In the girls' first year, the most prominent social institution in their lives has been the family, and the family has served as the sole mediator in their access to other institutions during this time: when the children have been touched by the health care system, or the community, or the state, that touch has been managed by the parents or other family members. Provisions for health care still differ substantially for Chloe and Kaylah, although Medicaid will continue to cover Kaylah's costs, ensuring that she receives necessary treatment if her parents are able to arrange it. The quality and safety of their accommodations also continue to differ, a difference that will have consequences for their health and well-being throughout childhood. The leading cause of injury and death among children is accidents, and as Kaylah begins to explore the world around her, she is more likely than Chloe to suffer injury or death from fire, traffic accidents, or poisoning.[27]

Moreover, in addition to the institutional differences between privileged and underprivileged households that were largely present when the girls were born, new types of institutional differences have emerged. Some of those new differences are particularly consequential for future opportunities because they occur in institutions that induce changes in both the biological self and the social self. One prominent difference between Chloe and Kaylah has to do with child care. In the first year, children are socialized into the family and the wider community; they are exposed to language, to the rules of social interaction, and to emotional support. Much of this training, although it may appear to be basic "rules of the game," is in fact essential for cognitive and behavioral development. It occurs deliberately, through targeted play and language teaching, but also unintentionally, in the course of normal day-to-day interactions. In both cases, the type of child care that the girls receive will affect their development. Where privileged parents themselves undertake child care, they can purchase all that is required to encourage child development and they also have the opportunity to devote time and concentration to training. When they outsource child care, money can purchase a higher quality of care, as well as greater control over the form of that care and training. While Kaylah's parents may have to rely on friends or relatives for care, Chloe's parents can afford one-on-one care in their own home or in a nursery setting.

Resources matter in these early years, both because they allow the acquisition of higher-quality child care, and because they make it possible for privileged parents to solve problems and pursue aims that go beyond concerns with basic survival. Chloe's parents can devote a great deal of cognitive bandwidth to "investing" in her development, precisely because they do not have to devote that bandwidth to remaining solvent and surviving.[28] Socioeconomic differences in the amount of time spent with children are greatest during these early years, and Chloe's mother is likely to spend an hour longer per day engaged in child care and developmentally important play activities than Kaylah's mother does.[29]

When privileged parents outsource child care to other institutions—notably, the labor market—they can trust that those institutions will similarly work to their child's benefit. If a particular arrangement fails in this regard, the parents can simply buy another. When underprivileged parents turn to the labor market for child care, they cannot afford care of similar quality. Kaylah's parents must again confront the fact that even if they carry out their child-training function perfectly, the web of institutions to which the family has access is flawed and fractured.

This problem is only compounded as the girls age and come into contact with more and more social institutions. As they gain independence, they spend more time outside of the family unit, and as time outside the family increases, so does the amount of contact that they have with other institutions. In particular, a growing child will soon spend more time interacting with the school than with her family. It is here that the coherent-vs.-fractured institutional web problem is perhaps most stark. Because public funding is tied to the tax base of the geographical areas in which schools are located, schools in poor neighborhoods have less funding than schools in rich neighborhoods.[30] The school is responsible for the crucial function of training young people for further education and the labor market, and the evidence suggests that a lack of money in poor school districts undermines that function.[31] Kaylah's school has high teacher turnover, large class sizes, and a lack of basic educational materials, even though it serves a very poor neighborhood where many of the children would benefit from additional educational support. In contrast to Kaylah's situation, Chloe's neighborhood is served by well-funded and high-quality schools, and if Chloe had not been able to access these schools, her parents would have either moved to a district with better schools or paid for private schooling.[32] Once Chloe's access to a high-quality school was secured, her parents could rest on the assumption that the school would (largely) function for the benefit of their child.

The neighborhood in which a child grows up usually determines the type of schooling that the child will receive, and it also determines the form of a number of other social institutions.[33] Along with schools, neighborhoods are strongly affected by decisions and policies imposed by the state, and since many of the amenities in poor neighborhoods are funded from the local tax base, a poor neighborhood has less money to spend on amenities than a richer neighborhood does.[34] A rich neighborhood, in contrast, offers amenities that aid the development of both the biological self and the social self: libraries, green spaces, and community theaters, to name but a few. Chloe's parents know that when their daughter is outside the family unit and interacting with the local community, she will be surrounded by institutions that safeguard her future opportunities. But Kaylah's parents cannot easily choose the neighborhood in which their daughter will grow up—though it is clear that their current neighborhood has flaws when compared to a rich neighborhood—and thus they live in the full knowledge that Kaylah's opportunities may be restricted even if the family works hard to protect them. Research evidence suggests that when poor families *are* given the opportunity to move to lower-poverty neighborhoods, their children grow up to have better educational and employment outcomes than those who did not have the same opportunity.[35] In other words, when resource constraints are removed, underprivileged families work to construct institutional webs that will protect the opportunities of their children in just the same way as privileged families do.

Webs of high-quality institutions are so beneficial to child development because they provide support for the development of all of the components of the biological and social self. The principle that there is substantial pay-off to the integration of developmental supports across institutions is well established in social science. Research shows, for example, that young children who experience supportive home *and* child care environments exhibit better-developed socio-emotional skills than children who experience just one supportive institution, while young children with neither of these supports do worst of all.[36] Reports produced by the National Academies of Sciences, Engineering, and Medicine that synthesize the evidence on healthy social and behavioral development similarly emphasize the importance of maximizing children's exposure to multiple high-quality institutional contexts.[37] Further, Rucker Johnson and Kirabo Jackson show that the beneficial developmental effects of multiple high-quality institutions persist into adulthood. In their study of the effects of Head Start on a range of outcomes in adulthood (including earnings), Johnson and Jackson found that Head Start participants experienced better outcomes when they subsequently attended well-funded K–12 schools. The study concludes: "For poor children, the combined benefits of growing up in districts/counties with *both* greater Head Start spending and K–12 per pupil spending are significantly greater than the sum of the independent effects of the two investments in isolation."[38]

Chloe's privileged access to a set of high-quality institutions offers her the maximum opportunity to develop her talents. At the point of transition to adulthood, the girls will gain further independence from the family, their socialization process all but complete. But Chloe and Kaylah are likely to make the transition to adulthood at different ages. Chloe is almost certain to go to college, where she will continue to receive her parents' support, and as a consequence of going to college she is likely to enter the labor market, marry, and have children later than most of her cohort. Kaylah, on the other hand, is unlikely to go to college, is more likely to enter the low-skilled and low-paid labor market after the end of compulsory schooling, and is more likely to marry and have children early.[39] During these transitions, dynamics similar to those already identified play out over and over again. Yet as the girls have grown in independence, a new feature of the institutional network has become more prominent, and it is a feature that will remain prominent throughout their adult lives: the safety net.

When we discuss the "safety net," we focus on the role of social welfare in supporting the underprivileged; the label is seen to be appropriate because these programs "catch" those who might otherwise "fall." But the most substantial safety net in this country is not a collection of government programs. Rather, it is the insurance that all privileged children can rely on from birth onward: the "insurance" that stems from being born into a privileged family.

As Chloe ages, her independence grows, and the direct control of the family over her life diminishes. She is likely to make mistakes on her path to adulthood, mistakes that could undermine all hopes of educational and occupational success. Perhaps Chloe misbehaves in high school, and receives warnings about bad grades. Perhaps the misbehavior tips into misdemeanor, and comes to the attention of law enforcement. In that event, Chloe's parents are likely to spring into action to prevent her from falling too far from the desired path. They will be aided in their efforts by the coherence of the institutional web surrounding the child. Because Chloe is likely to live in a privileged neighborhood, her behavior is more likely to be perceived as "out of character" or a "cry for help" rather than as an indicator of serious deviance. Because Chloe attends a school where behavioral problems are seen infrequently, the school is more likely to respond to the behavior with remedy rather than punishment. Because her parents belong to a dominant and high-status cultural group, they are more likely to be able to smooth over problems with the school and the police. All of the relevant institutions are operating together to protect Chloe's future: the safety net ensures that a privileged child's misbehavior is a blemish on, not a determinant of, the remainder of her life course.

After Chloe and Kaylah make the transition to adulthood, their quality of life and their life chances will chiefly be determined by their own occupational and economic attainments. But the safety net will appear periodically in Chloe's life, and has the potential to continue to ease her way through new transitions and interactions among institutions. It will be there when she needs help to purchase a house, or when she needs a contact to get a job, or when she needs to interact with a new institution in a new region. It will be available to her when her own children are born, and will support their development and well-being. Nevertheless, at this point the safety net is unlikely to substantially improve Chloe's life chances, because by adulthood the opportunities available to our two women are largely baked in. One of the ironies of the contemporary version of the American Dream is that almost all of the individual actions and decisions that are regarded as essential ingredients of success are frontloaded in childhood and adolescence, when the child is a dependent. Although in principle it would be possible to provide second chances for children who had experienced disrupted paths to adulthood, in practice second chances are few and far between. We have worked our way through but a fraction of these women's lives, but there will be only limited opportunities for them to achieve the Dream after this point.

Nothing that I have described as a feature of Kaylah's life allows us to predict with certainty that her future is compromised relative to those of other children. She may be unaffected by her experiences, she may be affected by some experiences but receive treatment at some other point in her life course that compensates for anything lost, or she may be affected by her experiences but luck into a good outcome.[40] Social science cannot yet predict what will unfold in any individual life course, but it does tell us that, on average, children who grow up in poverty have worse prospects than children who grow up in affluence. The descriptions of Chloe's and Kaylah's life courses make it crystal clear that even if a standard measure of equality of opportunity were to show no differences in eventual outcomes between privileged and underprivileged children, these children were not operating under equal *constraints*. Whether or not the institutional constraints can be compensated for later in life, one of our children faced barriers to flourishing that the other child did not.

The Institutional Web

The web of institutions within which our children sit is more properly described as an institutional network. In this section I will examine some of the sociological properties of this network in more detail, outline why the network is so important in the generation of inequality of constraints, and discuss the consequences for our inequality-of-opportunity policy agenda.

I have described a child's journey to adulthood as a series of interactions with a number of core social institutions. The quality of functions provided by each of these institutions is affected by resources, so that during each interaction with an institution a privileged child is likely to encounter better-quality functions than an underprivileged child does. It is the structure of institutions that generates inequality of constraints, by providing a clear path to educational and labor market opportunities for the privileged but not for the underprivileged. It is easy to recognize the malign influence of socioeconomic resources on institutions when we examine each institution individually. It is less easy to discern the interconnections among institutions, and the malign influence of resources on these interconnections.

Institutions are connected both through the focal child (an institution-child-institution link, labeled a "conveyance" link), and through the linkages that are formed when institutions are forced to "interact" (an institution-institution link, labeled a "fortification" link).[41] Figure 1.i provides a visual representation of the relationships between institutions and the child.

The conveyance link arises because one institution produces a change in an individual that then has consequences for the individual's interaction with other institutions. This change might be in the individual's biological or social self; in either case, because the individual has been changed, a subsequent institutional interaction will be affected.[42] As discussed earlier, socioeconomic resources influence institutions and the quality of functions that they provide: when an underprivileged individual interacts with one institution providing low-quality functions, she will suffer harm to her biological/social self, and her interactions with other social institutions will suffer as a consequence.[43] For example, if a child receives poor-quality health care from the medical system, her biological and neurological development may be inhibited, and her subsequent interaction with the education system will be disturbed. Even a more subtle outcome of low-quality health care, such as a prolonged recovery time from illness, will alter the child's experience of this otherwise unrelated social institution and reduce the chances of a good educational outcome.

Interventions almost always tackle part of the conveyance link. As Figure 1.ii shows, the conveyance link has two components: (a) a link that represents the effects of a single institution on a child; and (b) a link that represents the effects of the change in that child on her experience with a different institution. In the example above, the effects of the poor-quality health care on development are captured in the first link, while the subsequent disturbed interaction with the education system is captured in the second link. If an institution is failing, an intervention might aim to improve the quality of functions provided by the institution, and thereby improve the welfare of the child. The "replacement" interventions of Chapter 2 operate in this way, by improving the institution that is the origin of the conveyance effect. "Remediation" interventions that compensate for institutional failures instead operate at the destination of the first link: the child at the center of the institutional web. Replacement of what was lost in the interaction with an institution results in a break in the conveyance link, and the child is repaired in preparation for interaction with the next institution. Finally, interventions might target the second link, attempting to alter the changed child's interaction with a new institution. Many of the "nudge" interventions focus on this link, making no effort to alter either the institutions or the child.

All institutions with which a child interacts are linked through the conveyance mechanism. But interactions *among* institutions will be consequential for a child's opportunity. For a child to succeed, all of the core institutions surrounding her must work together to protect and nourish her biological self and protect and develop her social self through socialization, formal education, and skill development. The links among these institutions are therefore consequential for our child's future.[44] Figure 1.iii shows the proposed links among institutions, here labeled "fortification links." In this figure every institution is linked to every other institution: the entire network of institutions surrounding the child is interlinked. The institution of the family is placed at the apex of the network to indicate its special role in the formation of inequality of opportunity: the family is both the institution that children interact with most and the institution that can forge links among other institutions where those links have failed to emerge spontaneously. Two different

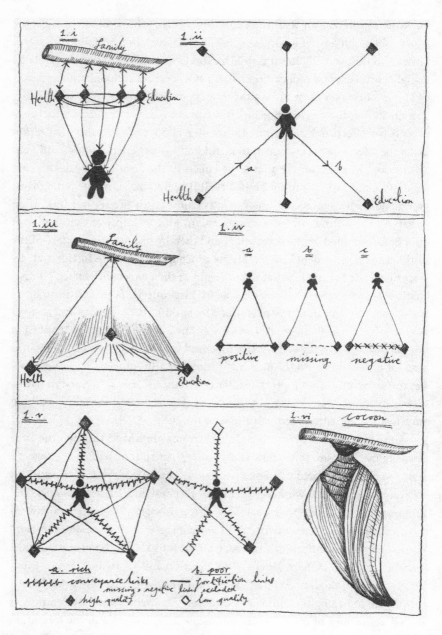

FIGURE 1.
SOURCE: Courtesy of Alexandra Wall.

types of fortification links might connect institutions: first, links that aid the *coordination* of functions that are split across institutions, and second, links that *smooth* the provision of distinct functions across different institutions.

When a child's opportunity rests on a network of core social institutions functioning effectively and collaboratively, a foremost problem is one of *coordination*. Although some institutional functions are provided primarily within a single institution (e.g., medical care is largely, though far from wholly, provided within the medical system), many institutional functions are spread across several institutions. A child's education, for example, is provided in both the family and the educational system, and in ideal circumstances the two social institutions will coordinate to provide complementary training. In the best of circumstances, the family will teach the child to read so that once the child enters school her reading ability is secure and she can focus on the development of other skills. Continuing coordination is an important—if often invisible—feature of a child's educational career. Teachers rely upon parents to help their children with homework that would be too challenging for the child to complete alone, or to help children prepare for standardized tests.

Resources buy productive coordination across institutions. Parents who have trained their child to read—either themselves or via high-quality child care—can buy private education that starts where they left off. Resources buy high-quality and coordinated training across the whole set of institutions that provide training, which promotes both effective learning throughout childhood and the development of more advanced skills than is possible when coordination is weaker. Resources also make it possible to bolster existing institutions with coordinated supplements, such as private tutoring, which will further enhance the child's achievement. Another feature that helps privileged parents to produce a coordinated web of institutions is that they have almost always acquired managerial or organizational skills in their occupation or educational career, skills that can be mobilized to produce coordination across institutions if effective coordination does not already exist. Although with resources it is viable to construct a coordinated network of social institutions from scratch, an alternative is to buy into a neighborhood in which a coordinated network of institutions already exists. As neighborhoods become ever more segregated by income, there is increasing pressure for all institutions in rich neighborhoods to provide the high-quality functions that the privileged have come to expect. A privileged family can therefore purchase a home in an appropriately developed neighborhood as a shortcut to constructing the coordinated network of institutions that will promote a child's opportunity.

Coordination describes the links across institutions providing the same function. In addition to the coordination of similar functions, linkages among institutions operate to smooth the provision of distinct functions. In a system with smooth linkages, schools can rely on medical institutions delivering to them a healthy child who can focus on learning, medical institutions can rely on families to provide safe and secure housing in which a child can recover from illness, and families can rely upon the neighborhood to protect and nurture the child when she is outside the household.[45] Smooth linkages are also in place when there is cross-institution contact with an eye toward compensating for problems in one particular institutional domain—for example, when schools provide medical accommodations to compensate for health problems that a child may be experiencing.[46] Being able to rely on other institutions offers certain efficiencies in the provision of functions; when smooth linkages are in place, institutions are closely matched to what the child needs to maximize her potential. Once again, resources assure these smooth links across institutions.

The fortification links that I have described substantially aid the coordination and smoothing of functions across institutions, to the benefit of the child's development. But there are two alternative relationships among institutions that will offer less protection for the child at the center of the institutional web. Figure 1.iv illustrates the differences between the fortification links so far described and other types of relationships among institutions. The fortification links thus far discussed are represented in Figure 1.iv.a, where a positive link exists between two institutions. In contrast, Figure 1.iv.b shows a missing link, indicating a low degree of coordination or smoothing across institutions. If there is a missing link, one institution takes no account of the quality of the functions provided by another institution. For example, a school might be set up to develop advanced skills when the family has failed to develop the child's basic reading ability, a situation that will inevitably lead to a worse educational outcome for the child. Or a doctor may work on the assumption that a child is well nourished, and provide medical advice that is actually ill-suited to the child's situation. If the two institutions in Figure 1.iv are both functioning well, the effect of a missing link may be small, but the child's outcomes would still be compromised relative to the ideal situation, in which a positive link exists. A trivial example might be where a family focuses on coaching their child in math at a time when the school assesses reading ability, and in reading when the school assesses math ability; the child of this family is likely to perform worse on the two assessments than if the coaching and assessments had been better coordinated. But the effects on a child's outcomes are likely to be far more substantial when some institutions in the child's network are functioning poorly and others are functioning well.[47] Here, a missing link has the potential to substantially undermine the positive effects of a well-functioning institution. If one of the two institutions is functioning poorly, the likelihood of a missing link is rather high.

The final type of link is a negative link, illustrated in Figure 1.iv.c. A negative link is a strong link among institutions in the child's network, but it is a link that operates to the child's disadvantage. In many underprivileged areas, for example, the education system is tightly linked to the institutions concerned with law and order, which puts poor children of color in contact with police officers throughout adolescence while their richer white peers go unscrutinized. Indeed, negative links appear to be particularly frequently documented for institutions concerned with law and order, most likely because the state responds to demands to "protect" the public from deviance and criminality, and it has the power to impose a negative link where that link might otherwise not arise. Through these strong and negative links, the previously incarcerated are blocked from full participation in other institutions such as the family or schools.[48] Similarly, laws that insist upon proof of vaccinations in order to access public schooling produce a strong link between the health and education systems. Although there are good reasons why communities might insist upon universal vaccination, children from less-privileged families are less likely to be vaccinated, and the link between the two institutions means that these children are not only at greater risk of childhood disease but are more likely to be excluded from educational opportunities.[49]

Technological developments have also played their part in creating negative links where previously no links existed. Matthew Desmond has documented, for example, the adverse consequences of making it possible for landlords to search for the eviction and arrest records of potential renters.[50] Technology ensures that problematic decisions and events follow individuals through life, transferring interactions with one institution to the rest of the institutional network. Negative institutional links provide strong linkages where missing links would be more valuable for an individual's opportunity.

There is continuous interplay between the conveyance links that operate through the child and the fortification links among institutions. Every interaction with an institution changes a child, and each change is carried to the child's next institutional interaction. If the fortification link between institutions is missing, the resulting mismatch between the child's needs and what the institutions provide will be reflected in subsequent changes to the child: each new institutional failure and each absence of a fortification link will change the child, and the conveyance link will then diffuse the effects of these institutional failures to the entire institutional network. A child's journey to adulthood is simply the playing out of a large number of these iterative processes.

Cocoons and Fractured Webs

The contrast between the institutional networks of privileged and underprivileged children could not be more stark. The privileged child is at the center of an institutional web designed to promote her opportunity. Her parents have constructed—through deliberate planning or through careful neighborhood choice or through a combination of both—a web of core institutions that will always operate to the benefit of the child. Each institution is likely to be of high quality, and each is linked to a whole network of high-quality institutions that work in cooperation to raise the child to adulthood (Figure 1.v.a). The underprivileged child is instead at the center of a fractured web of social institutions (Figure 1.v.b).

The fracturing arises from two different sources. First, because institutions are influenced by resources, an underprivileged child is likely to interact with many poorly functioning institutions; even if some institutions are functioning well, others will almost certainly be functioning poorly. Second, without resources it is extremely difficult to secure coordination or smoothing across all of the institutions with which the child interacts. While the privileged family is able to use resources to construct a network of functioning institutions, the underprivileged family must instead rely on the vagaries of chance to provide the network within which the child's opportunities will be determined, and the family will have little power to shape the linkages among those institutions. No matter what underprivileged parents are able to do to improve the quality of training and socialization within the family, on the path to adulthood their children are likely to encounter an institutional network that includes problematic institutions and that fails to operate as a coherent whole. When their child suffers bad luck, or needs additional help from an institution outside the family, the parents cannot assume that help will be forthcoming; the need for help may not be recognized outside the family, and even if it is recognized, the links fostering cooperation and smooth interactions among institutions may not be in place.

In highlighting the fractured institutional networks of underprivileged children I do not challenge the long-standing sociological finding that there is a substantial degree of social organization within poor communities. In contrast to the claims of some early and influential studies, poor neighborhoods have been shown to contain institutions that promote and support social cohesion, social solidarity, and social order.[51] Further, as Mario Small describes, those living in poor neighborhoods do sometimes see productive coordination across institutions; Small shows, for example, that some of the child care centers serving the poor in New York City are well-integrated with health organizations and other service providers.[52] The social problems that arise in socioeconomically disadvantaged neighborhoods do not derive, then, from an absence of social institutions or institutional structure per se. Rather, it is the full set of positive links among core social institutions that is missing in such communities. Underprivileged children are more likely to encounter missing links and negative links among the institutions that surround them. The positive linkages among the family, the health care and education systems, the neighborhood, and the state are likely to emerge only partially, haphazardly, and with low frequency. Underprivileged parents cannot rely upon a cocoon of core institutions operating as one to protect and promote their child's opportunity.

All of the actions and interactions that I have attributed to institutions are the macro-level result of a large number of micro-level decisions, actions, and interactions by and among individuals.[53] A web of institutions is not imposed from on high; rather, it occurs because resources make it possible to construct clusters of high-quality institutions. But the constructed cocoon of institutions within which the privileged child develops appears to the child to be something quite different. The institutional web is so coherent, so under the control of the privileged parents, that the set of functions being carried out could as reasonably be provided by a single institution as by a set of separate institutions. To the child, life in the cocoon is experienced as life in a total institution.

As described by Erving Goffman, a total institution has four key features. Individuals in a total institution (a) sleep, play, and work in the same physical location; (b) engage in daily activities with others who are required to engage in the same activities and who are treated similarly to them; (c) participate in a tightly scheduled sequence of activities imposed on them by others; and (d) through their participation in this sequence of activities are part of a "single rational plan purportedly designed to fulfill the official aims of the institution."[54] All but the first of these features apply to the cocoon of institutions that privileged children experience.

The tight-knit, coherent web of institutions that surrounds privileged children produces a great similarity in the experiences of those children: resources buy high-quality early childhood training, resources buy high-quality schools, resources buy high-quality neighborhoods, and so on. In short, resources buy consistency of high-quality functions across the institutions that children interact with. Given that there is substantial scientific and public agreement about what "high-quality" childrearing entails—at least with regard to the types of skills and personal characteristics that it is desirable to instill in one's child, and how such skills and personal characteristics should be developed— consistency of high-quality functions produces consistency of institutional experience.[55] The institutional cocoon of privileged children may not in fact be delivered through a single institution, but the level of coordination across the set of institutions with which the child interacts is such that the precise delivery mechanism becomes immaterial to the child's experience.

There has been resistance in the sociological literature to using the language of total institutions for the everyday environments that many of us experience.[56] The primary argument for maintaining a conceptual bright line between total institutions and other forms of social organization hinges upon the degree of differentiation and institutional specialization. Modern societies are characterized by substantial functional differentiation across institutions: whereas in preindustrial societies a single institution (e.g., the family) was responsible for providing a range of functions (e.g., health care, education, early socialization), in modern societies different functions are more frequently provided by separate institutions that specialize in providing those functions.[57] A total institution thus stands apart from the highly differentiated society, largely because it stands physically apart from society. But if the level of coordination of functions across institutions is so substantial that the institutional boundaries are not at all salient to the child, we may reasonably ask whether the insistence on physical separation in the definition of total institutions should be decisive.[58] The cocoon is not a prison, set apart from the everyday world, but it is a construction that is designed to protect privileged children from the possible uncertainties of institutional differentiation, with the aim of encouraging social reproduction. Furthermore, in a context of increasing institutional segregation, a definition of total institutions that insists on physical segregation might even be satisfied. Privileged and underprivileged children grow up in different physical locations, they attend different schools, churches, hospitals, and colleges, and they are surrounded by different institutional networks.

The existence of highly coordinated networks of well-functioning institutions has implications for inequality of constraints between privileged and underprivileged children, but it also has potential implications for our understanding of the move from preindustrial societies to modernity. Ferdinand Tönnies famously contrasted the modern-day *Gesellschaft* with a preindustrial *Gemeinschaft*, highlighting a move away from community-based social organization to society-based organization, in which the rational actions of individuals undermine long-standing customs and bonds.[59] Modernity is characterized by increased differentiation through specialization, which offers various efficiencies in the provision of social functions, but which also places demands on society because highly differentiated institutions must be somehow coordinated. As Eisenstadt summarizes the problem,

> differentiated and specialized institutional spheres become more interdependent and potentially complementary in their functioning. . . . But this very complementarity creates more difficult and complex problems of integration. The growing autonomy of each sphere of social activity, and the concomitant growth of interdependence and mutual interpretation among them, pose for each sphere more difficult problems . . . in regulating its normative and organizational relations with other spheres.[60]

As we have seen, raising a child to full flourishing entails negotiating multiple institutional spheres throughout the child's development and ensuring coordination across these spheres.

Social integration in the context of a highly differentiated society was assumed to be possible because shared norms and values operate to coordinate relationships among institutions.[61] In contrast, our society is one in which coordination among institutions is preferentially available to those with resources. Resources have solved the problem of integration: they provide the connective tissue that binds differentiated institutions together.

The highly constructed institutional networks of privileged children represent a type of social organization that prioritizes developing strong bonds among institutions in order to obtain an advantage. Rather than family and community diminishing in importance relative to a wider, bureaucratized society, the privileged family has pulled the institutions of society within its own sphere of influence to gain advantage for its children. Indeed, the advantage associated with an institutional cocoon is available only because other institutions have taken over functions that were previously the domain of the family and community. From this perspective, modern society is characterized not by differentiation per se, but by uneven differentiation, by differentiation for the poor but not for the rich. Resources allow the privileged to purchase islands of *Gemeinschaft* in a sea of *Gesellschaft*. The extent to which institutional networks can be constructed around privileged children therefore represents a challenge to standard treatments of societal and institutional change.

A Dream Undermined by Brutal Legacy

I have focused throughout on contrasting the lives of "privileged" and "underprivileged" individuals, and have suggested that the fracturing of institutional networks is a general feature of socioeconomic disadvantage in the contemporary United States. It is, however, important to emphasize that institutional flaws and unfavorable network conditions may be of special importance for children who face intersecting and multiple disadvantages. The institutional barriers stemming from economic disadvantage, for example, are likely to be even more substantial for people of color, women, and members of minority groups. Any demographic, economic, or social characteristic has the potential to alter the institutional landscape that determines inequality of constraints. In part, this is because once a characteristic is marked as relevant to a person's essential nature, that characteristic may become associated with cultural beliefs about status and esteem, and status shapes social institutions.[62]

Of the very many characteristics to which status may be attached in the contemporary United States, one characteristic is of particular importance in understanding inequality of constraints: race. As Nikole Hannah-Jones writes,

> The United States is a nation founded on both an ideal and a lie. . . . Anti-black racism runs in the very DNA of this country. . . . It is common, still, to point

to rates of black poverty, out-of-wedlock births, crime and college attendance, as if these conditions in a country built on a racial caste system are not utterly predictable. But crucially, you cannot view those statistics while ignoring another: that black people were enslaved here longer than we have been free.[63]

Hannah-Jones pushes us to recognize that race touches all of the institutions that are important for safeguarding a child's opportunities.[64] In particular, race is likely to create differences in the quality or form of institution that a child will encounter. During the period of school segregation, for example, African Americans were channeled to different schools from whites, and these schools were generally of lower quality.[65] Similar examples can be seen in the history of residential segregation and zoning, and in the de facto exclusion of African Americans from government programs.[66]

Race also produces differences in institutions because African Americans experience different treatment relative to whites within the *same* instantiation of a social institution (e.g., a single school, a single workplace). To take a simple and well-documented example, equivalently qualified Black and white candidates for jobs are not treated equally by employers: research shows that white job applicants receive 36 percent more callbacks than African American applicants, an inequality that has changed little in the past quarter century.[67] Whether the roots of differential treatment are to be found in straightforward discrimination, racial animus and unconscious bias, or elsewhere, the institution of the labor market is clearly affected by race and fails to offer equality of constraints to all those who interact with it. The parents of an African American child cannot trust that an institution is working to promote their child's opportunity, and even relatively affluent families must question whether or not an institution will protect their child.

If African American children are disadvantaged because they experience individual institutions that are flawed, they are further disadvantaged because they face a fractured network of institutions. Like poor parents, African American parents cannot operate on the assumption that every institution that their children interact with will promote opportunity.[68] African American students, for example, are more likely to attend schools with high proportions of low-income students, and these high-poverty schools have fewer resources than other schools.[69] Black students are also less likely to benefit from education-enhancing supports that are offered by other institutions. One striking example can be found in the use of educational disability accommodations: the

New York Times reported in 2019 that the richest school districts have rates of disability accommodations almost four times higher than the poorest school districts and that white students are more likely than Black students to obtain such accommodations. Educational accommodations can be used to obtain extra time for students who take SAT tests, and that extra time can pay off in higher scores.[70] The overwhelming conclusion from work covering a range of institutional domains is that for African American families, any privileges that economic resources might otherwise convey can be undone.[71]

Black children are yet further disadvantaged because they are more likely to confront a network that contains negative links. The criminal justice system offers an excellent example. As compared to whites, African Americans are more likely to be stopped by the police, are treated with less respect when they are stopped, are more likely to be charged and convicted, and are given harsher sentences by the courts.[72] Negative links exist between the criminal justice and education systems, placing adolescents of color at special risk. African American students who commit classroom infractions are treated more harshly than white students who commit similar infractions, and school-based arrests provide a direct pathway from school infractions to incarceration.[73] In the current social context, it would be a mistake—and sometimes a fatal one—for parents to assume that their children can rely on social institutions to promote their well-being.[74]

Pull Apart and Rebuild

The roots of inequality of constraints are to be found in social institutions. The roots of equality can be found there too.

The two themes that I have emphasized throughout this chapter on the sources of inequality of constraints are first, that socioeconomic resources change individual social institutions and the quality of the functions under the charge of those institutions, and second, that underprivileged children face a fractured web of social institutions, so that even if some institutions are working to support them, others may undermine that work. These structural qualities of the institutional network raise serious questions about how best to reduce the inequalities associated with socioeconomic background. An approach that tackles just part of the institutional network implicitly works on the assumption that changing one feature of a child's life has positive effects that will then cascade through the entire institutional network.

To take a concrete example, we know that unstable housing is a cause of poverty and inequality of opportunity.[75] Advocates of housing policy argue that providing secure housing would substantially improve the lives of the underprivileged, with predicted spin-off effects for underprivileged children, including increased chances of upward mobility. But spin-off effects depend upon an institutional web that will amplify the positive effects of a single institutional change, such that if housing is "fixed," children will carry the results of that fix to all of the other institutions in the network, and each of those institutional interactions will also be improved. Under this model, stable housing would set in motion a virtuous cycle whereby positive changes would beget further positive changes.[76]

The key problem with this model is that the underprivileged do not have a preexisting institutional network that would allow such effects to dominate. Stable housing in and of itself does not improve the quality of schooling, or the safety of a neighborhood, or access to health care. The fractured web means that gains in one institution can be undermined by continuing deficiencies in another. The child's life may well be markedly improved by stable housing, but if the other social institutions surrounding the child are misaligned, the housing intervention's potential to produce positive results is limited. We must also note that the provision of stable housing for all families would be a massive intervention by present-day standards. When we consider the potential of more-typical, modest interventions—such as "mind-set" interventions, or nudges—it becomes clear that any effects are likely to be small and short-lived.

Despite the strong claims made on behalf of any single intervention, the institutional structures in which underprivileged children are embedded act as impediments to long-lasting and transformative effects. Even the most extensive and enveloping policies, such as early childhood interventions, are vulnerable to being thwarted by the wider structure of the institutional network in the years following early childhood. The research findings on "washout" (or "fadeout") offer cautionary evidence in this regard.[77] Children who have made substantial gains in early childhood after participating in high-quality early intervention programs may nevertheless fall behind in later childhood and adolescence. Early intervention generates positive changes in children by building a network of support around them in the early years, but when this network disappears and is replaced with the fractured network that characterizes the institutional context of underprivileged children, the benign relationship between the individual and the surrounding institutions comes to an end. The achievements of the early institutional network may be diminished when new institutional failures occur, and when these failures are transmitted to other institutions around the child.[78] Transformative effects of any policy should not be anticipated unless the institutional networks surrounding underprivileged children continue to nurture the child until she reaches adulthood.

Transformative reforms cannot, therefore, treat a flawed institutional network as binding and fixed. Any transformative policy must ask how the building blocks of inequality can be remodeled and recombined to produce new institutional structures that will protect the opportunities of the underprivileged just as our current structures protect the privileged. Rebuilding and restructuring the institutions that organize the path from childhood to adulthood will inevitably require radical policy solutions. In Chapter 4 I ask whether there are models from other countries that might serve as a starting point for these radical solutions in the United States.

CHAPTER 4

GRASP BY THE ROOT

radical
A.2.b. Of action, change, an idea, etc.: going to the root or origin;
pertaining to or affecting what is fundamental; far-reaching, thorough.

There may be few words in political discourse as widely and haphazardly applied as the word "radical." The term has been used to describe politicians on the left and the right, social scientists subscribing to a variety of academic schools of thought, and followers of fundamentalist religions. It is commonly applied to policy proposals that recommend little more than a change to the status quo.

In this chapter, I describe in detail a number of concrete policies that I believe to be radical. To what, then, do I refer when I use the term "radical"? Here I take the lead from Marx, who embraced the origins of the word and determined that "to be radical is to grasp things by the root."[1] My interest is in policies that tackle the root causes of inequality of constraints, policies that improve the outcomes of underprivileged individuals by addressing the web of social institutions that produces inequality of opportunity. I will not use the term "radical" as shorthand for "extreme," "left-field," or "outlandish." These are value judgments that may be applied to the policies that I will discuss, but that will necessarily differ among readers, depending upon those readers' ideological commitments and partisanship. Note, however, that I will be presenting examples of policies that have already been implemented in many parts of the world; indeed, some have been implemented in parts of the United States. This emphasizes that what is viewed as extreme, left-field, or outlandish is likely to vary substantially over time, across countries, and across social groups within countries.

The purpose of this chapter is to assess whether various concrete proposals are truly radical and what types of revisions to them might make them more or less radical. I will not consider whether these proposals meet *all* of the criteria that one might legitimately consider when deciding upon what constitutes a "good" society. As I define them, radical proposals are oriented toward reducing inequality of constraints, not toward maximizing liberty, or minimizing taxes, or prioritizing family bonds. In focusing on the question of whether a proposal is or is not radical, I do not suggest that other objectives are unimportant, but only that they are beyond the scope of this analysis.

I begin the chapter by outlining the general principles that must be at the foundation of a radical policy agenda. These principles are derived from the argument presented in the previous chapters about the roots of inequality of opportunity. If specific forms of institutional constraint can account for observed inequalities of opportunity, it is these constraints that radical policy must address. I next draw upon examples of radical policy initiatives from other countries, and from the United States, that tackle institutional constraints. I describe how these radical policies are consistent with my general principles, and ask how such initiatives might be further adapted to fulfill the promise of radical reform. In describing these policies, I hope to demonstrate both the feasibility and the promise of a policy agenda that would truly grasp at the roots of inequality of constraints. I conclude by pointing toward possible avenues for further policy development.

Roots and Branches

Our current level of inequality of constraints is neither inevitable nor insurmountable. It is the consequence of socioeconomic resources shaping individual social institutions and the institutional network surrounding each child. Here I lay out the general principles that lie behind any effort to dismantle inequality of constraints.

In Chapter 3, I identified the roots of inequality of constraints in social institutions and argued that underprivileged children face two important problems. First, because socioeconomic resources influence the quality of the functions that core social institutions provide, children who are born into families without resources will necessarily be disadvantaged relative to those who originate in families with resources. For example, underprivileged families may be able to provide only low-quality early child care, and as a result, when formal education begins, the children will be disadvantaged relative to their privileged counterparts. Second, the schools, neighborhoods, and other institutions surrounding underprivileged families all tend to be poorly resourced, and these families are unable to develop high-quality connective tissue to link institutions together. Consequently, underprivileged children encounter a fractured network of institutions rather than the coherent network that promotes the growth and opportunity of privileged children.

Transformative reforms must break the links connecting family resources, the quality of institutions, and the coherence of the institutional network. Logically, this implies that to reduce inequality of constraints we would need either (a) to impose a substantially flatter (i.e., more equal) distribution of socioeconomic resources or (b) to eliminate the effects of family resources on the quality and coherence of institutional networks. Either of these approaches to reform could be addressed by using existing policy levers.

The flatter resource distribution solution to inequality of constraints, attractive in its simplicity, is perhaps the obvious solution if we believe that the barriers to success are sustained primarily by inequality on the economic dimension. It is, after all, relatively straightforward to redistribute money from the top to the bottom (and middle) of the income distribution.[2] If the United States were to commit to deeply progressive tax policy, such redistribution could happen very quickly, and all else being equal, we would expect an increase in the incomes of the poor along with a decrease in the incomes of the rich to reduce the level of inequality of constraints. But two practical issues arise with this approach, issues that any radical policy agenda must address.

The first is that although there are simple policy levers that can be used to effect income redistribution, it is more difficult to redistribute other forms of socioeconomic resources. Social status, race, gender, and power, for example, cannot be redistributed by using tax policy, although no doubt the redistribution of income and wealth would have consequences for the distribution of at least some other forms of socioeconomic resources. But even in the extreme condition of complete income and wealth equality, we would still expect to see inequality of constraints with respect to other dimensions of inequality. Even if the racial wealth gap could be eliminated, for example, racism and racial discrimination would persist, and we would observe racial inequalities in access to housing and to neighborhoods that are associated with improved child outcomes.

A second issue that arises with the flatter resource distribution approach is just as fundamental, and highlights a general point about the nature of social institutions. Assuming that the income distribution is not *completely* flat, resource inequality will always produce inequality of constraints. Because many inequality-generating mechanisms rest on relative differences among people, rather than on absolute differences, we may see swift adaptation by the relatively advantaged to the new distribution of resources. Insofar as access to "better" neighborhoods is rationed by cost, access to these neighborhoods will still be preferentially available to the relatively advantaged. In the worst case, institutions may simply respond to ever finer resource distinctions among families; in this situation, even if the top and bottom of the resource distribution were much closer together in absolute terms, the stability of their relative ranking would preserve all of the current structures of inequality. This worst-case scenario is unlikely to be on the mark, given that absolute levels of resources matter for a great many institutions. We must, though, be cognizant that some of the positive effects of a flatter income distribution might be reduced if the children of relatively disadvantaged families still lack access to a coherent network of institutions all working in harmony.

The foregoing would suggest that the redistribution route is likely to fail in delivering full equality of constraints unless it is paired with further reform. An alternative route is to instead reduce the power of resources to shape the institutional web and the quality of institutional functions. Breaking the link between resources and social institutions in the absence of resource equalization usually requires state action. For example, the state might persuade or force institutions to operate differently by introducing antidiscrimination legislation to prevent socioeconomic resources from being taken into account when individuals interact with institutions. Or the state might step in to provide the functions that would otherwise be susceptible to market influence. There are already many instances of this latter form of state action. The early education system is perhaps the most prominent example, but the argument around single-payer vs. market-based health care is also, at its core, an argument about whether the state or the market should provide the health care function. In the past, the state played a substantial role in providing public goods, and it would be quite feasible for the state to fulfill that role again today.[3]

Policy can, then, tackle the tainting of individual institutions by socioeconomic resources. But radical policy must also be mindful of the fractured-network problem; therefore, a focus on how institutions fit together is necessary. This will be particularly important if policy fails to ensure that *all* institutions work well for those without resources.

The state could guarantee institutional coherence by simply taking over the functions of each and every institution: if all functions are embedded in a single organization, inter-function coordination is in principle facilitated. Under such a radical model, the state would be responsible for all of the functions that arise when raising children from birth to adulthood. Child care responsibilities would be centralized, and thus the nuclear family as it exists today would disappear. All education and socialization would be undertaken by the state, thus eliminating the need for coordination among the family, community, and school. The task of satisfying the physical and emotional needs of the child would be removed from the family, community, schools, and health care systems, and embodied in the state. The state's taking on all institutional functions would be an efficient solution to the coordination problem, but even the most radical of radical policy advocates is unlikely to support state provision of all social functions from birth to death.[4]

State centralization is but one approach to building coherent institutional networks. There are many ways to achieve coordination of networks without relying on the state to provide all social functions. It could in fact be encouraged through relatively modest policy interventions. One solution to the problem of coordination across highly differentiated institutions would be to set up a coordinative entity to manage the set of social institutions. This entity could be part of the social services infrastructure, but coordination could also be provided by non-state entities, such as individuals or nonprofits. For example, what if when a school was failing, the family and community were to automatically receive extra resources (both financial and non-financial) to ensure that the affected child could continue to learn? What if when families were in difficulty, and had decreased capacity to help their children to learn, the community would respond by offering additional support? An entity that coordinated institutions to seamlessly step in when other institutions were in difficulty would go some distance toward offering the network coherence that underprivileged children currently lack. Mentoring programs, technological innovations, and community-based service delivery are all examples of non-state entities performing the coordinative role.

In the abstract, it is relatively straightforward to imagine how a radical policy agenda might produce a coherent and well-functioning institutional network around all children. The challenge is in translating such abstractions into concrete policies, a task to which I now turn.

The Road Traveled

According to standard measures of equality of opportunity, countries vary enormously in the extent to which the socioeconomic position of parents determines a child's life chances.[5] Countries with relatively low levels of income inequality, for example, have lower levels of educational inequality, and weaker correlations between parent's and child's income.[6] Few social scientists believe that such variation is random, and few believe that it can be attributed to differences in the fundamental nature of the individuals who live in different countries. In searching for policies that have the potential to break the link between parent's and child's socioeconomic position, therefore, a natural place for social scientists to begin is to look to the policies of other countries. As is the case with U.S. domestic policy, many of the policies in other countries are small-scale and incremental. But that is not always the case, and other countries have much to offer when it comes to imagining a radical reshaping of societal institutions.

The existing policy reforms that I discuss here might be classified as radical, since they grasp at one or more of the roots of inequality of constraints. Radical reforms must, at minimum, involve serious efforts to impose a flatter income distribution, break the link between resources and the quality of institutional functions, and break the link between resources and the coherence of institutional networks. Substantial reductions in inequality might be achieved if any one of these approaches were to be embraced wholeheartedly, and I therefore include in the following discussion examples of more-circumscribed reforms that nevertheless have the potential to greatly reduce inequality of constraints, particularly when adapted to fit local contexts and incentive structures.

I will begin by considering two models of reform that rely upon a flattening of the income distribution—either wholly or in part—for their effects on inequality of constraints. I then move to consider radical models that operate more directly to address the fractured-network problem and to produce institutional change.

One for All

A simple change in tax policy could produce a completely flat income distribution within a matter of days. There is no technical obstacle to accomplishing this. That there are other obstacles is undeniable, but cross-national variation in the degree of post-market redistribution indicates that many people could tolerate rather higher tax rates than obtain in the present-day United States.[7] Even if no country has yet committed to the level of redistribution that would be necessary to eliminate inequality of constraints, in recent years we have seen a surprising takeoff in popularity for the concept of a universal (also known as "unconditional") basic income (UBI).

In its most radical form, UBI proposes that a sum of money be paid to every individual in a country, financed by tax increases on the rich. Although most discussions of UBI focus on the sum to be paid to all, the real potential of the idea with respect to reducing inequality of constraints comes both from the absolute increase in the incomes of the poor and from the reduction in income inequality via the redistribution that would be required to fund UBI. For this reason, radical UBI proposals should be treated as distinct from UBI proposals that do not redistribute (e.g., Alaska's Permanent Fund, which pays out an annual dividend from oil revenues). A radical UBI reform breaks the link between resources and institutions through a flattening of the income distribution.

The potential impact of UBI on inequality of constraints depends on the extent of redistribution, and it is here that there is ambiguity in the policy prescription. Observers of the contemporary discussion of UBI may be mildly surprised to see the breadth of support for the policy; UBI has strong supporters on both the left and the right of the political spectrum, has outspoken advocates among both "firebrand" academics and tech billionaires, and is being proposed in countries on almost every continent. In part, the widespread support can be explained by differences across constituencies in the precise details of the UBI being proposed: some of the supporters are in favor of basic income as a repackaged commitment to substantial redistribution; some are in favor of welfare reform, whereby a single UBI payment would replace existing welfare programs; and still others have in mind a middle-distance future in which automation has rendered most jobs obsolete and people must instead be supported by the state.[8] If UBI either replaces existing welfare arrangements or adds but a small sum to the incomes of the poor, relatively small effects on inequality of constraints might be expected. In contrast, if UBI were funded via redistributive tax policy, and substantial amounts were transferred from the top half of the income distribution to the bottom, larger declines in inequality of constraints would be expected. This is an unusual case in which a proposal can become more radical simply by being scaled up.

Trials of basic income are under way in several countries, although on a much smaller scale than that envisioned by the policy's proponents. Most importantly, relatively few people are enrolled in the trials, and the amounts paid to participants are smaller than the amounts discussed in much of the UBI literature. Furthermore, the funding for the vast majority of these trials comes either from philanthropic organizations or special funds assigned for the purpose of carrying out the experiment. Given that effects on inequality of constraints would be expected to be stronger in the context of whole communities receiving money, stronger when larger sums are provided, and stronger in the context of UBI's being funded through redistribution, the current design of the experiments potentially undermines the possibility of finding large effects of UBI on inequality of constraints.[9] Nevertheless, results from earlier trials of basic income (and similar policies) show that poorer children can expect to be healthier, better educated, and richer in adulthood when their families receive a basic income.[10] These trials suggest that a fully implemented UBI might be effective in translating absolute improvements in the income of the poor into increased opportunity for children, even in the context of an unchanging institutional structure.

There are two paths to securing UBI as a radical reform. First, UBI could be scaled up to the point that it is profoundly redistributive. In the absence of serious redistribution, it will also be necessary to make additional changes to the institutional structure if UBI is to fulfill its radical promise. Critics of narrow basic income proposals have already made this case, with advocates of broader UBI programs arguing that basic services—such as health care, education, shelter, and food—should be provided alongside any monetary sum.[11] The latter broadening of the discussion on UBI is to be welcomed, given the danger that without additional changes to the wider institutional structure UBI simply legitimates the effects of socioeconomic resources on institutions. Rather than tackling the roots of inequality of constraints, a poorly implemented and narrow UBI would only solidify our existing institutional arrangements. Universal basic income may currently be the Rorschach of policy proposals, but those wishing to represent UBI as anything more than a business-as-usual "intervention" must either find a way to scale up, or to combine UBI with authentic institutional change.

To Each according to His Needs

Universal basic income aims to reduce inequality of constraints through its effects on the distribution of income. Any further effects on institutional structures would come only if UBI ushered forth a new policy agenda that addressed institutions directly. In searching for a policy that combines equalization of the resource distribution with innovative institutional design, the most obvious reform to consider is socialism. Is socialism the radical reform that has the best chance of delivering on the American Dream?

The words "radical" and "socialism" may be virtual synonyms in the ears of many, but socialism in fact only partially grasps at the roots of inequality of constraints, even if some elements of socialism do have the potential to influence institutions in directions that might be productive. Although socialism is typically associated with communal ownership of the means of production, a very partial and limited version of it might take the form of mandated representation of workers on corporate boards, as championed by Elizabeth Warren during her 2020 presidential campaign. There is, then, much variation in the types of institutional configurations and societal arrangements that might be viewed as having socialist elements.

How would socialism address the inequality of constraints that I previously described? Most obviously, it would produce a flatter distribution of resources, although the extent of the flattening would depend on the precise type of socialism embraced. In very weak versions, such as Warren's proposed corporate board reform, we would expect to see only marginal effects on the distribution of resources. In its authentic and full-throated form, the scale of the flattening would likely have substantial effects on breaking the link between resources and institutions.

Authentic socialism also breaks that link through institutional design. In a society committed to socialist principles, it is essential that institutions be able to function in the absence of income differences, and many countries therefore introduced universal health care, education, and pension systems to ensure that individuals and families were supported. In some countries, further steps were taken to promote the opportunities of the less well-off. For example, China and some countries in Eastern Europe employed the policy of "counter-selection," whereby a number of slots in higher education were reserved for the children of manual workers.[12] Not only were socialist institutions designed to operate successfully in the context of a very flat resource distribution, but some were explicitly designed to counteract the effects of economic resources on a child's life chances. Importantly, though, in a socialist society, little explicit attention is paid to a coherent web of institutions, because the priority is instead to completely break the link between resources and institutions. If this link is broken across the board, the fractured network problem should become moot.

This lack of attention to the institutional web lies at the heart of one of the well-documented failings of socialism, notably that the children of party members received privileged treatment by institutions such as the education system and the labor market.[13] Institutions responded to party membership in much the same way as our current institutions respond to other dimensions of socio-economic position (e.g., income, gender, or race). Inequality of constraints still existed, then, but it existed because institutions privileged the children of party members, and because there was a coherent web of social institutions in place around those children. This is not to say that socialist societies failed to reduce inequalities of constraints related to economic resources. On the contrary, evidence from Eastern Europe suggests that class structures were more fluid in communist times, and that social mobility has declined in the post-communist era.[14] Rather, the evidence is consistent with a failure to fully tackle the issue of how institutions respond to all forms of socioeconomic advantage—whether economic, social, or political—which then opened the door to new forms of inequality of constraints once one dimension of advantage was replaced with another. For those concerned with promoting opportunity, socialism highlights both the dangers of legislating for a narrow conception of socioeconomic advantage and the dangers of ignoring the power of socioeconomic advantage to grant differential access to coherent institutional webs.

A United States that embraces authentic socialism is unlikely in the fore-seeable future, although the Council of Economic Advisers was concerned enough that it released a report in 2018 warning of the perils of taking this path.[15] But socialist ideas have inspired—and still inspire—scholars and advocates to build alternative models of society and social institutions. One notable contemporary example is found in the Real Utopias Project, and particularly in Erik Olin Wright's influential work, *Envisioning Real Utopias*, which urges institutional reform following socialist principles while steering away from a wholesale reimagining of society along socialist lines.[16] The most important legacy of socialism is likely this commitment to deliberative institutional design. Although socialist societies have historically paid little explicit attention to installing coherent webs of institutions, they did at least remind us that social institutions can in principle be harnessed toward building a better and more equal society.

I will now discuss examples of institutional reform that address the fractured institutional web directly. These models of reform attempt to break the links between resources and the coherence of institutional networks by building the connective tissue linking institutions that the underprivileged would otherwise lack. I will consider several examples of reform that differ in their degree of expansiveness: the first tackles coordination across a small number of institutions that affect only adults, the second addresses the coherence of institutions early in a child's life, and the third puts institutional coherence at the heart of the vision of a good society. I begin with the relatively narrow approach to constructing a coherent network of institutions: flexicurity.

Den Gyldne Trekant

A contemporary sympathy for the social democratic model, evident among both public commentators and social scientists, has elevated the social systems of Denmark and Sweden to quasi-mythical status in the search for a land of opportunity. These countries have lower levels of income inequality and higher rates of social mobility than the United States, and regularly appear on lists of the happiest and healthiest countries.[17] The lauding of the Scandinavian countries has provoked the inevitable backlash by social scientists, but Scandinavia does offer many examples of institutional design that—if adopted and applied in other countries—might help to reduce inequality of constraints.[18]

One such institutional form is the Danish model of "flexicurity," which is now one of the central planks of European Union labor market policy. A flexicurity system is one that offers the "golden triangle" of flexible employment relationships, unemployment security, and an active labor market policy that emphasizes lifelong learning and retraining. The main aim of flexicurity is to promote employment security and thereby economic security. This goal is achieved not by tying employees to any particular job or employer, but by offering substantial financial support for the unemployed, committing to continuous retraining, and smoothing the transition between employment and unemployment.[19] The precise nature of the economic and social supports and the administration of the program have varied across the decades since the introduction of the concept, but the policy is generally regarded as a success.[20]

Flexicurity shares the two aims that should be part of any radical policy program. First, the program breaks the links between resources and the quality of institutional functions: adults are entitled to unemployment benefits should they need them, and job training programs and counseling are available to all. This emphasis on lifelong learning lies in sharp contrast to countries such as the United States, where investments in education are frontloaded to occur during the childhood and adolescent years.[21] The ease with which adults can undertake later-life training is particularly important in promoting equality of constraints, given the disruptive childhoods experienced by many of those born into underprivileged families. Second, flexicurity builds a coherent network of institutions around an individual, with strong links among labor market, training system, and social safety net. When an individual experiences failure in the labor market, the training system and the social safety net stop the failure from spiraling out to other areas of life. All three of the golden triangle institutions are working together to protect the individual.

Despite these benefits, the policy has limited potential to influence inequality of constraints simply because flexicurity is situated too late in the life course to have large effects on an individual's opportunity. To be sure, flexicurity raises the floor of societal welfare and improves individual lives, but without institutional reform that touches the earlier stages of life, inequalities relating to socioeconomic background will remain. Indeed, the main influence of flexicurity on inequality of constraints may primarily operate for the next generation, as the improvement in the lives of adults who participate is likely to lead to improvements in children's outcomes should those adults be (or later become) parents. Thus, from the perspective of tackling inequality of constraints, flexicurity and similar policies ought to be considered seriously by those in favor of a radical policy agenda, even if these policies are likely to be most successful when combined with other policies that produce institutional coherence earlier in life. If nothing else, flexicurity is a useful model for consciously implemented institutional coordination.

A Time to Build

Early childhood intervention is an institutional reform that takes seriously the charge of shaping the early part of the life course. This policy has gained much prominence in the United States in recent years, and one might therefore wonder why it should appear in a discussion of radical models of institutional design. Despite its ubiquity, early childhood intervention fulfills the criteria for radical reform, and indeed, full-throated early childhood intervention is among the most radical of the available policy models.

"Early intervention" is used as a catch-all term to describe a set of policy prescriptions for young children and their families. Their features include, but are not limited to, unconditional cash transfers to the families of young children in the form of tax credits or cash payments; conditional cash transfers in which families receive payments in exchange for engaging in certain behaviors, such as participating in preschool programs or taking advantage of medical checkups; food stamps, free school meals, and nutritional supplements for pregnant women; home visits by nurses; and the provision of free and high-quality child care and preschool.[22] As this list demonstrates, early intervention policies often improve or replace the functions provided by the institutions that surround the child: the family, the neighborhood, the medical system, the educational system, and so forth. The key tenet of the early intervention approach is that investments made early in a child's life provide the greatest return: it is economically inefficient to invest a dollar in adulthood if that same dollar could have been invested in the early years instead.[23] Early investment raises the productivity of later investments, as young children develop skills that can be used as a foundation for later skill development.[24]

The focus on "investment" and "skill development" by proponents of early childhood intervention emphasizes the continuity between this policy prescription and other forms of intervention. But the extent to which early childhood intervention is truly a radical policy prescription is deemphasized. At its most expansive, early childhood intervention builds a cocoon of institutions around children from underprivileged families: financial, emotional, and parenting support for the family is integrated with medical support, educational support, and the contextual support that results from all families in the neighborhood having access to resources. Further, as program administrators directly intervene to produce improvements in the crucial institutions with which young children come into contact, the underprivileged gain greater access to high-quality institutions. Early childhood intervention therefore works toward satisfying both of the criteria that I identified for radical reform. Evaluations of early childhood intervention programs are on the whole positive, although the magnitude of the effects differs substantially across programs.[25] It appears that it is only in its most expansive form—what Heckman labels the "gold standard" of early childhood intervention—that substantial effects are found.[26] This result is consistent with the hypothesis that effects on inequality of constraints are strongest when both criteria for radical reform are addressed.

A long-established criticism of early childhood intervention is that the effects "wash out" during later childhood and adolescence in the absence of further policy intervention.[27] Other policy programs in the "wraparound" mold therefore address the whole "pipeline" from early childhood through to adulthood, putting in place supports for all of the crucial points in a child's development. The best-known example of a more comprehensive approach is the Harlem Children's Zone, a community-based initiative that brings together a range of different programs with the aim of creating a "pipeline of support."[28] At the center of this program is a set of well-funded charter schools that also provide food and health services.[29] Parents are supported, particularly during the early childhood years, with parenting programs and Single Stop sites that provide legal and financial services, and information on eligibility for public benefits. Harlem Children's Zone has shown positive results, particularly with respect to test scores, although it is still too early to provide a full assessment of the effects of the pipeline approach.[30] Nevertheless, the program inspired President Obama to establish a set of "Promise Neighborhoods," with the similar aim of transforming whole communities and thereby improving children's opportunities.

Both early childhood intervention and Harlem Children's Zone provide services that low-income families could not otherwise afford, and both aim (whether explicitly or not) to build a coherent web of institutions around children. These qualities bring the policies into the realm of the radical reform that I have been advocating.[31] And yet these policies still fall short, because the links among resources, institutions, and the institutional web are never fully broken. These interventions primarily touch the institutions of the poor, and even then only partially. Instead of making access to high-quality health care universal, for example, so that privileged and underprivileged alike are accessing the same institutions, these programs provide substantially better care for underprivileged communities by augmenting the institutions already in place. Although there is an increase in the range of services provided by schools, this takes place within an existing model of the educational system, and without any restructuring of these institutions. Nevertheless, it must be emphasized that early childhood intervention and Harlem Children's Zone are the two domestic programs that come closest to the type of radical reform that I am proposing.

From Cradle to Grave

The two reforms to institutional networks that I have discussed to this point are partial, in that they focus on specific life course moments. My final example of a reform at the level of the institutional network comes from post–World War II Britain, where the Labour government led by Prime Minister Clement Attlee attempted to build an entire society on a foundation of coherent webs of institutions, so that at every stage of the life course individuals would be supported by all of the institutions that surrounded them.

The Attlee government introduced a system of democratic socialism, largely through the nationalization of key industries and the construction of a system of social support that would protect and nurture individuals throughout their lives. Importantly, this system was not a halfway point between capitalism and communism, but a fresh attempt to refashion existing institutions to promote the common welfare.[32] The rationale behind the refashioning is highly consistent with the criteria that I laid out for radical reform, in that attempts were made to break the link between resources and institutions, and to create a coherent network of institutions around individuals.

The Beveridge Report, which described the proposed reforms, identified five "giants" that the new welfare state needed to tackle simultaneously: want, disease, ignorance, squalor, and idleness.[33] The reformers insisted that true social progress could be made only with an integrated approach, and they stressed that directing money to the poor and jobless would be but a partial solution. Thus, a comprehensive system of unemployment insurance and pensions was paired with the introduction of the National Health Service, a free and compulsory state education system, and substantial investment in public housing and subsidized loan schemes to improve rates of home ownership.[34] The reforms were generally viewed as a success. The National Health Service ensured that all had access to health care, and other reforms gave low-income families access to housing and the right to free education. Unemployment fell substantially from prewar levels, and Britain's economy recovered from its wartime battering.[35] In sum, the "welfare state," as it came to be known, targeted inequality of constraints by making access to institutions universal and by recognizing that individuals needed to be supported by a network of institutions if they were to reach their potential.

Although some of these reforms were later undone or altered beyond recognition in the subsequent decades, many of the original welfare state structures persisted and provided ready levers for new policy and reform. When the New Labour government implemented a plan to reduce child poverty, it was able to repurpose existing institutions rather than having to start from scratch. The integration of institutions that was a feature of the postwar period was also mimicked in new institutional forms, notably in the Sure Start centers that provided integrated health care, education, and support to children under the age of five.[36] The reduction in child poverty achieved through the New Labour reforms was substantial.[37]

Although the Attlee reforms were achieved only through substantial state action, similar coherent webs of institutions can be built at the local level by non-state actors. One example of this may be found in the long history of company towns in the United States. Company towns arose in the nineteenth and early-twentieth centuries when American industrialists decided to provide amenities to workers alongside wages. Some industrialists were motivated by ideological commitments to their workers' welfare, while others were motivated by profit, but they had in common the view that workers would be most productive when they were living in an environment that offered a complementary set of well-functioning institutions. In the best examples of such towns, workers and their families were given access to subsidized housing, schools, medical care, public parks, libraries, and retirement benefits.[38] At a local community level, and well before the European social model was established, capitalists were introducing coherent webs of institutions to families across the United States.

The dangers of relying on individual capitalists to design institutional structures for workers and their families are obvious. The history of company towns provides many examples of exploitative relationships between management and workers, of misaligned incentives and interests, and of antidemocratic practices that undermined the utopian ideals of these communities.[39] But one lesson that we should draw from the example of company towns is that, like many European states, private enterprises with an eye toward profit might anticipate significant returns to building coherent institutional webs around workers and their families.

Rolling the Dice

Up to this point I have discussed a number of models that produce changes in inequality of constraints either by addressing the distribution of resources or by addressing the structure and quality of the institutional network. Given that I have argued in favor of a set of policies that limit the power of resources to shape institutions and the institutional network, one might assume that radical reform must always involve direct intervention in the institutional structure. But there is an alternative approach. In contrast to direct intervention through careful, visible-hand "institutional design," we might instead consider exploit-ing randomization as a very minimalist form of design.

The randomization approach works to break the link between resources and institutional structures by making access to institutions dependent on chance. Rather than assigning children to schools on the basis of geographi-cal area, for example, children could be assigned at random to one of sev-eral possible schools. Where access to institutions is determined by chance, institutions may still differ in quality, but children from different socioeco-nomic backgrounds have equal chances of access to those institutions. At the extreme, where access to all institutions is governed by chance, children of the privileged would no longer be cocooned by institutions, because the chances of gaining access to a set of high-quality institutions would be determined only by the associated probability distributions.

Randomization would be expected to have two effects relevant to equality of constraints. First, we would expect the link between resources and institu-tional quality to be broken as a result of this policy. Privileged parents would no longer be able to choose which institutions their children would interact with, because that choice would be made by the state through a lottery. Sec-ond, as a result we would expect to see equalization of institutional quality, because privileged families would no longer be clustered within particular institutions.

An example of access through randomization can be found in South Korea, where the state regulated access to the education system with a lottery. The school lottery was introduced for middle schools in the late 1960s by the Ministry of Education, and was extended to high schools (High School Equal-ization Policy) a few years later. The policy was designed to address severe inequalities in access to high-quality and well-resourced schools in urban areas, both within and between the regions of Korea. Students were assigned at random to middle and high schools in their local district by means of a computerized lottery, and both public and private schools were required to accept the students assigned to them.[40] Evaluation studies have shown that the implementation of the randomization policy was associated with an equaliza-tion of socioeconomic composition across schools and a subsequent reduction in educational inequality.[41]

One concern with policies of this type is that they achieve their goals, in part, by taking something away from those already advantaged. Equaliza-tion is expected here because the performance of weaker schools is improved, but also because the performance of stronger schools may deteriorate. If one assumes, as many do, that total output is maximized when high-quality schools train well-resourced and high-performing children, a randomization policy will reduce total educational output. It is therefore possible that the gains in equity from the randomization policy will occur in a context of declining average levels of achievement, with important consequences for economic growth. The evidence from Korea is inconclusive on this question. Although some studies have shown declines in average achievement as a result of the randomization policy, others show no change or even improvements in average achievement.[42]

The key problem with using randomization to eliminate inequality of constraints is that while random allocation can be relatively easily introduced to the education system, random allocation to *all* social institutions would be difficult to implement in the context of our current economic and social system. It is not at all obvious, for example, how random allocation might be applied to the institution of the family. Randomization can be effective in equalizing social institutions partly because privileged families have an interest in improving all institutions if their children may come into contact with them. Once the stork drops us into a particular family, we "belong" to that family. If a reformer proposed seizing children immediately after birth and randomly assigning them to a new family, it would cause substantial social turmoil. If a reformer instead proposed to implant randomly selected embryos into the wombs of would-be mothers, it is hard to imagine that the reception would be terribly positive, but more importantly, it would not engender any special incentive for privileged families to improve the lives of the underprivileged families into which their child might otherwise have been born. This may be contrasted to the South Korean case, where privileged families are motivated to support *all* schools, as they do not know the school to which their child will be assigned.[43] Randomization cannot, then, be relied upon to break all links between socioeconomic resources and institutions, although it may still have a role to play in combination with more thoroughgoing institutional design.

The Other Road

To this point I have considered radical models from around the world that would likely reduce inequality of constraints. But in considering the institutional arrangements of other countries as possible models, it is important to acknowledge that we have already moved away from the most extreme examples of possible reforms. Although levels of inequality and estimates of inequality of opportunity vary substantially across countries, there are no countries that offer anything approaching perfect equality of constraints. There is, then, an obligation to consider institutional reforms that do not already exist in other countries.

In the remainder of this chapter I propose several radical reforms that would alter the structure of social institutions and thereby reduce inequality of constraints. As it is so straightforward to flatten the income distribution through tax policy, I instead focus on reforms that equalize access to coherent and high-quality institutional networks among children of different socioeconomic backgrounds. I discuss four categories of reform that are likely to have particular payoffs in this respect: social exchange, network, computational, and legal.

The Rubber Band

Although we are fortunate to live in a society with a well-established state and laws that guarantee certain types of reciprocity, privileged parents nonetheless have inadequate incentives to assist underprivileged parents. Socioeconomic resources have an effect on the quality of institutions in large part because parents are willing to use resources to improve the chances that their own child will do well, and they are not willing to use resources to improve the chances that other children will do well. Consequently, privileged children have access to institutions that underprivileged children do not, and the child of a privileged family has the opportunity to be cocooned by institutions in a way that the underprivileged child does not. It would be beneficial to find ways to incentivize privileged parents to give all children access to high-quality social institutions.

Self-interest with respect to our children is an expected behavior that should probably be encouraged, even if it increases inequality of constraints. Recent work, such as Richard Reeves's *Dream Hoarders*, uses moral appeals in attempts to persuade the families from the top income quintile that the advantages that their children enjoy are illegitimate and unfair. His recommendations include a set of actions—not ticking the "alumni" box on college applications, a call for the top 20 percent to "check our privilege"—that explicitly ask the privileged to accept that their children are advantaged, and to take action against their own interests.[44] But perhaps instead of trying to persuade privileged parents to act against their own self-interest, we might find ways to harness self-interest to reduce inequality. The randomization policy discussed above is one example of reform that relies on self-interested behavior, in part, for its positive effects: privileged families have an incentive to raise school quality for all children if they do not know ahead of time which school their children will attend.[45]

Another possibility is to directly tie the outcomes of privileged children to those of the underprivileged. Consider, for example, a policy that might be labeled the "rubber band." The "rubber band" policy would make the educational and labor market success of a privileged child conditional upon the success of an underprivileged child. Up until adulthood, for example, each rich child could be bound to a child much lower in the income distribution: if one child drops out of high school, so must the other; if one child wishes to attend an elite college, she may do so only if the other can also attend. The "rubber band" binding rich and poor children together could connect two specific children or it could operate at the societal level. In the former case, each poor child would be matched at random to a rich child in a similar region of the country, and the opportunities of the rich child would depend entirely on the partner's success. In the latter case, opportunities for rich children would be rationed according to how many poor children had taken up those opportunities. If one thousand poor children were accepted to elite colleges, for example, no more than one thousand rich children could be accepted to those colleges. The rationing approach would tie the success of rich children to that of poor children without insisting that a particular rich child's success depends on the success of a particular poor child.

The rubber band policy relies on self-interest for its beneficial effects. If the self-interest of the privileged depends directly upon the outcomes for the underprivileged, privileged families have a strong incentive to improve the lives of underprivileged families. We might expect improvements to the health care system, the education system, neighborhoods, and other public goods to follow. Institutional cocoons would be built for underprivileged children just as for the privileged.

But a further consequence of rubber band reform would be to emphasize the extent to which the destinies of our children are linked. Under current institutional arrangements, their destinies are already linked, although it is a linkage in which privileged children benefit from restricting the opportunities of others. For example, the returns to schooling in the United States are high, in part, because there are too few people with college degrees: if more people obtained degrees, the competition for jobs requiring high levels of education would increase, and the premium associated with a college degree would be expected to fall.[46] Given that almost all of the children of the privileged already attend college, the only way to increase the numbers of those with a college degree is to increase the numbers of underprivileged children attending college.[47] Returns to schooling are high, therefore, because underprivileged children do not attend college in large enough numbers. A contrasting example comes from the "rising tide lifts all boats" analogy. Those who subscribe to this position believe that economic growth should be encouraged through very high individual rewards for the "growth promoters," because that growth will "trickle down" to those at the bottom of the income distribution, improving the utility of all in the society. Those in favor of trickle-down economics are already promoting a version of a rubber band solution to societal problems: the welfare of the poor is assumed to depend on the economic success of the rich.

The objections to the rubber band policy are obvious. Issues of liberty and self-determination loom large, particularly where individual children are tied to each other until adulthood. Why should my life's trajectory depend on another person over whom I have no control? Implementation of the individual-pairs rubber band policy would be extremely difficult to achieve and would require cooperation from educational and other institutions that would not necessarily regard the policy as operating in their interests. We might also have strong concerns about the rubber band policy inhibiting economic growth. Although one possible outcome of the policy is that talented poor children would be more likely to achieve academic and occupational success, and subsequently go on to drive growth, another possible outcome is that some talented rich children may be blocked from opportunities that they would have taken up with enthusiasm. We may currently be willing to accept rubber bands that tie children to their parental circumstances, and the negative consequences of these ties for economic growth, but an individualized rubber band policy of the type that I have proposed would likely be seen as a step too far.

Why should we even discuss the rubber band policy when it has little chance of implementation? First, highlighting the interdependence of children from different socioeconomic backgrounds helps to emphasize the trade-offs integral to our current social system. When these trade-offs cannot be ignored, action of the sort that Reeves calls for becomes more likely. And second, although an individualized rubber band policy is unlikely to be realized, a societal-level policy perhaps holds more promise, particularly when recast as a type of affirmative action. If profound inequalities in opportunity were to become delegitimated as being inconsistent with the Dream, sufficient support might be found to preserve prestigious educational and labor market slots for those from poorly resourced social backgrounds. We already see, for example, proposals to undertake affirmative action in college admissions with respect to first-generation status or income.[48] Alternative forms of "offsets" might also be considered, such as those used to good effect in the environmental realm: under this model, privileged parents who wished to send their child to an elite college might be required to contribute to a fund that would support underprivileged children on the pathway to elite college acceptance. If even a small number of educational or labor market institutions were to embrace such reforms, we would likely see further delegitimation of current resource-tainted institutional processes and practices.

The rubber band policy underscores some of the contradictions that lie at the heart of the current inequality of opportunity policy agenda. We recoil from the interdependence imposed by this approach, while accepting the interdependence imposed by the current structure of inequality. We are troubled by the intrusions into institutional practices that we might require of the state in order to provide opportunity to some individuals, while accepting those institutional practices that were shaped by different powerful interests and that provide opportunity to other individuals. The rubber band policy lays bare these contradictions, and encourages deliberative decision making with respect to inequality of constraints.

Constructed Communities

The key premise of the preceding proposal is that successful institutional reform requires introducing incentives for the privileged to care more about the underprivileged. I next consider a reform that targets community rather than incentives. In June 2017, *New York Times* columnist David Brooks asked the question "What would I do if I had a billion bucks to use for good?"[49] He answered that he would "start with the premise that the most important task before us is to reweave the social fabric. People in disorganized neighborhoods need to grow up enmeshed in the loving relationships that will help them rise. The elites need to be reintegrated with their own countrymen."[50]

Brooks's premise brings to mind the definition of radical policy that I laid out above, although when it comes to specific prescriptions he pulls back toward a less ambitious project of establishing twenty-five-person "collectives" that meet once a week to "discuss life." But if we push Brooks's vision to its most radical conclusion, we reach a society founded on artificial families and constructed communities.

The social institution of the family plays a special role in the intergenerational inheritance of inequality, largely because it is difficult to separate children from their families and the associated resources. There are examples of alternative family forms, such as the traditional kibbutz, but these communities are distinctive for being economically and socially autonomous from the wider society.[51] Instead of challenging the nuclear family, a constructed communities reform would add a layer of new family forms to our existing institutional structures, and extend the number of ties that a child could draw upon for resources, advice, and support. Ideally, such a reform would be paired with substantial economic desegregation, so that rich and poor would once again live alongside each other. But in the absence of economic desegregation, the constructed communities could draw from a wide range of socioeconomic groups. Even if rich and poor did not live together, the constructed community would ensure that every individual was exposed to different types of people, and over time, members of the constructed community would develop ties analogous to kinship that held emotional resonance and expectations of mutual exchange. These ties are valuable both because they emphasize the interdependence of members of the group and because they are associated with resources that will help children succeed.

The constructed communities reform is an attempt to intervene in the individual-level networks within which children are raised. Given existing social science research, we would expect two types of effects to follow for inequality of constraints. First, the networks within which we are embedded have consequences for our opportunities and economic success. As Mark Granovetter famously argued, opportunities for mobility are enhanced when individuals have contact with people outside of their close family and friends, because there is an increased likelihood of hearing "new" information about jobs and other opportunities.[52] By artificially extending the number and quality of weak ties among individuals, constructed communities would increase underprivileged children's access to educational, occupational, and economic opportunities. These would be strong ties that offered many of the benefits that weak ties currently provide.

The second effect of the constructed communities reform would be more subtle, but it also has the potential to be more transformative. By interacting with people from a range of socioeconomic backgrounds, community members would be in constant contact with both poverty and affluence: poverty and its effects would no longer be hidden from the privileged, and affluence would be displayed to the underprivileged.[53] Increased interaction might be expected to lead to increased empathy for the challenges of others, and increased investment in shared dreams of prosperity and success.[54] Privileged parents would also have incentives to improve the lives of the underprivileged children in their constructed community, because their own children would be held in a network that included less-privileged children: if poverty puts constraints on the opportunities of underprivileged children, network effects may transmit their disadvantages to privileged children, too. Without the opportunity to live entirely segregated lives, therefore, the privileged may choose to embrace collective goods to a much greater extent than at present. It follows that a network-based reform might exert indirect effects on incentives and interests as well.

Once again, this radical proposal raises issues of liberty and self-determination. The proverbial caution that "you can't pick your family, but you can pick your friends" may turn out to capture two especially popular features of the status quo: we like to be able to pick our friends, but privileged children also benefit from their close family ties being limited to the family within which they were born or adopted. And yet we see many examples of people collaborating in ways that would be expected to reduce inequality of constraints, particularly if those collaborations could be encouraged on a larger scale. The long-standing Big Brothers Big Sisters program demonstrates that ties among different types of people can be created and nurtured, with positive benefits for the children who are matched to supportive mentors.[55] Canada's program to resettle refugees similarly demonstrates the power of close ties: under the Private Sponsorship of Refugees Program, communities can apply to sponsor a refugee for one year, during which time community members commit to provide emotional and financial support for refugees to help them settle into Canadian society. These community ties often persist long past the initial year, and privately sponsored refugees appear to fare better than government-sponsored refugees.[56] Although a truly radical proposal would entail a far greater degree of engagement and many more ties among different types of people, our communities are seemingly already open to some types of planful integration, and this openness could be exploited by the radical policy agenda.

The Engine

Technological development has had profound implications for stratification processes and for economic growth.[57] One of the central questions of our time is how future technological development will change how we live and work, particularly since growing automation appears to have a greater potential (at least in the short term) to increase economic inequalities than to reduce them.[58] Although it is unlikely that any single technological development will dramatically reduce inequality of constraints, might there be ways to harness a set of technological developments within a radical policy initiative?

Two important features of technology hold promise in this regard. First, socioeconomic resources affect institutions in many ways, but one important effect operates through information asymmetries. The underprivileged are locked out of social networks that might provide information about economic opportunities, they attend schools that have insufficient resources to provide information about college applications or financial aid, and they may be unaware of their eligibility for state aid programs. Technology can fill these information voids, both by identifying information relevant to underprivileged individuals and their current circumstances and by delivering information directly to the person who needs it. Technology can also reduce the burden of any interaction between people and institutions, by prefilling application forms or automating the transfer of information from people to institutions without any intervention from humans.[59] Such techniques are frequently applied in many nudge interventions, but technological innovations could also be used alongside some of the radical policy models that have been implemented in other countries. Flexicurity, for example, eases an individual's transitions among the education system, the labor market, and the safety net. Automation would make it possible to link individuals to training programs the moment that they became unemployed, to push well-trained individuals into appropriate vacancies, and to ensure that welfare benefits would begin and end as needed. Examples of this type of technological innovation are already being developed by governments as a key part of labor market policy.

The second feature of technology that may aid the radical policy agenda is its capacity to knit together institutions without any human intervention. Underprivileged children may be provided with a coherent web through technology: if they suffer ill health, for example, technology might be harnessed to provide an automatic exemption from school assignments, or an automatic application for the appropriate accommodations. Conversely, some of the advantages that the privileged enjoy could be undermined. Automation of the recruitment process has the potential to reduce discrimination against disadvantaged groups, since taking people out of the process reduces the likelihood that high-status cultural signals will compensate for weaknesses in the résumé.[60] Artificial intelligence of this type, therefore, can build links among institutions for the underprivileged or break down the barriers created when the privileged are cocooned by institutions.

A technological solution to inequality of constraints has attractions. Solving information problems should encourage growth (by cutting out market distortions) in addition to reducing inequality. It is less clear that a technological solution could guarantee equality of constraints in the absence of other radical policy reforms. The best available research suggests that information constraints cannot fully account for inequalities in educational or occupational opportunities, although these studies never consider the possibility that *all* information constraints could be eliminated.[61] Another serious concern relates to the construction and design of technology. Automated systems are designed by humans and are likely to take on some of the biases of those humans. Contemporary examples include facial recognition software that recognizes white skin but will not operate for people of color, and a chatbot that "unexpectedly turned into a Hitler-loving, feminist-bashing troll."[62] It would therefore be naïve to rely upon technology to take on inequality of constraints. But it would also be unwise to build radical policy without taking advantage of the techniques and systems that may arise from technological innovation.

Rightful Liberty

In the United States, we are immensely tolerant of freedom being limited by parental resources, but immensely intolerant of legal constraints limiting our day-to-day behaviors. If this balance were ever to shift, we might see a pathway for the law to guarantee equality of constraints. Legislation has been used both in this country and in others in support of the principle of equality of opportunity; laws operate either by prohibiting behavior that obstructs equality, such as discrimination, or by promoting equality more directly.

The latter type of law—in which positive action is taken to promote equality—is built into the constitutions of a number of countries, among them countries (such as Finland) that are widely praised for their approach to poverty and inequality. Martha Nussbaum and Amartya Sen have long argued that countries engaged in constitutional reform should embed in their legal statutes guarantees that a core set of "capabilities" will be supported for all citizens. In supporting these capabilities, laws might be designed to protect and promote rights to life, health, bodily integrity, and education.[63] More recently, Darrick Hamilton, Mark Paul, and William Darity Jr. have proposed that the United States should introduce an economic "Bill of Rights," which would extend the current legislation to the protection of economic rights.[64]

A radical reform built on a foundation of positive law would almost certainly require the United States to alter its Constitution, as conventional interpretations of the equal protection clause would rule out extensive changes to existing arrangements in order to promote equality of constraints. But if an amendment were passed that promised equality of constraints to all citizens, many of the current arrangements that encourage inequality could be challenged in the courts. Segregation in housing and schooling could be addressed through changes in zoning laws and school finance reform. Income inequality could be addressed through redistributive policies and reparations for past harms, both of which would increase the incomes of the poor.

An alternative to using the law to *promote* equality of constraints is instead to *outlaw* inequality-generating practices. Antidiscrimination law gives the courts the power to punish problematic behaviors, and we would therefore expect organizational practices and personnel policies to be shaped by the intent of the law. In the United States, a well-known example of antidiscrimination law being used to address equality of constraints is the decision in *Brown v. Board of Education*, in which racial segregation in U.S. public schools was deemed to be unconstitutional. The main difficulty in using current antidiscrimination law to address equality of constraints is again that family socioeconomic status is not a protected class in the United States, and it would therefore be difficult to address either disparate treatment (e.g., direct discrimination against low-income job candidates) or disparate impact (e.g., a preference for local workers in a high-income region) to reduce inequality of constraints across all dimensions of socioeconomic inequality. Radical reform based on antidiscrimination provisions would therefore require that new protected classes be added to the existing list.

Both types of legal reform—whether the introduction of laws promoting equality of constraints or the use of antidiscrimination law to outlaw inequality-generating practices—would place the ultimate responsibility for reducing inequality of constraints on the courts. As is clear from the above examples, a wide range of policies might be considered if such laws were established, with the precise policies implemented dependent on a court's interpretation of the law, and the interpretation of the law by private and state institutions. This interpretive process, however, opens the door to the possibility that the original intent of the law might be undermined, or the chance that unforeseen negative consequences might result from the law being applied appropriately.[65] As Frank Dobbin has documented for the period immediately following the introduction of laws mandating equal treatment in employment, the "laws were mute on the nuts and bolts of compliance," and company personnel officers therefore had a great deal of freedom in determining what "compliance" looked like.[66] Thus, a purely legal approach to equality of constraints would require both new laws and strong guidance in interpreting those laws to ensure that the relationships among parents, children, and social institutions are properly regulated.

The policies that I have proposed in this section are fantastical. They have obvious weaknesses, and some of them challenge values that we hold dear. The point of this discussion was not to propose models that might be implemented wholesale, but to highlight the types of institutional reform that would be needed to address inequality of constraints. The path to equality may be taken only after it has been imagined and constructed.

What is notable is that whether the policies discussed in this chapter are fantastical or real, they have little in common with the interventions actively pursued by contemporary policymakers. Even where we see bureaucratic and institutional support for particular incarnations of radical policy, those incarnations exist outside of a more ambitious radical agenda. But the roots of a radical policy agenda can be found in other countries, and even in the history of this country, should we look for them.

CHAPTER 5

WONDERING, FEARING

Let America be the dream the dreamers dreamed—
Let it be that great strong land of love
Where never kings connive nor tyrants scheme
That any man be crushed by one above.
                    —Langston Hughes, "Let America Be America Again"

The American Dream is a dream about society. It describes a society without barriers, a society where children are free to pursue economic opportunities without regard to the circumstances into which they were born. The Dream is not a dream about individuals, for no individual can fulfill its promise.

The Dream of this country is not its reality. Individuals are constrained by their socioeconomic origins, and the set of opportunities on offer differs according to the circumstances of birth. This country does not offer equality of opportunity to its citizens because it does not offer equality of constraints: the barriers that the underprivileged face are more substantial than those faced by the privileged. These are human-made barriers, embodied and reproduced in our social institutions, institutions that hold and protect the children of the privileged while leaving those of the underprivileged to confront institutional indifference and neglect.

When we enact policy to reduce inequalities in access to desirable educational and economic opportunities, we do not start from the position that we should eliminate these institutional constraints. Instead, we attempt to remediate, to improve the lives of the underprivileged, all the while moving further away from addressing the root causes of inequality of opportunity. We at once hold on to the Dream as a guiding commitment and work on the assumption that it cannot be realized.

In this final chapter, I advocate an emboldened social science, a social science that embraces the radical reforms that would be required to tackle inequality of constraints. A social science of radical reform can be built, I argue, on firm scientific foundations, but to accomplish that goal we must address three fundamental beliefs. When we address these beliefs head-on, we find that there is more potential for radical reform than is ordinarily imagined.

Small Steps Forge Giant Leaps

A common reaction to a call for radical reform is to insist that change is more likely to come gradually, through small reforms, and that radicals will undermine the possible by aiming for the ideal. Pragmatism consequently demands that we focus on small reforms to obtain any improvement at all: it is only if these are successful that we can consider adding further reforms that will likely produce additional incremental improvements. And supporters of incrementalism have an arsenal of data to assist their case. Cass Sunstein, for example, in his spirited defense of nudge interventions, writes, "It is true, of course, that for countless problems, nudges are hardly enough. They cannot eliminate poverty, unemployment, and corruption. But by itself, any individual initiative—whether it is a tax, a subsidy, a mandate, or a ban—is unlikely to solve large problems. Denting them counts as an achievement."[1]

A reasonable utilitarian position might be that we will come closer to achieving equality of constraints if we chip away at the problem rather than demand a wholesale reform that is unlikely to be realized. In this context, an advocate for radical reform risks undermining all of the good work that could be done by a set of incremental reforms.

As I argued in Chapter 2, this belief is widespread. It may be correct. It would be reasonable to argue that people are committed to the status quo, that changing political attitudes can be difficult, and that there are powerful vested interests that will resist the type of radical change that I am proposing. But in considering these issues social scientists have already moved away from what are supposed to be our central scientific commitments: to describe the extent of inequality, to explain how it is reproduced, and to leave no doubt about the extent of the reforms that would be required to call a halt to this reproduction. We have accepted the unspoken assumptions that radical change is impossible and that our job is to work within the narrow range of what has been deemed plausible. Our focus moves to nudges and narrow reforms, and we let the possibility of more substantial changes fade into the distance.

There are two important reasons why those concerned about undermining incremental improvements by considering radical reform might nevertheless wish to create room for the more extreme conversation.

First, high-profile scientific discussions of radical reforms are likely to highlight the research finding that inequality of constraints is a substantial problem. Inequality of constraints has deep roots, and to eliminate it completely would require a wholesale attack upon the cultural, economic, and social structures that maintain it. Inequality of constraints violates a cherished American value, it is at odds with the principles of social justice that are the moral foundations of most late-industrial societies, and it is economically inefficient. Social scientists are reticent about making such statements for fear of being perceived as "not objective"—a damning verdict for a scientist, because if research is not conducted according to standard scientific principles, there would be good reason to question its reliability, validity, and generalizability. And yet these statements are all rooted in scientific fact. That we do not loudly and frequently state such facts means that we undermine the science of inequality itself. It means that we are complicit in a falsehood. Even for those social scientists who have no interest in engaging with policy, outlining just what types of reform would eliminate inequality-generating institutions and practices would help to emphasize the extent of the inequality problem. It is up to the public to decide whether or not to support reforms that would mitigate or eliminate inequality of constraints. If, after thorough discussion, the public decides not to support such reforms, the decision is at least taken in full knowledge of the extent of the problem.

The second reason why proposals for radical reform should be welcomed even among those who support smaller interventions is the existence of the "radical flank effect." The radical flank effect describes the increase in the palatability of moderate ideas as a consequence of the introduction of more-radical voices. The term originates in the social movement literature, particularly in research examining the fights for racial and gender equality in the second half of the twentieth century.[2] Herbert Haines, for example, describes how the presence of Black radicalism during the civil rights era increased the attractiveness of more-moderate organizations, which were viewed as offering a more "reasonable" vision in comparison. During the radicalized period, corporate interests discovered a new enthusiasm for moderate organizations such as the NAACP, and the money poured in.[3] Far from generating a backlash against the general cause of racial equality, radical flank effects instead consolidated support for moderate reform.[4] This dynamic has been observed in various contexts, and would be expected to apply in the case of inequality as well. If social scientists aim to produce change—any change at all—in the level of inequality of constraints, even those without a taste for radical reform may wish to encourage their more-radical colleagues to speak up.

The contrast with climate science is instructive here. As the science tells us, global temperatures have been rising over the past 150 years, a change that is attributable to human activity (primarily the burning of fossil fuels).[5] Although this is a highly politicized issue, and our attention is often drawn to those who deny that climate change is happening, a clear majority of Americans are worried about global warming, believe that its effects are already being felt, and attribute temperature changes to human activity rather than to natural causes.[6]

The science of climate change has much in common with the science of inequality, perhaps most especially that researchers in both fields share a deep conviction that their subject of study reveals a significant problem and that there will be consequences for social stability if the problem is not addressed.[7] Both fields must find ways to communicate complex scientific ideas to a non-specialist public. In both cases, the policy response must weigh the potential social benefits of reform against the possible negative effects on personal liberty and on economic growth.

But where the climate change science has been more successful, I would argue, is in emphasizing the scientific consensus around global warming, and in highlighting the need for structural reform.[8] In 2019, more than 11,000 climate scientists collaborated to publish a warning that the world is facing a clear and unequivocal climate emergency. They did not entertain the possibility that small-scale or incremental reforms would be enough to overcome the challenges of global warming. Rather, they stated, "We must change how we live . . . we need bold and drastic transformations regarding economic and population policies."[9] This recent consensus well represents the policy discussions that now dominate the climate change field. These discussions focus on institutional and technological changes, and it is understood that when such structural changes occur, individual behavior will respond. If it is difficult to persuade people to stop driving, the aim must instead be to build cars that do not pollute and to provide more attractive public transport solutions. If it is difficult to persuade people to use less energy, the aim must instead be to find new sources of energy and to invest in green technology. And if individuals in one country cannot be persuaded to force their government to act, the aim must be to work toward cross-national cooperation on these issues.

The push toward radical reform has been aided by the radical flank of the environmental movement. In a paper examining radical flank effects of the fossil fuels divestment movement, Todd Schifeling and Andrew Hoffman observe that while the movement did not significantly affect the economic viability of fossil fuel companies, it did influence mainstream discussions of climate change. The divestment movement helped to neutralize the "no-change" positions while making space for a discussion of "moderate" institutional reforms. Schifeling and Hoffman conclude that radical and moderate reform movements might have a "symbiotic dynamic, where radicals strengthen the negotiating position of moderates, who in turn provide a pathway for central issues to move towards radical goals."[10] As the experience of the environmental movement demonstrates, a push for radical reform highlights the argument that the problem to be solved is immense, while at the same time clearing space in the policy arena for moderate (but still transformative) ideas to be heard.

Strangers in Our Own Land

A fundamental belief that holds social scientists back from proposing radical reform is a fear that there is little public appetite for substantial social change. As I have argued, a lack of public appetite for reform is not, in itself, a good reason for social scientists to back away. But if we accept the proposition that social scientists should respond to public desires, we need to take seriously the task of judging the public's openness (and potential openness) to radical policy solutions. After all, the vast majority of Americans believe that society should do "what is necessary" to deliver equal opportunity to everyone.[11]

Before the 2016 presidential election campaign, there would perhaps have been skepticism that the public desired anything more than campaign slogans making gestures toward change, or relatively modest tweaks to the tax code and welfare policy.[12] Leslie McCall's detailed analysis of Americans' attitudes toward inequality in recent decades finds no evidence that they have become more sympathetic to redistributive tax policy or increased antipoverty spending as income inequality has risen. Although there is evidence that when income inequality is higher, support for government spending on some social services (particularly education) is also higher, it would be difficult to make a case from the attitudinal data that the American public is anxious for the government to undertake a radical attack on existing inequalities of outcome or constraints.[13]

And yet.

We have now lived through multiple election campaigns in which it has become startlingly clear that a substantial proportion of the U.S. population is not only open to the idea of radical change, but is demanding it. If the greatest failure of contemporary economics has been the failure to predict devastating economic downturns, the greatest failure of contemporary sociology must surely be the failure to appreciate the substantial proportion of the U.S. population that is experiencing profound alienation, loss, and economic despair.[14] To be sure, sociologists of inequality have documented the difficult socioeconomic circumstances of those who are losing out in today's economy, and scholars such as Arlie Hochschild were remarkably prescient in identifying the anger and pain of the "left behind."[15] But whatever the detailed autopsies of the 2016 presidential election might come to reveal, it is impossible to ignore the fact that many people in this country were willing to cast their vote either for a man who became president on the basis of a promise to overhaul the "system" or for a Democratic Party candidate who was a self-proclaimed socialist.

The years following have provided only further confirmation that a large number of voters are attracted to political platforms that commit to sweeping change, with the 2020 Democratic party primary contest swiftly cast as a battle between centrists and those with a more radical vision.[16] Outside of the narrow political process, we see increased enthusiasm for social movements such as Me Too and Black Lives Matter. The latter movement in particular has been highly successful in emphasizing the importance of tackling structures and systems of inequality rather than focusing on individual behaviors. If ever there has been a time for social scientists to question their conviction that radical policy reforms could not gain any ground in the United States, this is it.

There is a seeming inconsistency, then, between the stasis revealed in conventional attitudinal data and the growing support for more-radical political candidates and social movements. Even if the public can be persuaded to vote for a candidate who promises societal overhaul, a reasonable concern would be that the evidence from attitudinal measures is at odds with the claim that there is a groundswell of support for such overhaul. But as McCall noted, perhaps we are simply asking the wrong questions to elicit public opinion on this topic. She argues that "the highest priority for future research . . . is to take American public opinion about inequality seriously enough to find out exactly how it is related to policy preferences."[17] Recent experimental work offers support for the idea that the public would express support for policies to address structural inequalities if only we measured these policy preferences properly.[18]

Even if we were to assume that there remains but a small constituency for radical reform at present, should we continue to push for incremental policy proposals alone? It is clear that we should not. First, as I have argued, it is a scientific and professional responsibility to propose reforms that actually address the problems that we identify: if we believe that radical policies will work, we must argue on behalf of them. But perhaps more importantly, it is difficult to predict what the future will hold. If we cannot predict with accuracy the types of policies that the public will demand in ten years, or five years, or even next year, we cannot assume that radical policies will always be regarded as beyond the pale.

It is well known that public opinion may change, and it may change quickly. A prominent recent example of this phenomenon is the increasing enthusiasm for marriage equality and gay rights in the United States. In the early 2000s, 57 percent of the public opposed marriage equality. By 2017, 62 percent were in favor of it.[19] This change did not come about through processes of cohort replacement, but because attitudes became more favorable among people of all ages and social groups.[20] Similar shifts in public opinion can be seen with respect to implementing a single-payer health care system in the United States and with respect to support for police reform.[21] Cass Sunstein has described rapid changes of this sort as "norm cascades," a phenomenon in which what is regarded as deviant or acceptable changes rapidly, from one moment to the next, often because there is a disjuncture between what people feel privately and what they are willing to express publicly.[22] Norm cascades may be provoked by random or unexpected events (e.g., experience of a hurricane might generate a sudden change in attitudes toward climate change, or new technology might make the previously unthinkable possible) or because "norm entrepreneurs" have initiated actions with the specific intention of producing a change in norms (e.g., a politician or charismatic social movement leader).[23]

The effects of unexpected events are of particular interest in the context of attitudes toward inequality. Much of the momentum behind post-WWII changes to the welfare state in the United Kingdom, for example, came from an understanding among the public and political elites alike that the sacrifices of the working classes during wartime must be recognized: all of those who had contributed to the wartime integrity of the country had a right to benefit from its resources.[24] War is generally an equalizing force, in part because workers are diverted from productive activity to the war effort, and assets are destroyed and redeployed. But in the aftermath of war, the specter of exchange often rises, and political exigencies call for the restructuring of economic and social policy in favor of the socioeconomically disadvantaged.[25]

A new world war does not appear to be on the horizon. But plagues have historically had far-reaching consequences too.[26] Within weeks of the Covid-19 pandemic striking the United States, public discussion turned to weaknesses in the U.S. social and economic system that were causing some social groups to bear the brunt of both the economic disruption and the disease. Bernie Sanders, for example, wrote in the *New York Times*:

> Disparity in outcomes from exposure to the virus is a direct reflection not only of a broken and unjust health care system but also an economy that punishes, in terrible ways, the poor and working class of this country. . . . If there is any silver lining in the horrible pandemic and economic collapse we're experiencing, it is that many in our country are now beginning to rethink the basic assumptions underlying the American value system.[27]

Sanders's conviction that the pandemic might rupture American values to positive effect may turn out to be all too sanguine given the possible alternatives; there are, after all, many Americans who wish simply to return to the prior status quo, and others who might embrace greater inequality in preference to a radical restructuring.

Nevertheless, the clear lesson from history is that unpredicted and extreme events have the potential to upset contemporary understandings of what are acceptable (or appropriate) levels of inequality and government intervention. The potential is there because unfair exchange relationships are at the heart of society, underpinning economic and social relationships among individuals.[28] If enough people come to appreciate that their sacrifices and investments in society are not valued or repaid, the current social arrangements may be called into question.[29]All institutions exist because of generations of investments by our parents, grandparents, and more-distant ancestors. In almost all cases these investments were not voluntary, meaning that our present-day institutional structures rest on the subjugation and sacrifices of earlier generations. The clearest example of exploitation can be found in the United States' history of slavery, and as Ta-Nehisi Coates observes, "The laments about 'black pathology,' the criticism of black family structures by pundits and intellectuals, ring hollow in a country whose existence was predicated on the torture of black fathers, on the rape of black mothers, on the sale of black children."[30] The exploitation of indigenous peoples, immigrants, and labor is similarly inseverable from our current institutional structure. Our institutions are more vulnerable than we generally appreciate, for the exploitation upon which most of our institutions are built is thinly disguised. It is not a large step from "business as usual" to an appreciation that all institutions rest on exploitative exchange and should be reimagined to work to the benefit of all people.

The existence of unpredicted events, associated norm cascades, and similar phenomena indicates that reforms that are now considered to be unpalatable and infeasible might not always be considered to be so. In societies with very high levels of socioeconomic inequality and where most people are relatively disadvantaged, it is particularly unwise to assume that private beliefs about inequality will always match the current normative, public expressions. If contemporary norms around the appropriate institutional responses to inequality of constraints change rapidly, social science needs to be ready to weigh in on the viability of alternative institutional arrangements.

Scientific Revolutions

An important objection to an agenda for radical reform is that such reform is difficult to test in advance. As I described in Chapter 2, part of the reticence in proposing radical reform originates in the difficulties of pointing to a body of research evidence that can be used to justify a substantial overhaul of existing institutions. Without a science of radical reform, it will therefore be difficult to generate support from the scientific mainstream. Can such a science be developed?

One way to respond to this question is to point out that such a science already exists, albeit on a small scale. Economists, for example, have exploited to great effect some of the visionary and inventive experiments of the War on Poverty period. This was a time during which there were "experiments, hopes, new beginnings," as Martin Luther King described it.[31] Importantly, many of the more-radical policy initiatives that feature in current public debate draw upon research that was initiated in this period: the negative income tax experiments of the 1960s and 1970s are referenced by supporters of a universal basic income, while the early childhood literature relies heavily upon the high-quality data collected in the Carolina Abecedarian Project, the Perry Preschool Program, and Head Start. The contemporary period offers further examples of experiments with radical reform, but the impetus and funding for such experiments increasingly originates in the nonprofit sector.[32]

The existing evidence base on radical reform relies to a large extent, therefore, upon our more-radical forebears and on the present-day enthusiasms of entrepreneurs and foundations.[33] It relies upon the social scientists of the past who acted as advocates for change and who planned the ambitious and evidence-informed modifications to existing social institutions. A key point is that the institutional modifications were evidence-informed, but they could never be evidence-*determined*, because until the radical reforms were implemented it was impossible to predict precisely what might happen: in a package of reforms, one reform might undermine another, reforms might turn out to be less effective in a real-world context than in the laboratory, or particular combinations of reforms might produce particularly strong or weak effects on outcomes. As with all predictions about intervention and change, evidence on individual components of the package of radical reform must be assessed in the light of existing theories about these components and the relationships among them. In the case of early childhood reforms, for example, Bronfenbrenner's theory about interrelationships among individuals, proximate institutions, and the wider society was used to inform the design of a program of interventions that would support the development of very young children.[34] The theory had never been tested in full, but there was sufficient evidence on behalf of some of its main elements that Head Start and other early childhood programs could be developed and subsequently tested. This interplay between empirical evidence and theory is at the heart of a science of radical reform.

How might this interplay best be managed? In the shorter term, the aim must be to maximize the reliance upon strong empirical evidence while using theory to make predictions in the absence of such evidence.[35] In the case of the types of radical reform that were discussed in Chapter 4, many of the elements of reform packages have been rigorously tested in other countries, and we have strong evidence about the type of institutional design that might pay off. For example, in building a coherent web of institutions around underprivileged children, we can look to existing research on the design of health care systems, schools, neighborhoods, public services, and tax policy, and bring these elements together to design a reform package. We may be missing data and evidence on some of the links among these elements—we may not know, for example, how changing a health care system might alter the effects of changing a school system—but existing theory can be used to make reasonable predictions about the combined effects.

A longer-term aim should be to amass evidence on the effects of both the design of individual institutions and the web of institutions. Despite sociology's long-standing intellectual interest in understanding the workings of social systems, our empirical attention is strangely divided between examining individual institutions and examining the outcomes of entire systems. Much less attention has been paid to interactions among institutions, although insofar as these interactions are of interest, it is the interaction between the family and another institution that is most frequently studied.[36] It is the tools to identify the effects of institutional linkages that must be developed to provide an underpinning for radical reform.

Such tools can be found in the engineering field, which has an interest in examining systems and system coherence. Integration testing, for example, breaks systems down into distinct "modules" and tests whether interactions between modules produce the expected results. A final stage, known as "system testing," examines integration across all systems, to ensure that the entire process operates as expected. These kinds of tests are crucial in fields where failure would be costly or dangerous. Take aircraft construction, for example. The definitive test of whether or not a newly designed aircraft can fly is to attempt to fly it. But if it cannot fly, or cannot fly for long, the result could be potentially disastrous consequences for the pilot, for the company, and for the general public. Integration and system testing ensure that the first test flight is low risk, because it is known that each component integrates with the others as theorized.

The model of integration and system testing currently used in engineering was in fact taken up for a time by social policy analysts. As the Cold War progressed, the United States invested significant human and physical capital in the development of scientific systems; a single technological innovation was less valuable than a functioning missile system, or an entire satellite network. The RAND Corporation, a key player in the development of full-system evaluation methods, realized that the same style of analysis could be extended to the social world, and "systems analysis" was applied to all manner of social and policy problems.[37]

Although systems analysis was used extensively by policy analysts, particularly at RAND, it soon fell out of fashion. In part, this failure can be explained by a lack of appropriately trained personnel: many of the practitioners were not social scientists, but engineers or military personnel applying systems analysis methods to the social world. But there were also three other important reasons why systems analysis did not fulfill its promise. First, there is more uncertainty around the operation of each system component in a social context than in an engineering context. Uncertainty makes it difficult to obtain precise estimates of the effects of any individual component (i.e., a social institution, or part of an institution), a problem that is inevitably magnified when assessing effects of institutions in combination. Second, systems analysts were forced to settle for crude assumptions about links among social system components in the absence of rigorous data and measurement. And third, the field was highly quantitative, and system features that could not be quantified were overlooked or minimized in the analysis.[38] Although elements of systems analysis remain in present-day policy analysis, the approach is no longer in favor.[39] Is it wise to build a science of radical reform on such foundations?

One of the difficulties in working in scientific fields that operate in a quasi-cumulative fashion is that methodological and theoretical approaches with significant potential are abandoned and not necessarily revived. Given that many social scientists subscribe to a systems-like model of the social world, an approach to policy design that recognizes the interconnectedness of different social institutions should not be permanently discarded if advances in social science make it possible to overcome the failings of previous approaches. Since the heyday of systems analysis passed, we have had half a century of social scientific progress: social scientists have built a more substantial body of knowledge about the interactions among individuals and institutions, we are starting to gain access to administrative and commercial data systems that hold information on the intricacies of individual lives, we have developed methodological techniques to more convincingly identify causal effects, and we recognize the value of mixed-methods approaches to the understanding of social problems. These scientific advances, when combined with an approach that highlights the interconnectedness of social institutions, offer a rather firmer foundation for a science of radical reform.

It is after radical policy reforms have been tested and implemented that incremental reform might be most useful. Work in the field of evolutionary operation (EVOP) describes how alterations can be made to existing systems to improve performance, while allowing those systems to operate on a day-to-day basis. Although this might appear to be a more general argument in support of incrementalism, proponents of the approach are clear that it should be applied only after the implementation of careful system design. In their discussion of the design of industrial process, the statisticians Box and Draper describe a process of system refinement, in which fine-tuning the newly implemented system is combined with collecting data to produce further improvements.[40]

Evolutionary operation in the context of social system design would certainly benefit from the use of high-quality administrative data to identify where improvements should be introduced. Experimentation and data collection are deliberately built into the reform process, so that where theory and deliberative design have failed to produce the optimal outcome, improvements can still be made. In the context of a national health service, for example, what are the best techniques for ensuring compliance with a treatment regimen? What is the most effective means of disseminating information about job opportunities in the context of a flexicurity-style system? What is the optimal amount of money to be provided via universal basic income? The process of policy implementation will almost always require that such tweaks to policy programs be made along the way.

This outline of a potential social science of radical reform highlights the extent to which the roots of such a science might be found both in our own disciplinary history and in the system-evaluation methods that are currently central to other scientific and engineering disciplines. Radical reform in a social scientific context may require us to develop methodological and empirical techniques that we do not currently rely upon in our scientific work, but alternative disciplinary models provide a foundation for work on deliberative system design and evaluation.

Building a successful science of radical reform will require not just that social scientists consider new models and techniques. We must also address those ills that have long haunted our scientific inquiry. Increasing differentiation and specialization is a feature of contemporary social science, just as it is a feature of other institutions, and it has had some problematic consequences for scientific inquiry. Two consequences in particular are of special concern.

First, scientists face conflicting incentives when undertaking research. Although science is a collective endeavor, rewards are assigned to individuals, and those rewards are unequally distributed. Incremental and specialized studies add value to the body of scientific knowledge, but individual career rewards are likely to be highest for work that is recognized to be innovative and audacious. This, in turn, reduces the career value of replications, increases the incentives to find "interesting" results, and increases the chances of incremental work being represented as revolutionary. These conflicting incentives have culminated in a crisis of science, in which "it can be proven that most claimed research findings are false," as John Ioannidis memorably put it.[41] A successful science of radical reform must insist upon transparency and replicability in evaluating research, and must tamp down the urge to reward incremental novelty at the expense of the cumulation of reliable data.

A second negative effect of scientific differentiation and specialization occurs because many social sciences operate in quasi-cumulative fashion. In a fully cumulative science, the accumulation of studies should provide robust evidence within specialist areas of study, and highlight commonalities across those areas. Cumulation makes visible the links among specialist areas, with theory providing the connective tissue necessary to make sense of the whole. But in fields that operate in a quasi-cumulative fashion, it is less easy to identify commonalities, and links between areas can be missed. Researchers have little incentive to carry out cross-institution studies, or to draw links among multiple fields, because this work is time-consuming, data-intensive, difficult to summarize in article-length form, and more likely to be vulnerable in the peer review process.[42] Changing incentives to encourage the synthesis of research evidence across different specialist areas of study is therefore an important step toward developing a science of radical reform.

The future of a science of radical reform will depend upon the skills and contributions of a great many different types of social scientists. Discrimination and bias within the academy—with respect to race, gender, institution, and other characteristics—distort decisions as to which studies command attention and limit the possibility of accumulating reliable evidence. A science of radical reform also depends upon multiple and diverse sources of evidence, although the analysis of administrative data is likely to be of particular importance. Administrative data offer the possibility of tracking individuals over time and across multiple social institutions, and it is therefore essential that access is straightforward and widespread. The current concentration of administrative data in the hands of a small number of social scientists is not sustainable if science is to develop to its fullest capacity. Radical policy demands a science that exploits the strengths of all scientists and all sources of data.

The Words of a Dream

We use the language of "opportunity" when we discuss the substantial inequalities in access to education and to high-paying occupations. We should be using the language of "constraints." If we wish to equalize access to valued outcomes, we must remove the constraints placed on individuals by social institutions. This is the true American Dream. It is a belief in a society without the barriers that hold some groups back while granting others a clear path. It is a belief in the power of individuals to succeed when they are not curtailed by the social institutions that surround them. It is a belief in the central fairness of a system that was built to capitalize on the talents of all individuals, a system that was built in opposition to the titles and privileges of the Old World.

We use the language of "chance" when we describe differences in the fortunes of those from different socioeconomic groups. We should be using the language of "design." We may indeed be lucky if the customary stork drops us into a privileged household rather than an underprivileged household, but from that moment on our destiny is shaped by the social institutions in which we find ourselves. Insofar as a privileged child suffers bad luck, the cocoon of institutions will soften the blow. In contrast, the fractured web in which an underprivileged child is embedded makes failure likely, even when bad luck does not further intervene.

Social institutions may give the appearance of permanence and longevity, but the web of institutions surrounding children is a construction and it can be reshaped. If we ever needed confirmation that institutions could be altered, we would only have to look to the effect of socioeconomic resources on social institutions: resources alter both the quality of institutions and the strength of the connections between institutions. If resources alter social institutions, deliberative policy surely can.

We use the language of "increments" when we consider policies to tackle inequality of constraints. We should be using the language of "radical reform." An emphasis on radical reform would help to highlight how inequality of constraints is constructed by society, and it would highlight the extent of the changes needed to attack those constraints. Until we confront the fact that our current policies have no hope of eliminating inequality of constraints, we are unlikely to make great headway in achieving this goal. It may be that the goal is an unreasonable one, because it would require too great a sacrifice of economic growth, or too great a privileging of the goal of equality over other goals such as liberty. But without social scientists making the case for radical reform just as powerfully as the proponents of "economic growth at all costs" or "liberty at all costs" make their cases, we may never discover the optimal mix of policies that would maximize across all of these outcomes.

We, the people, built the social institutions within which inequality of constraints is produced. We built the economic strength and national security that disproportionately benefit some in our society. But we also built the science that allows us to document the extent of inequality, the policy infrastructure that transforms proposals into real-world reforms, and the bureaucratic apparatus that would allow policies to be brought to scale. We learned from our experience of the Old World that social institutions can be corrupted, and that a new world without corruptions can be imagined. The sooner that we begin to imagine that new world, the sooner we can begin to build it.

NOTES

PREFACE

1. Elizabeth Warren, speech to the Democratic National Congress, San Francisco, Saturday, June 1, 2019.

2. Alexandria Ocasio-Cortez, news conference, Washington, DC, Thursday, February 7, 2019.

3. Roth 2002.

4. Duflo 2017, 5. See Duflo and Banerjee (2019) for a more recent defense of this approach in light of public and political demands for non-incremental policies.

5. Durkheim [1908] 1982, 245.

CHAPTER 1

1. Alexis de Tocqueville writes of the founders of New England: "In their hands, political principles, laws, and human institutions seem to be malleable things that can be shaped and combined at will. The barriers that imprisoned the society where they were born fall before them; old opinions that for centuries ruled the world vanish; an almost limitless course and a field without horizons opens" ([1835] 2010, 69–70). See also Bellah et al. 1985, highlighting the communitarian nature of early American culture (Chapter 2, "The Biblical and Republican Strands" section, and Chapter 11); McClay 1994. Sarah Churchwell similarly emphasizes the differences between the original Dream and modern interpretations. In her view, the original Dream was collectively oriented, such that "individual success would not redeem collective failure" (2018, 28).

2. Adams [1931] 2001, 405.

3. Jennifer Hochschild, who has written extensively on the modern-day Dream, identifies individualism and the pursuit of success as key features of it. She does not distinguish between the current incarnation of the Dream and previous versions, but states that the contemporary Dream is "broadly individual in its focus on persons rather than on structures, processes, or historical patterns. Indeed, it not only focuses on individual agency, it insists that agency is all that matters in the end" (1996, 252). On the importance of individualism in U.S. policy, see Eppard, Rank, and Bullock 2020.

4. Obama 2014a.

5. See, for example, Chetty, Grusky et al. 2017.

6. See Jennifer L. Hochschild 1996.

7. Granovetter 1985; Coleman 1990.

8. Bowles, Gintis, and Osborne-Groves 2005; Arrow, Bowles, and Durlauf 2000; Fischer et al. 1996.

9. Social scientists might highlight, for example, the importance of respect, or happiness, as an outcome that could be prioritized over income, wealth, or socioeconomic status. On the materialistic focus of the American Dream, see Lamont 2019, and for useful discussions of the many and diverse concepts of personal worth, see Lamont 2012 and 2018.

10. The "where you start should not determine where you end up" formulation is common in the social sciences, but a range of interpretations of this concept exists (particularly in political philosophy). See below for further discussion of this point.

11. I follow W.E.B. Du Bois in capitalizing "Black" when the word is used to refer to a group of people. See also Tharps 2014.

12. See, respectively, Chetty et al. 2020; Bonnie and Backes 2019, table 4.1; Chetty and Hendren 2018.

13. Hodgson 2006, 2.

14. The term "total institution" was used by the sociologist Erving Goffman to describe "a place of residence and work where a large number of like-situated individuals cut off from the society for an appreciable period of time together lead an enclosed, formally administered round of life" (1961, xiii). Goffman described how the individual "self" became subordinated in such institutions. I further discuss the concept of total institutions in Chapter 3.

15. There are, of course, other environmental influences that may operate independently of social institutions. A natural disaster has the potential to change or end a life even in the absence of social institutions (see Torche 2011 on the effects of an earthquake on birth outcomes). Note, however, that the effects of natural disasters only rarely operate independently of social institutions: the chances of experiencing a natural disaster (which are dependent on geographical location), the likely effects of the disaster on a person (which are partially dependent on quality of housing and infrastructure), and the chances of a recovery (which are partially dependent on disaster response) will all be bound up with the social institutions in which a person is embedded. The Covid-19 pandemic provides a sobering example of the unequal consequences of natural disaster. Those classified as "essential workers" (e.g., grocery store workers and health aides) are among the lowest-paid workers in our economy. These workers were required to continue working outside the home, which put them at high risk of contracting the disease, while others worked from the safety of quarantine. Covid-19 was a natural disaster, another zoonotic virus to be added to the list of viruses that have threatened human health and well-being over the centuries. When it was introduced to a society with preexisting inequalities, however, the effects were devastating for those who were already socioeconomically disadvantaged. For a discussion of natural disasters and socioeconomic inequality, see Arcaya, Raker, and Waters 2020.

16. UNICEF 2004.

17. Bonnie and Backes 2019.

18. For a useful summary of the cumulative effects of early advantage (and disadvantage), see Heckman 2007; on dynamic complementarities, see Grusky, Hall, and Markus 2019; DiPrete and Eirich 2006.

19. See, for example, Härkönen et al. 2012; Persico, Figlio, and Roth 2016; Torche and Sirois 2019.

20. Salesses, Schechtner, and Hidalgo 2013.

21. Bonam, Bergsieker, and Eberhardt 2016.

22. In deciding on appropriate terminology, it is hard to avoid the conclusion that the available terms are not fit for the purpose. The terms "rich" and "poor" fail to capture multidimensional inequalities. The same is true of terms related to "class." The terms "advantaged" and "disadvantaged" carry a tone of happenstance. I settle on terms relating to privilege, as "privilege" highlights the extent to which membership in social groups carries special advantages that are conferred upon individuals by society. Although I contrast privileged and underprivileged groups to illustrate the profound differences in the institutional contexts experienced by children born into very different socioeconomic circumstances, differences in institutional structures would also be expected for groups more closely matched on socioeconomic resources, even if those differences are more subtle. Note that I will continue to employ the terms "rich" and "poor" when referring to group differences characterized by differences in income or wealth See Fields and Fields 2012 for a discussion of race and language related to inequality.

23. Varner, Mattingly, and Grusky 2017; Grusky and Hill 2017; Grusky and MacLean 2016.

24. On neighborhoods, see Sampson 2012 and Sánchez-Jankowski 2008; on the demand for public goods, see Verba and Nie 1972.

25. Author calculation from CDC WONDER database linked birth and infant death records 2007–15.

26. Author calculation from figure 3 of Chetty et al. 2014.

27. Chetty et al. 2016. For a detailed discussion of socioeconomic inequalities in mortality in the United States, see Case and Deaton 2020.

28. The classic exposition of this position is Okun [1975] 2015; cf. Berg and Ostry 2011; Ostry, Berg, and Tsangarides 2014.

29. Friedman and Friedman 1990, 137.

30. Corak 2013; Krueger 2012.

31. Results from analyses comparing inequalities of opportunity over time, or across states within the United States, provide further evidence that inequality of opportunity is undermined by inequality of outcome. See Kenworthy 2016; Mitnik, Cumberworth, and Grusky 2016; Davis and Mazumder 2017; Jackson and Holzman 2020; Chetty et al. 2014; Bloome 2015. See Neckerman and Torche 2007 for a discussion.

32. See Bellah 1995 for a discussion of the individualistic focus of the "opportunity" concept; Bellah et al. 1985.

33. For useful discussions of this issue, see Swift 2004; Kanbur and Wagstaff 2014.

34. Brand and Xie 2010; DeLuca, Clampet-Lundquist, and Edin 2016.

35. Deary et al. 2004; Rönnlund, Sundström, and Nilsson 2015; Cunha and Heckman 2007.

36. Alon and Tienda 2007.

37. Although the SAT is used in the admissions process for the majority of four-year colleges, a small (but increasing) number of colleges are moving toward SAT-optional admissions (Furuta 2017). In these colleges, greater weight is placed on the quality of the candidate's written application materials in determining whether or not an offer will be made.

38. Dynarski and Wiederspan 2012; Bettinger et al. 2012.

39. DiPrete, Eirich, and Pittinsky 2010.

40. Goldrick-Rab et al. 2016.

41. Torche and Sirois 2019.

42. Young 2017.

43. Okbay et al. 2016.

44. The estimate of 3.2 percent is derived from an analysis of the power of a polygenic score to predict educational attainment. The analyses of individual SNPs (i.e., the 74 SNPs described in the paper) showed a lower predictive power: around 0.43 percent of variation in educational attainment was explained by a model including the SNPs (Okbay et al. 2016). A more recent study in the UK found that polygenic scores could explain 9 percent of the variance in educational attainment at age sixteen (Selzam et al. 2017). Both estimates are somewhat lower than previous estimates based on twin studies (e.g., Taubman 1976; Branigan, McCallum, and Freese 2013; Colodro-Conde et al. 2015).

45. See especially Freese 2008; Dickens and Flynn 2001; Jencks 1980.

46. Freese 2008, S24.

47. Okbay et al. 2016, supplementary information; also FAQs for Okbay et al. 2016. See also Keers and Pluess 2017 and Figlio et al. 2017.

48. Agar and Tate 1936, 1.

CHAPTER 2

The definition at the beginning of this chapter comes from Lexico.com.

1. I use the term "inequality of opportunity" rather than "inequality of constraints" here in deference to the fact that policymakers would themselves describe their approach as one that addresses inequality of opportunity, not inequality of constraints.

2. It should be unnecessary to emphasize that use of the term "damage" carries no normative implications.

3. See LaLonde 2003 for a good history of these programs.

4. For a useful summary of the research findings on EITC, see Hoynes 2017. For evidence on labor market participation, see Hoynes and Patel 2018; Nichols and Rothstein 2015; on smoking, see Averett and Wang 2013; Cowan and Tefft 2012; on maternal health, see Evans and Garthwaite 2014.

5. Hoynes and Patel 2018; Manoli and Turner 2018.

6. Food stamps are distributed under the Supplemental Nutrition Assistance Program (SNAP). For a description of SNAP and an assessment of the program's effects on

poverty and other outcomes, see Bartfeld et al. 2015. See Bailey et al. 2020 for evidence that food stamps improve children's long-term outcomes.

7. York, Loeb, and Doss 2019.

8. E.g., Fryer 2013; Castleman and Page 2014.

9. Herd and Moynihan 2018; see also Porter 2020. During the first month of the Covid-19-induced economic crisis, these administrative hurdles proved to be barriers to the smooth distribution of stimulus and unemployment benefits (Herd and Moynihan 2020).

10. The data on household income are drawn from the supplemental information to the Congressional Budget Office's June 2016 report *The Distribution of Household Income and Federal Taxes, 2013* (Congressional Budget Office 2016, supplemental information, table 14). I use these data to be able to examine the distribution of household income for households with children; later versions of this report do not provide data by household type. I compare "market income" to "income after taxes and transfers" for two groups of households with children: one in the bottom quintile and the other in the 91st–95th percentiles of (before-tax) household income. For those in the bottom quintile, before-tax income is $24,000 and post-tax/transfer income is $34,200; for those in the 91st–95th percentiles, before-tax income is $257,500 and post-tax income is $197,000. The difference in pre-tax income between rich and poor households is $233,500, while the difference in post-tax/transfer income is $162,800. Sammartino and Francis (2016, table 1) provide estimates of state tax burdens by income quintile (for individuals): the average state tax rate is 0 percent for the bottom quintile and 2.5 percent for the 90th–95th percentiles. On an income of $257,500, the average state tax difference between rich and poor would be $6,437.50. Note that some states, such as California, have highly progressive state tax systems, and the tax burden would be substantially higher. Vericker et al. (2012) present estimates of per-child state/local expenditures for high- and low-income children. They report a difference of $2,596 (in 2009) in state/local expenditures between the two groups of children. I estimate that families with a low-income child will have an income of around $37,000, which may be compared to the median income for family households of $75,062 in 2016 (Semega et al. 2019).

11. Coleman-Jensen et al. 2018, 34. The cited report provides a detailed account of how frequently individuals and families had difficulties buying food, involuntarily went without meals, went hungry, or lost weight because of lack of food.

12. Coleman-Jensen et al. 2019.

13. Edin and Shaefer 2015. See Bartfeld et al. 2015 for a useful discussion of the benefits of the food stamp program, and for a summary of debates on the future of the program.

14. Sharkey 2010; Sharkey et al. 2014; Sharkey and Sampson 2015; see Sharkey 2018 for a review. See Bell 2019 for a discussion of safety and violence in marginalized communities.

15. Whitmore 2002, 5. See also Edin and Lein 1997.

16. Edin and Lein write: "Typically, mothers traded food stamps for cash only when they were short on the rent—a common occurrence in cities where rent alone often cost as much as the family received from welfare" (1997, 220). See also Desmond 2016.

17. Thaler and Sunstein 2008, 6.

18. See Richburg-Hayes et al. (2017) for a report on behavioral policy interventions in the United States; see also Benartzi et al. (2017) for an argument in favor of government investment in nudging.

19. Castleman and Page 2014, 2015.

20. Richburg-Hayes et al. 2017, 37–40.

21. Bhargava and Manoli 2015.

22. Evidence from research on climate change policy, for example, shows that nudges can undermine support for more-high-impact reforms. Hagmann, Ho, and Loewenstein (2019) show that when people believe a "quick fix" solution is possible, they are less likely to support larger-scale policies of proven efficacy. The authors conclude that "an ideal world would have a place for both nudges and more heavy-handed interventions to combat climate change. However, our results indicate that an effort to deploy both can backfire by reducing the likelihood that the most effective policies will be implemented" (488).

23. For a useful introduction to the scientific method, see Andersen and Hepburn 2016. There is much debate about whether science does indeed adhere closely to the scientific method (e.g., Knorr-Cetina 1981; for a recent example, see Peterson 2016). I am not here making a general claim that all social scientists are committed to a hypothetico-deductive approach. Instead, I am making the simple claim that social scientists and applied policy researchers in the inequality field are very likely to be committed to the basic principles of science.

24. One example of such a reform can be found in the postwar development of the welfare state (see Chapter 4).

25. A large-scale basic income experiment in Oakland, California, for example, is funded by the technology start-up Y Combinator.

26. On the growth of the use of experiments in social science, see Jackson and Cox 2013.

27. Herbert Simon identified the problem of satisficing, which he describes as follows: "Since there did not seem to be any word in English for decision methods that look for good or satisfactory solutions instead of optimal ones, some years ago I introduced the term 'satisficing' to refer to such procedures. Now no one in his right mind will satisfice if he can equally well optimize; no one will settle for good or better if he can have best. But that is not the way the problem usually poses itself " (1996, 118).

28. See Campbell 2002 for a discussion of some of the ideological commitments of policymakers and the effects of these commitments on policy proposals. See Hausman, McPherson, and Satz 2016 for an outline of the competing ideological principles that are at stake.

29. E.g., Gordon 2016.

30. Rogoff 2012. Note that Rogoff is not proposing that growth should be the sole focus of policy. Rather he is characterizing the contemporary focus on growth by those macroeconomists engaged in policy work.

31. The view that growth is generally welfare-increasing has been questioned. Easterlin, for example, highlights the research finding that increasing growth is not generally

associated with increasing happiness, while Throsby, in the same volume, takes issue with the widely held view that "a rising tide raises all boats" (2017). One might also raise concerns about the negative effects of growth on the environment, insofar as growth is delivered via industry and the exploitation of natural resources. The negative externalities of climate change are subsequently likely to disproportionately affect less-privileged communities (Diffenbaugh and Burke 2019).

32. The relationship between inequality and economic growth is an active area of research, but concerns about high levels of inequality having negative effects on growth are prominent in the economic literature. See, for example, Herzer and Vollmer 2013; Banerjee and Duflo 2003; Persson and Tabellini 1994. For a concise discussion of an alternative position, see Fuest 2017.

33. Brighouse and Swift 2014.

34. Brighouse and Swift 2014; Munoz-Dardé 1999; Fishkin 1983; Rawls 1971.

35. These estimates of the child poverty rate are provided by the U.S. Census Bureau, which reports that 19.5 percent of all U.S. children live below the federal poverty threshold (American Community Survey 2016, one-year estimates). See Jiang, Granja, and Koball 2017 for a brief outline of the basic facts on child poverty.

36. Work in political philosophy questions to what extent familial relationships should be seen as legitimate (and therefore undeserving of state attention) if those relationships in turn generate inequality of opportunity (see especially Fishkin 1983; Brighouse and Swift 2014). Note that John Rawls, despite his focus on inequality of opportunity and the "basic structure" of society, was taken to task for his failure to address the institution of the family in sufficient detail (1971, 1993); see also Munoz-Dardé 1998.

37. E.g., Huber and Malhotra 2017; Iyengar and Westwood 2015; Green, Palmquist, and Schickler 2002.

38. See Gross and Simmons 2014 for a discussion of the political commitments of professors; see also Gross 2013 on why professors are more likely to be liberal.

39. Given the dominance of economists within the policy discussion, we might be particularly interested in the ideological coherence of economics. Although economics is rather more conservative than the other social sciences, Democrat economists still outnumber Republican economists by almost three to one (Cardiff and Klein 2005, 239); see also Jelveh, Kogut, and Naidu 2018, who find a 3–2 split in Democratic-Republican campaign contributions by economists. Nevertheless, research shows that there is substantial agreement within the discipline around a "core" set of economic beliefs (Reay 2012; also Fourcade 2010, who describes differences in core beliefs and practices across countries).

40. Weber's position, as summarized by Dahrendorf (1987).

41. The extent to which ideological positions influence the positions of economists on academic issues is contested. For example, Gordon and Dahl (2013) find no evidence that political ideology influences leading economists' answers to economic questions, while Jelveh, Kogut, and Naidu (2018) find a correlation between ideology and published research results. These studies do not, however, evaluate the extent to which economists might be willing to trade off progress on one policy dimension for progress

on another, which is the main concern when "choosing" between growth and inequality. See Krugman 2016 for a useful short discussion of the types of trade-offs that might need to be evaluated when considering policy solutions.

42. A cautionary example can be found in the treatment of the economist Gabriel Zucman. Zucman and his colleague, Emmanuel Saez, have documented the growing inequalities in income and wealth in the United States, and have proposed new taxes on wealth to ameliorate these inequalities (e.g., Saez and Zucman 2019). When Zucman was under consideration for a tenured faculty position at Harvard, the *New York Times* reported that "Harvard's president and provost nixed the offer, partly over fears that Mr. Zucman's research could not support the arguments he was making in the political arena, according to people involved in the process" (Tankersley and Casselman 2020).

43. Horowitz, Haynor, and Kickham (2018), for example, report that more than three-quarters of the sociologists who identify as "radical" disagree with the statement "A dispassionate attitude in research [is] important for accuracy" (as compared with the 15 percent of self-identified "moderates" who disagree).

44. In his 2014 State of the Union address, President Obama drew on Heckman's research to make the case for high-quality early childhood education (Obama 2014b; see also Heckman's 2014 response).

45. See Hamilton et al. 2015; Hamilton, Paul, and Darity 2018; Darity and Mullen 2020; Saez and Zucman 2019; Tankersley and Casselman 2020.

46. E.g., García et al. 2016; Heckman 2006; Heckman et al. 2010; Doyle et al. 2009; Carneiro and Heckman 2003.

47. Work on political persuasion demonstrates that arguments are more effective in changing minds if those arguments are framed to appeal to the ideological concerns of the audience. For example, although liberals are less supportive of military spending than conservatives, liberals view an appeal for increased military spending much more favorably when it is framed in terms of reducing inequality rather than in terms of national loyalty (Feinberg and Willer 2015).

48. The average salary for a full professor in the 2018–19 academic year was $136,506 (AAUP 2019, table 1), as compared to U.S. median earnings of $55,291 and $45,097 for men and women, respectively (for those who worked full-time); Semega et al. 2019, 9.

49. Jonsson et al. 2017.

CHAPTER 3

1. Tax evasion provides one example of subversion in the context of relatively small-scale policy change. Recent research describes how strategies to evade or avoid tax evolve alongside changes in tax law (De Simone, Lester, and Markle 2020). De Simone summarized the findings in an interview, stating, "It's always a cat-and-mouse game. . . . Any time you shut down one evasion tactic, you open up another. . . . As long as these individuals have alternative channels to evade taxes, it's going to happen" (Andrews 2019). See Alm 2012 for a review of research on tax evasion, and Saez and Zucman 2019 for a discussion of tax evasion by the very rich.

2. For the sake of clarity, I am not taking the position that we should focus on theory development and the construction of elegant theories at the expense of empirical testing (see Ellis and Silk 2014 for a useful rejection of such an argument in the context of physics, a field in which elegant theories are not always well matched with empirical analysis). Rather, I wish to argue for the importance of attending to theory and covering laws in an area of social science and policy analysis that is predominantly empirical (e.g., Hempel 1965).

3. Turner 1997, 6. The problems referred to include ensuring reproduction and the socialization of children; providing food, safety, and shelter; preventing and curing ill health and disease; and maintaining the smooth running of daily life.

4. "Core" social institutions, as I label them here, have substantial overlap with what sociologists refer to as "primary" institutions (Sumner and Keller 1927). Primary social institutions are defined as those that pertain to the fundamental problems and aspects of life. I use the term "core" institutions to highlight those institutions that pertain to the problems and aspects of life that are most important for child development (note that most of the "core" institutions that I identify can also be found in Bronfenbrenner's "microsystem" [Bronfenbrenner 1979]).

5. See Galster and Sharkey 2017 for a similar description of neighborhood effects on individuals; also Boudon 1974.

6. I here embrace something analogous to the standard Cartesian distinction between body and mind. As Freese reasonably points out, although the Cartesian distinction feels natural to most all of us, our mind is not biologically separate from our body. I must therefore explicitly acknowledge that the "social self" is fully embodied within the "biological self."

7. See Center on the Developing Child 2007 for a basic overview of brain development in early childhood.

8. World Health Organization 2010, 22–23.

9. Duncan and Magnuson 2005.

10. Klinenberg 2018.

11. Jackson, Johnson, and Persico 2016.

12. As I described in Chapter 1, I use "privileged" as shorthand for "privileged with respect to socioeconomic resources."

13. Chloe and Kaylah are fictional, but the descriptions of their lives are based on empirical facts documented in the social science literature. I used random assignment to determine whether the hypothetical child would be a boy or a girl.

14. See Aizer and Currie 2014 for a review. Differences in prenatal conditions may be viewed as an indirect institutional effect: the mother's quality of health and nutrition, as well as her stress level, will be strongly influenced by the institutional context of her own life.

15. The Lucile Packard Children's Hospital at Stanford, for example, advertises "post-delivery care tailored to meet your and your baby's needs," and "optimal mother-infant bonding, personalized care, hands-on patient teaching, [and] lactation initiation

and breastfeeding" (http://www.stanfordchildrens.org/en/service/pregnancy-newborn/maternity-care). Other amenities include room service meals, free wireless Internet, flat-screen televisions, and on-demand movies.

16. On the benefits of cultural match and the comfort gained from interactions with similar others, see Collins 2004; Lareau 2011.

17. At the time of writing, Medicaid covered maternity care for the poor. See Markus et al. 2013 for an overview of Medicaid-covered births.

18. See Polsky et al. 2015, table 2, for a comparison of appointment availability for Medicaid and private patients. A brief summary of some of the constraints imposed by Medicaid on treatment availability and quality is provided in Renter 2015.

19. See Blumenshine et al. 2010 for a systematic review of adverse birth outcomes by socioeconomic status; Fiscella et al. 2000 for a general review of inequalities in health care with respect to socioeconomic status; Nagahawatte and Goldenberg 2008 and Larson 2007 on the maternal health of poor women; Declercq et al. 2013 on differences in the birth experiences of Medicaid patients and private patients. The chances of adverse birth outcomes for poor women are increased for women of color (Braveman et al. 2015).

20. E.g., Desmond 2016; Edin and Lein 1997.

21. Just as with other social institutions, access to the institution of marriage is influenced by socioeconomic resources. This means that children born into underprivileged families are more likely to grow up in single-parent families or to experience a parental divorce in childhood (e.g., Cherlin 2009, 2010; Edin and Kefalas 2005). The effects on children of growing up in single-parent families (and of experiencing instability in family structure) are widely understood to be negative, and family structure is recognized as an important mechanism through which inequality is reproduced across generations (see McLanahan and Percheski 2008 for a review; Lee and McLanahan 2015; Crosnoe et al. 2014; Magnuson and Berger 2009).

22. See Grusky and MacLean 2016; Grusky and Hill 2017; Grusky, Hall, and Markus 2019; and Milanovic 2019 for more on marketization (also known as "commodification").

23. On differences in speech patterns by socioeconomic origin, see Ellis 1967; Bernstein 1971; Kraus, Park, and Tan 2017; on self-presentation, see Kraus and Mendes 2014; on social interaction, see Bourdieu 1984; Fiske and Markus 2012.

24. See Deming 2017; Rivera 2015; Jackson, Goldthorpe, and Mills 2005.

25. The literature on "institutional betrayal" suggests that where institutions have failed to protect individuals, those subject to the "betrayal" will experience reduced psychological well-being (Smith and Freyd 2014).

26. E.g., Doyle et al. 2009; Heckman 2007.

27. E.g., Whitney et al. 2015; Consumer Federation of America 2013; Krieger et al. 2005.

28. Shah, Mullainathan, and Shafir 2012; Mani et al. 2013; Mullainathan and Shafir 2013.

29. Kalil, Ryan, and Corey (2012) show that college-educated mothers with a child aged 0–2 years old spend just under 190 minutes per weekend day on child care (1372), while high-school-educated mothers spend around 120 minutes; see also Guryan, Hurst,

and Kearney 2008. Differences in time spent with children cannot be accounted for by differences in hours worked by parents (Guryan, Hurst, and Kearney 2008). Evidence suggests that differences between high- and low-educated parents in time spent with children have only increased over time (Bianchi 2000; Ramey and Ramey 2010). Spending gaps between rich and poor parents are also large in the preschool years, and these gaps have similarly increased over the decades (Kornrich and Furstenberg 2013; see also Schneider, Hastings, and LaBriola 2018).

30. The Department of Education estimates that high-poverty school districts receive almost 16 percent less funding per student than low-poverty districts (U.S. Department of Education 2013; see also Semuels 2016 for a useful summary).

31. There has been much research on the extent to which school funding affects student outcomes, with the most recent evidence showing that increased K–12 spending leads to higher school completion rates, higher wages, and reduced rates of poverty in adulthood (Jackson, Johnson, and Persico 2016).

32. See Murnane and Reardon 2018 for evidence of increasing inequality between high-income and middle-income families in private school enrollments over the past five decades.

33. E.g., Sharkey 2013.

34. Note that local governments receive transfers from state and federal governments to support local services (e.g., support for elementary and secondary education). See Urban Institute 2011 for a useful set of "backgrounders" outlining state and local revenues and expenditures.

35. Chetty, Hendren, and Katz 2016. This study examines families who were part of the Moving to Opportunity experiment, in which families living in poor neighborhoods were randomly selected to receive a housing voucher that facilitated movement to a lower-poverty neighborhood. Although the research literature evaluating the effects of the experiment could be characterized as mixed—with many examples of relatively weak effects on outcomes including the earnings and employment of adults who moved—Chetty, Hendren, and Katz 2016 show substantial improvements in long-term outcomes for the *children* of families who participated in the experiment. See Chetty and Hendren 2018 for similar findings based on a quasi-experimental analysis of the effects of changing neighborhoods during childhood.

36. Watamura et al. 2011. See also NICHD Early Child Care Research Network 2002; Phillips 2013.

37. Shonkoff and Phillips 2000; Bonnie and Backes 2019; Bonnie, Stroud, and Breiner 2014.

38. Johnson and Jackson 2019; see also Currie and Thomas 2000. Note that there is disagreement in the literature with respect to whether or not dynamic complementarities of the type identified by Johnson and Jackson predominate. The term "dynamic complementarities" refers to the cumulative advantage process whereby early gains are transformed into later gains, summarized by Heckman as "skill begets skill" (2008). A useful summary of the questions at issue can be found in Magnuson and Duncan 2016.

39. On college enrollment, see Chetty, Friedman et al. 2017; Jackson and Holzman 2020; on the transition to adulthood, see Furstenberg 2008.

40. On unforeseen consequences and access to social networks, see Small 2009.

41. Throughout this section I will use language that implies that inanimate institutions are acting. I of course recognize that inanimate objects do not act or interact, and merely use this language as shorthand for the very many individual-level decisions and behaviors (both rational and irrational) that are implicated when a child encounters a social institution.

42. The conveyance link is the mechanism called upon in the "dynamic complementarities" account outlined in the economics literature (see particularly Cunha and Heckman 2007; Johnson and Jackson 2019). A key difference, however, is that discussions of dynamic complementarities focus on comparisons of relatively substantial inputs over relatively substantial periods of time. Cunha et al., for example, focus on the effects of investments in skill development in early childhood relative to the effects of the same investments made in the later childhood years (2006). The model presented here, in contrast, places emphasis on the continuous and ongoing nature of the changes in individuals that institutions produce. The conveyance mechanism could perhaps be summarized as "dynamic complementarities on steroids."

43. It is not necessary to embrace an "oversocialized" view of human action, as criticized by Mark Granovetter (1985), to admit that institutions have effects on individuals. Insofar as changes to behavior result from interactions with institutions, those changes are likely to be the result of rational responses to the structural circumstances as defined by institutions.

44. This conceptualization of child development through interaction with social institutions has much in common with Bronfenbrenner's "ecological" theory of child development, which in turn had much in common with Lewin's analysis (see Bronfenbrenner 1974, 1977, 1979; also Lewin 1935, 1936; Shipler 2011; see Reskin 2012 for a related account of racial discrimination). Analogous arguments can be found in the literature on the relationship between genetics or biology and the environment (e.g., Dickens and Flynn 2001; Freese 2008; see also Van Der Maas et al. 2006; Borsboom and Cramer 2013), and similar themes appear in the organizational ecology literature (Weick 1976). In contrast to the account given here, Bronfenbrenner and related accounts place less emphasis on the potential for socioeconomic resources to alter the strength and nature of linkages among social institutions.

45. James Coleman and Thomas Hoffer, for example, highlight the value of living in a "functional community," where community members will cooperate in the process of socializing children, thus aiding in both "coordination" and "smoothing" across the school and the family/community (Coleman and Hoffer 1987). Coleman and Hoffer's discussion of inter-institutional linkages is very limited relative to the current analysis, in that it is primarily focused on the complementarities between schools and neighborhoods, and the effects of those complementarities on educational attainment.

46. See also work on ADHD medication and standardized tests. As King, Jennings, and Fletcher (2014) show, high-SES students are more likely to take stimulants during

the school year, a practice that is then likely to pay off in higher test scores. In this case, the medical system provides aid with the aim of improving the child's interaction with an entirely separate social institution, i.e., the school.

47. Note that in our day-to-day understanding of institutions we are frequently willing to take into account the level of coordination and smoothing when we assess the quality of a single institution. So, for example, a school serving an underprivileged area might be coded as a "good school" when it takes actions to compensate for failures in another institution, independent of whether or not the school effectively performs the functions that it is actually responsible for (e.g., the school provides snacks and school materials where families have been unable to provide these items).

48. On schools and policing, see Shedd 2015; Flores 2016, Davis 2003. On the relationship between the criminal justice system and the child support system, see Haney 2018. See also Haskins (2014, 2017), who shows that the *children* of the incarcerated are more frequently found in poor-quality schools. See Soss and Weaver 2017 on the policing of "race-class subjugated" communities, and the ease of installing police in institutional settings unrelated to law and order (also Bell 2020).

49. There has been much focus on the child vaccination practices of the worried rich, but research shows that vaccination rates for children living below the poverty line are substantially lower than the rates for children at or above poverty level (Elam-Evans et al. 2014).

50. Desmond 2016. See also Eubanks 2018.

51. See Sánchez-Jankowski (2008, Introduction), for a useful summary of early research; see Wilson [1987] 2012 for an example of an argument that focuses on the social disorganization of poor communities; cf. Pattillo-McCoy 1999. For recent evidence on social organization within poor neighborhoods, see, e.g., Sánchez-Jankowski 2008 and Small 2009.

52. Small 2006, 2009; see also Marwell and McQuarrie 2013.

53. See Granovetter 1973 on the importance of linking micro- and macro-levels of analysis.

54. Goffman 1961, 5–6.

55. My claim here is not that scientific and public consensus as regards high-quality childrearing and the development of skills/personal characteristics is always correct. Indeed, some of the activities that privileged parents engage in might actively inhibit the development of desirable characteristics such as self-reliance (e.g., Lareau 2011). My claim is rather that the consistency of beliefs about what it takes to deliver high-quality functions leads to consistency in the institutional experiences of children.

56. See Davies 1989 for a strong critique of non-standard applications of the "total institution" term; also Coser 1974 for the introduction of the concept of "greedy institutions," a term that is designed specifically to describe institutions with some but not all of the "total" characteristics identified by Goffman (e.g., some religious organizations).

57. See Weber [1922] 1978, Chapter 2, on specialization and differentiation of functions. See also Lockwood 1964 on social and system integration.

58. The extent to which the term "total institution" can be applied to the institutional networks of privileged children could alternatively be treated as a simple empirical question. A comparison of the functional differentiation experienced by (a) privileged children and (b) patients in a mental institution, for example, would provide important empirical context for judging whether or not the term is reasonably applied. The empirical test is particularly important if, as is likely, the daily life of a patient in a mental institution is in practice less regimented than the definition of a total institution might require.

59. Tönnies [1887] 2001. A more recent example may be found in Coleman 1987, 1993.

60. Eisenstadt 1964, 377. Note that Eisenstadt breaks from traditional functionalist arguments with respect to differentiation, arguing that differentiation through specialization is not a necessary feature of modernization. He highlights, in particular, the possibility of dedifferentiation following differentiation, and the possibility of differential differentiation across (and within) institutional spheres. On differentiation and modernity, see also Granovetter 1979.

61. Parsons 1937, 1964; Durkheim [1893] 2014.

62. See Ridgeway 2014 and 2019 for a detailed discussion of status. See Crenshaw 1989 for a discussion of intersecting disadvantages; see Collins and Bilge 2016 for an overview of the concept of "intersectionality."

63. Hannah-Jones 2019.

64. See Darity and Mullen 2020, Shelby 2016, and Reskin 2012 for detailed discussions of the institutional sources of racial inequality. There is a substantial literature on the effects of race on individual institutions. For example, on education, see Alexander and Morgan 2016, Carter and Welner 2013, Kao and Thompson 2003; on health, see Williams, Lawrence, and Davis 2019, Shavers et al. 2012, Williams and Mohammed 2009; on labor market discrimination, see Quillian et al. 2017; Pager, Western, and Bonikowski 2009; on residential segregation and housing, see Massey, Rothwell, and Domina 2009, Pager and Shepherd 2008. See Ray 2019 for a discussion of whiteness as a "credential."

65. See Ashenfelter, Collins, and Yoon 2006 on why "separate but equal" was a myth.

66. On the history of segregation with respect to race, see Rothstein 2017. On the de facto exclusion of African Americans from government programs, see Katznelson 2005.

67. Quillian et al. 2017.

68. Hamilton et al. 2015.

69. Reardon et al. 2019.

70. Goldstein and Patel 2019; Sireci, Scarpati, and Li 2005. See also the 2000 report of the California State Auditor, which concluded that "although few students receive extra time on standardized tests, some may not deserve it while other students may not be getting the assistance they need. Less than 1.2 percent of California seniors graduating in 1999 who took the SAT received extra time. However, these students were disproportionately white, or were more likely to come from an affluent family or to attend a private school."

71. Chetty et al. 2020.

72. See Goel, Rao, and Shroff 2016; Epp, Maynard-Moody, and Haider-Markel 2014; Voigt et al. 2017; Eberhardt et al. 2006.

73. ACLU 2014.

74. In recent years, serious concerns have been raised about the use of force by police. As highlighted by the Black Lives Matter movement, African Americans are more likely to be subject to force during interactions with police (Goff et al. 2016), and work from psychology suggests that police officers are more likely to see Black and minority individuals as a threat (as compared to whites) (e.g., Correll et al. 2002).

75. E.g., Desmond 2016.

76. Merton 1968.

77. Puma et al. 2012; Bailey et al. 2017; cf. Heckman 2017. See Chapter 4 for a detailed discussion of early childhood intervention and fadeout effects.

78. Johnson and Jackson 2019; Currie and Thomas 2000.

CHAPTER 4

The definition at the beginning of this chapter comes from *The Shorter Oxford English Dictionary* (Volume 2 N-Z).

1. Marx [1843] 1970, introduction.

2. See Piketty 2013; Atkinson 2015; Young 2017; Saez and Zucman 2019, for advocates of this approach to reducing inequality of constraints.

3. Grusky and Hill 2017; Varner, Mattingly, and Grusky 2017; Grusky, Hall, and Markus 2019. Note that Grusky and colleagues distinguish between public goods that were available to all for free in the past (e.g., parks) and amenities that were variable in quality (e.g., desirable neighborhoods) but where access did not depend on money.

4. As political philosophers have discussed, such a situation is likely to be intolerable given current societal sensibilities, and it would require trampling many of our other most cherished values: self-determination, liberty, and community would all be threatened if we were to embrace this solution to the equality of constraints problem (see, e.g., Rawls 1971; Brighouse and Swift 2014).

5. E.g., Breen 2004; Shavit, Arum, and Gamoran 2007; Jackson 2013; Jerrim and Macmillan 2015; Landersø and Heckman 2017; Bukodi, Paskov, and Nolan 2020.

6. Jerrim and Macmillan 2015; Corak 2013.

7. Atkinson 2015; Piketty 2013; Saez and Zucman 2019.

8. For more detail on basic income proposals, see Standing 2017; Rogers 2017; Booth 2017; Murray 2016; Reed and Lansley 2016; Wright 2010.

9. Many of the positive effects predicted for UBI are not directly related to inequality of constraints. Even if UBI has no or little effect on inequality of constraints, we might expect positive impacts on a whole range of desirable outcomes, including happiness, family stability, and labor market behavior. See Marinescu 2018 for a recent summary of some of the positive effects of UBI. Negative effects of UBI are also possible. One troubling scenario is that UBI recipients might reduce their labor supply because of a reduced incentive to work, which might subsequently have consequences for the country's economic and social stability. Large-scale trials will clearly be important in

evaluating the likelihood of negative effects. See Milanovic 2019 for a discussion of some of the problems in implementing UBI.

10. On health, see Aizer et al. 2016; Forget 2011; on educational attainment, see Aizer et al. 2016; Maynard and Murnane 1979; on income returns in adulthood, see Aizer et al. 2016.

11. See, for example, Institute for Global Prosperity 2017; Rogers 2017.

12. Li and Walder 2001; Szelényi 1998.

13. E.g., Li and Walder 2001; Hanley and McKeever 1997.

14. Gerber and Hout 2004; Jackson and Evans 2017. Comparisons of current European mobility regimes suggest that while some postcommunist countries (including Estonia, Latvia, and Russia) are still among the most fluid countries in Europe, others (Bulgaria, Hungary, and Poland) are among the least fluid (Bukodi, Paskov, and Nolan 2020).

15. Council of Economic Advisers 2018.

16. The examples provided by Wright range from universal basic income to collective projects such as Wikipedia. See Fourcade 2012 for a critical appraisal of Wright's approach. See also Edwards, Crain, and Kalleberg 2007 for a range of practical but ambitious proposals to eliminate poverty in the United States.

17. E.g., Helliwell, et al. 2020.

18. Social scientists have argued that while the social democratic model doubtless has some positive consequences for inequality and social mobility, it is not a panacea. For example, Landersø and Heckman (2017) find that Denmark has higher rates of income mobility than the United States, but very similar rates of educational mobility, which they attribute to Denmark's high rates of neighborhood segregation and weak incentives to pursue higher levels of education. This finding was recently called into question by Andrade and Thomsen (2018), who demonstrate that Landersø and Heckman's conclusions with respect to educational mobility cannot be supported by the data. For a detailed and convincing case in favor of U.S. adoption of social democratic institutions, see Kenworthy 2014, 2019.

19. See Moller, Misra, and Strader 2013 and Cohen and Sabel 2009 for descriptions of flexicurity; European Commission 2007 for a detailed discussion of flexicurity and its application in the EU context.

20. See Bredgaard, Larsen, and Madsen 2005 for a review.

21. For a critique of a narrow vision of higher education as four-year college, and a discussion of alternative visions for the United States, see Stevens 2014; also Kirst and Stevens 2015.

22. See Currie and Almond 2011 for a good review.

23. In the United States, programs such as the Perry Preschool Project, the Abecedarian Project, and Head Start are well-known examples of early intervention policies. Analysis of the outcomes for children who participated in these programs, alongside results from both experimental and non-experimental research, provides the evidentiary basis for the claims about the economic benefits, costs, and efficacy of early intervention policies. Important studies include Currie and Thomas 1995; Garces, Thomas, and Cur-

rie 2002; Heckman 2006. See Reynolds et al. 2010 for a thorough discussion and evaluation of early childhood interventions in the United States.

24. E.g., Doyle et al. 2009.

25. See Camilli et al. 2010 for a meta-analysis; see Barr and Gibbs 2019 on the intergenerational effects of early childhood education.

26. The "gold-standard" studies include the Abecedarian Project, the Perry Preschool Project, and the Chicago Child-Parent Centers.

27. Puma et al. 2012; Schweinhart et al. 2005; see Bailey et al. 2017 for a discussion of early childhood interventions and washout (also known as "fadeout").

28. See http://hcz.org/; Tough 2008. For a different example of a "wraparound" approach, see Communities in Schools, https://www.communitiesinschools.org; Figlio 2015.

29. For a description of services, see Harlem Children's Zone 2009, 2010.

30. Hanson 2013; Page and Stone 2010.

31. It is perhaps unsurprising that these policy prescriptions compare favorably with the criteria that I have laid out for radical reform, given that one of the founders of Head Start was Urie Bronfenbrenner. Bronfenbrenner's "ecological systems" model proposes that individuals are embedded in an ecosystem of linked institutions, with the family at the center of it. As noted in Chapter 3, Bronfenbrenner's model is not primarily concerned with the effects of resources on institutions, although the type of intervention that he designed in Head Start has much in common with the "cocoon" that I have argued already characterizes the lives of privileged children.

32. Bevan 1952, 101; see also Bevan 1944.

33. Beveridge 1942; see also Abel-Smith 1992; Perrin 1992.

34. See Addison 2011 for a detailed discussion of this period. Similar policy elements can be found in the New Deal reforms in the United States. In contrast to the development of the British welfare state, New Deal policies did not attempt to build a coherent web of institutions around individuals from cradle to grave. But the New Deal did represent a break with earlier policy thinking, in that domains that were previously considered out of bounds for federal policy (e.g., retirement and housing) were now firmly within bounds (Hofstadter 1955, chapter 7).

35. Addison 2011; also Thorpe 1997, chapter 6; Lindsey 1962; Gorsky 2008.

36. See Lupton et al. 2013, table 2, for a useful list of social policy reforms introduced by New Labour.

37. Lupton et al. 2013; Waldfogel 2010. Sadly, the austerity policies introduced in 2010 reversed the gains of the New Labour years. In summarizing a report on the effects of austerity policies in the United Kingdom, the United Nations special rapporteur on extreme poverty and human rights wrote that "much of the glue that has held British society together since the Second World War has been deliberately removed and replaced with a harsh and uncaring ethos" (Alston 2019, 1).

38. For useful introductions to company towns in the United States and elsewhere, see Crawford 1995; Dinius and Vergara 2011; Green 2010.

39. E.g., Green 2010, chapter 3.

40. For descriptions of the policy, see Choi, Moon, and Ridder 2019; Byun, Kim, and Park 2012; Kim and Lee 2003.

41. Choi, Moon, and Ridder 2019; Byun, Kim, and Park 2012; Kim and Lee 2003.

42. See Byun, Kim, and Park 2012 for analysis and a review.

43. Note, though, that even in Korea randomization is applied to only *part* of the education system. Entry to higher education is non-randomized and highly competitive. College entry is based primarily on test scores, which increases the incentives for parents to invest in private tutoring (and to find ways to bypass the middle- and high-school randomization policy). The evidence from Korea therefore demonstrates how a radical policy like randomization can be undermined when applied to just part of a single institution.

44. Reeves 2017.

45. Rawls 1971.

46. E.g., Grusky 2012.

47. See Chetty, Friedman et al. 2017 for differences in the proportions of rich and poor children attending college.

48. Grusky, Hall, and Markus 2019.

49. Brooks 2017.

50. Brooks 2017.

51. See Aviezer et al. 1994 for a discussion of the traditional kibbutz. Note that modern examples of the kibbutz may differ substantially from the traditional form.

52. Granovetter 1973, 1974, 1983. See also Lin 2001.

53. See Sherman 2017 on the unease that the rich feel in displaying their affluence to those who are poorer than they are.

54. See Waal 2008 for a review of the relationship between empathy and altruism; also see Ordabayeva and Fernandes 2017; Eisenberg et al. 2002; Eisenberg 1986; Underwood and Moore 1982; see Simpson and Willer 2015 on prosocial behavior.

55. See Tierney, Grossman, and Resch 1995.

56. Beiser 2003.

57. Goldin and Katz 2008; Kalleberg 2011.

58. E.g., Katz and Krueger 2019; Arntz, Gregory, and Zierahn 2016; Eubanks 2018. As I discuss in Chapter 3, alongside its effects on economic inequality, technology also has effects on inequality of opportunity, for example, by establishing negative links among institutions.

59. The nonprofit organization Single Stop, for example, provides a "one-stop shop" for the whole range of safety net and other programs, which it characterizes as "the nation's first Amazon.com, for social services" (see singlestopusa.org). Other nonprofits, such as the National Alliance to End Homelessness, emphasize the importance of a coordinated approach to cross-system data linkage if policy interventions are to be effective. See Herd and Moynihan 2018, chapter 10, for a discussion of auto-enrollment in government programs.

60. See Rivera and Tilcsik 2016 on class discrimination in hiring.

61. E.g., Scott-Clayton 2012; Goldrick-Rab et al. 2016; Lochner and Monge-Naranjo 2012; Grodsky and Jones 2007.

62. The chatbot was designed by Microsoft, and was withdrawn soon after its turn to Nazism (Reese 2016). On unintended biases in technology, see Buolamwini 2016; Gershgorn 2017; Hutson 2017.

63. Nussbaum 2003, 2007, 2011; Sen 1999.

64. Hamilton,Paul, and Darity 2018.

65. E.g., Jackson and Buckner 2016.

66. Dobbin 2009, chapter 9.

CHAPTER 5

1. Sunstein 2017, 10. See also Correll 2017 on the value of "small wins."

2. Freeman 1975; Haines 1984; see also descriptions of the "Overton window" (e.g., Lehman 2010).

3. Haines 1984: 41–42.

4. It is also undeniable that a radical flank movement risks discrediting the wider push toward social change. The type of radical flank that I envision having positive effects in the current inequality policy environment is a flank arguing in favor of science-based radical reform, similar to that outlined here.

5. Wuebbles, Fahey, and Hibbard 2017.

6. Leiserowitz et al. 2020.

7. The World Economic Forum, for example, produces assessments of leading global risks and challenges, as identified by experts. Inequality and climate change are routinely identified as being among the greatest threats to society and world stability (e.g., World Economic Forum 2015, 2019).

8. There is evidence that emphasizing scientific consensus among experts is helpful in persuading the public that a consensus exists. Linden, Leiserowitz, and Maibach 2018, for example, use experimental data to show that when the extent of the scientific consensus around climate change is highlighted, audiences respond by updating their prior beliefs about the science.

9. Ripple et al. 2020, 10.

10. Schifeling and Hoffman 2019, 228; see also Roberts 2017; Conner and Epstein 2007.

11. Rosentiel 2011. Rosentiel writes of the Pew Research survey results: "In May 1987, 90% agreed with the statement: 'Our society should do what is necessary to make sure everyone has an equal opportunity to succeed.' This percentage has remained at about 90% ever since (87% in the most recent political values survey)."

12. E.g., Page and Shapiro 1992, chapter 4.

13. McCall 2013, chapter 4. Adam Levine (2015) provides one possible explanation for why increasing income inequality has not led to increased calls for measures to reduce inequality. He shows that when individuals experience the feeling of economic insecurity, they become more aware of their lack of resources, and less rather than more likely to expend those scarce resources supporting policies that might reduce inequality. McCall's study was published in 2013, but with respect to measures of standard attitudes, there is no evidence that much has changed since then, with the exception of some

partisan shifts that are consistent with conventional models of public opinion (Newport 2015, 2016).

14. Jackson and Grusky 2017.

15. Arlie R. Hochschild 2016.

16. The *Los Angeles Times*, for example, described the contest between Biden and Warren as follows: "They bring to the 2020 campaign very different worldviews and goals: Warren is aiming not just to beat Trump but to rid the U.S. of structural inequities that she believes contributed to Trump's rise. Biden is aiming to focus Democrats' energy on getting rid of Trump, calling for more incremental policy changes and a return to the normality of the Obama era" (August 29, 2019).

17. McCall 2013, 218.

18. McCall et al. 2017; see also Becker 2020.

19. Pew Research Center 2017; see also Rosenfeld 2017.

20. Baunach 2012; Rosenfeld 2017.

21. Newport 2017; Byler 2020.

22. Sunstein 1996; see also Kuran and Sunstein 1999.

23. Sunstein 1996; see also Jackson and Grusky 2017 on norm entrepreneurs and the political exploitation of social inequality.

24. Bevan 1944; Morgan 2001.

25. Scheidel 2017; Piketty 2013; Piketty and Saez 2003; Scheve and Stasavage 2010.

26. Scheidel 2017; see Scheidel 2020 for a discussion of Covid-19 in historical context.

27. Sanders 2020. A similar theme was—unexpectedly—struck by the *Financial Times* editorial board, who argued, "If there is a silver lining to the Covid-19 pandemic, it is that it has injected a sense of togetherness into polarised societies. But the virus, and the economic lockdowns needed to combat it, also shine a glaring light on existing inequalities—and even create new ones. Beyond defeating the disease, the great test all countries will soon face is whether current feelings of common purpose will shape society after the crisis. As Western leaders learnt in the Great Depression, and after World War 2, to demand collective sacrifice you must offer a social contract that benefits everyone" (*Financial Times*, April 5, 2020). There is some evidence that support for universal social policies did indeed increase in the early months of the Covid-19 pandemic (Thomas, Kalkstein, and Walton 2020).

28. Granovetter 2017.

29. One striking example of sacrifice and exchange was provided by David Ansell, in a moving opinion piece in the *Washington Post*. He writes of his time in hospitals serving low-income and minority patients, "In my 27 years at these two safety-net hospitals, not one of my patients received an organ or bone marrow transplant. Yet the organs that fed the transplant centers across the region came from the dying patients in these hospitals. Our patients—the poorest of the poor—gave, but they never received" (Ansell 2017).

30. Coates 2014; see also Beckert and Rockman 2016; Porter 2020. The United States' history of slavery has provided the moral foundation for arguments in favor of reparations for African Americans. (e.g. Coates 2014; Darity and Mullen 2020).

31. King 1967.

32. Note that foundation-driven projects frequently draw on academic support from teams of social scientists who can advise on randomization, clear treatment protocols, and careful measurement.

33. See Reich 2016 on the dangers to democracy of foundation-driven social policy.

34. Bronfenbrenner 1974, 1979; see also Ramey, MacPhee, and Yeates 1982; Bertalanffy 1968.

35. E.g., Roth 2002; cf. Duflo 2017.

36. There are active areas of research examining the knock-on effects of institutional failures, even when those failures are not described as such. A clear example of this can be found in research that highlights the links between health care/nutrition and the education system, where the effects on individuals of poor health care or nutrition are shown to have subsequent negative effects on achievement test scores and educational outcomes (e.g., Frisvold 2015; Basch 2011; Currie 2009; Fiscella and Kitzman 2009; Hair et al. 2015).

37. For useful descriptions of the history of systems analysis and the RAND Corporation, see Levien 2000; Gibson and Scherer 2007; Quade 1972.

38. See Hoos 1972 for a thorough critique of systems analysis.

39. Note that contemporary policy researchers frequently refer to a "systems" approach to policy analysis, which focuses on examining the functioning of government-provided systems such as the education system, the juvenile justice system, the child welfare system, and so on. This approach is distinct from the "systems analysis" that is discussed here.

40. Box and Draper 1969; see Hare 2015 for an introduction to EVOP.

41. Ioannidis 2005, 696. For recent discussions of proposals to improve the situation, see Freese and King 2018; Gelman 2018; Young 2018.

42. Heckman and Moktan (2020), for example, argue that a reliance on the top five journals in economics in tenure and promotion procedures encourages careerism over creativity.

REFERENCES

Abel-Smith, Brian. 1992. "The Beveridge Report: Its Origins and Outcomes." *International Social Security Review* 45 (1–2): 5–16.

ACLU. 2014. *School to Prison Pipeline*. https://www.aclu.org/issues/juvenile- justice/school- prison- pipeline/school-prison-pipeline-infographic.

Adams, James Truslow. (1931) 2001. *The Epic of America*. Boston: Little, Brown.

Addison, Paul. 2011. *The Road to 1945: British Politics and the Second World War*. Rev. ed. New York: Random House.

Agar, Herbert, and Allen Tate, eds. 1936. *Who Owns America? A New Declaration of Independence*. Boston: Houghton Mifflin.

Aizer, Anna, and Janet Currie. 2014. "The Intergenerational Transmission of Inequality: Maternal Disadvantage and Health at Birth." *Science* 344 (6186): 856–61.

Aizer, Anna, Shari Eli, Joseph Ferrie, and Adriana Lleras-Muney. 2016. "The Long-Run Impact of Cash Transfers to Poor Families." *American Economic Review* 106 (4): 935–71.

Alexander, Karl, and Stephen L. Morgan. 2016. "The Coleman Report at Fifty: Its Legacy and Implications for Future Research on Equality of Opportunity." *RSF: The Russell Sage Foundation Journal of the Social Sciences* 2 (5): 1–16.

Alm, James. 2012. "Measuring, Explaining, and Controlling Tax Evasion: Lessons from Theory, Experiments, and Field Studies." *International Tax and Public Finance* 19 (1): 54–77.

Alon, Sigal, and Marta Tienda. 2007. "Diversity, Opportunity, and the Shifting Meritocracy in Higher Education." *American Sociological Review* 72 (4): 487–511.

Alston, P. 2019. *Visit to the United Kingdom of Great Britain and Northern Ireland: Report of the Special Rapporteur on Extreme Poverty and Human Rights*. https://digitallibrary.un.org/record/3806308

American Association of University Professors (AAUP). 2019. *The Annual Report on the Economic Status of the Profession, 2018–19*. Washington, DC: Committee on Economic Status of the Profession, American Association of University Professors.

Andersen, Hanne, and Brian Hepburn. 2016. "Scientific Method." In *The Stanford Encyclopedia of Philosophy* (Summer 2016), edited by Edward N. Zalta. https://plato.stanford.edu/archives/sum2016/entries/scientificmethod/.

Andrade, Stefan B., and Jens-Peter Thomsen. 2018. "Intergenerational Educational Mobility in Denmark and the United States." *Sociological Science* 5 (5): 93–113.

Andrews, Edmund L. 2019. "Good News and Bad News on Tax Evasion." *Insights by Stanford Business*, July 22, 2019.

Ansell, David A. 2017. "I Watched My Patients Die of Poverty for 40 Years: It's Time for Single-Payer." *Washington Post*, September 13, 2017.

Arcaya, Mariana, Ethan J. Raker, and Mary C. Waters. 2020. "The Social Consequences of Disasters: Individual and Community Change." *Annual Review of Sociology* 46: 1.

Arntz, Melanie, Terry Gregory, and Ulrich Zierahn. 2016. "The Risk of Automation for Jobs in OECD Countries: A Comparative Analysis." OECD Social, Employment, and Migration Working Papers, no. 189. Paris: OECD Publishing.

Arrow, Kenneth, Samuel Bowles, and Steven N. Durlauf, eds. 2000. *Meritocracy and Economic Inequality*. Princeton, NJ: Princeton University Press.

Ashenfelter, Orley, William J. Collins, and Albert Yoon. 2006. "Evaluating the Role of *Brown v. Board of Education* in School Equalization, Desegregation, and the Income of African Americans." *American Law and Economics Review* 8 (2): 213–48.

Atkinson, Anthony B. 2015. *Inequality*. Cambridge, MA: Harvard University Press.

Averett, Susan, and Yang Wang. 2013. "The Effects of Earned Income Tax Credit Payment Expansion on Maternal Smoking." *Health Economics* 22 (11): 1344–59.

Aviezer, Ora, Marinus H. van IJzendoorn, Abraham Sagi, and Carlo Schuengel. 1994. "'Children of the Dream' Revisited: 70 years of Collective Early Child Care in Israeli Kibbutzim." *Psychological Bulletin* 116 (1): 99–116.

Bailey, Drew, Greg J. Duncan, Candice L. Odgers, and Winnie Yu. 2017. "Persistence and Fadeout in the Impacts of Child and Adolescent Interventions." *Journal of Research on Educational Effectiveness* 10 (1): 7–39.

Bailey, Martha J., Hilary W. Hoynes, Maya Rossin-Slater, and Reed Walker. 2020. "Is the Social Safety Net a Long-Term Investment? Large-Scale Evidence from the Food Stamps Program." NBER Working Paper Series 26942, National Bureau of Economic Research.

Banerjee, Abhijit V., and Esther Duflo. 2003. "Inequality and Growth: What Can the Data Say?" Working paper. https://economics.mit.edu/files/753.

Barr, Andrew, and Chloe R. Gibbs. 2019. "Breaking the Cycle? Intergenerational Effects of an Anti-poverty Program in Early Childhood." EdWorkingPaper Series 19–141, Annenberg Institute at Brown University.

Bartfeld, Judith, Craig Gundersen, Timothy M. Smeeding, and James P. Ziliak, eds. 2015. *SNAP Matters: How Food Stamps Affect Health and Well-Being*. Stanford, CA: Stanford University Press.

Basch, Charles E. 2011. "Breakfast and the Achievement Gap among Urban Minority Youth." *Journal of School Health* 81 (10): 635–40.

Baunach, Dawn Michelle. 2012. "Changing Same-Sex Marriage Attitudes in America from 1988 through 2010." *Public Opinion Quarterly* 76 (2): 364–78.

Becker, Bastian. 2020. "Mind the Income Gaps? Experimental Evidence of Information's Lasting Effect on Redistributive Preferences." *Social Justice Research* (33): 94–137.

Beckert, Sven, and Seth Rockman, eds. 2016. *Slavery's Capitalism: A New History of American Economic Development*. Philadelphia: University of Pennsylvania Press.

Beiser, Morton. 2003. "Sponsorship and Resettlement Success." *Journal of International Migration and Integration/Revue de l'integration et de la migration internationale* 4 (2): 203–15.

Bell, Monica C. 2019. "Safety, Friendship, and Dreams." *Harvard Civil Rights-Civil Liberties Law Review* 54: 703–739.

———. "Located Institutions: Neighborhood Frames, Residential Preferences, and the Case of Policing." *American Journal of Sociology* 125 (4): 917–973.

Bellah, Robert N. 1995. "Individualism and Commitment: America's Cultural Conversation." http://www.robertbellah.com/lectures_6.htm.

Bellah, Robert N., Richard Madsen, William M. Sullivan, Ann Swidler, and Steven M. Tipton. 1985. *Habits of the Heart: Individualism and Commitment in American Life*. Berkeley: University of California Press.

Benartzi, Shlomo, John Beshears, Katherine L. Milkman, Cass R. Sunstein, Richard H. Thaler, Maya Shankar, Will Tucker-Ray, William J. Congdon, and Steven Galing. 2017. "Should Governments Invest More in Nudging?" *Psychological Science* 28 (8): 1041–55.

Berg, Andrew G., and Jonathan D. Ostry. 2011. "Inequality and Unsustainable Growth: Two Sides of the Same Coin?" IMF Staff Discussion Note SDN/11/08.

Bernstein, Basil. 1971. *Class, Codes and Control: Theoretical Studies towards a Sociology of Language*. London: Routledge and Kegan Paul.

Bertalanffy, Ludwig von. 1968. *General System Theory: Foundation, Development, Applications*. New York: George Braziller.

Bettinger, Eric P., Bridget Terry Long, Philip Oreopoulos, and Lisa Sanbonmatsu. 2012. "The Role of Application Assistance and Information in College Decisions: Results from the H&R Block FAFSA Experiment." *The Quarterly Journal of Economics* 127 (3): 1205–42.

Bevan, Aneurin. 1944. *Why Not Trust the Tories?* London: Victor Gollancz.

———. 1952. *In Place of Fear*. London: William Heinemann.

Beveridge, William H. 1942. *Social Insurance and Allied Services: Report by Sir William Beveridge*. London: Her Majesty's Stationery Office.

Bhargava, Saurabh, and Dayanand Manoli. 2015. "Psychological Frictions and the In-complete Take-Up of Social Benefits: Evidence from an IRS Field Experiment." *American Economic Review* 105 (11): 3489–3529.

Bianchi, Suzanne M. 2000. "Maternal Employment and Time with Children: Dramatic Change or Surprising Continuity?" *Demography* 37 (4): 401–14.

Bloome, Deirdre. 2015. "Income Inequality and Intergenerational Income Mobility in the United States." *Social Forces* 93 (3): 1047–80.

Blumenshine, Philip, Susan Egerter, Colleen J. Barclay, Catherine Cubbin, and Paula A. Braveman. 2010. "Socioeconomic Disparities in Adverse Birth Outcomes: A System-atic Review." *American Journal of Preventive Medicine* 39 (3): 263–72.

Bonam, Courtney M., Hilary B. Bergsieker, and Jennifer L. Eberhardt. 2016. "Polluting Black Space." *Journal of Experimental Psychology: General* 145 (11): 1561–82.

Bonnie, Richard J., and Emily P. Backes, eds. 2019. *The Promise of Adolescence: Realizing Opportunity for All Youth.* Washington, DC: National Academies Press.

Bonnie, Richard J., Clare Stroud, and Heather Breiner, eds. 2014. *Investing in the Health and Well-Being of Young Adults.* Washington, DC: National Academies Press.

Booth, Adam. 2017. "Universal Basic Income: Utopian Dream or Libertarian Night-mare?" *Socialist Appeal*, February 9, 2017.

Borsboom, Denny, and Angélique O. J. Cramer. 2013. "Network Analysis: An Integrative Approach to the Structure of Psychopathology." *Annual Review of Clinical Psychol-ogy* 9 (1): 91–121.

Boudon, Raymond. 1974. *Education, Opportunity, and Social Inequality: Changing Pros-pects in Western Society.* New York: Wiley.

Bourdieu, Pierre. 1984. *Distinction: A Social Critique of the Judgement of Taste.* Cam-bridge, MA: Harvard University Press.

Bowles, Samuel, Herbert Gintis, and Melissa Osborne-Groves, eds. 2005. *Unequal Chances: Family Background and Economic Success.* Princeton, NJ: Princeton Uni-versity Press.

Box, George E. P., and Norman R. Draper. 1969. *Evolutionary Operation: A Statistical Method for Process Improvement.* New York: Wiley.

Brand, Jennie E., and Yu Xie. 2010. "Who Benefits Most from College? Evidence for Negative Selection in Heterogeneous Economic Returns to Higher Education." *American Sociological Review* 75 (2): 273–302.

Branigan, Amelia R., Kenneth J. McCallum, and Jeremy Freese. 2013. "Variation in the Heritability of Educational Attainment: An International Meta-analysis." *Social Forces* 92 (1): 109–40.

Braveman, Paula A., Katherine Heck, Susan Egerter, Kristen S. Marchi, Tyan Parker Dominguez, Catherine Cubbin, Kathryn Fingar, Jay A. Pearson, and Michael Cur-tis. 2015. "The Role of Socioeconomic Factors in Black-White Disparities in Preterm Birth." *American Journal of Public Health* 105 (4): 694–702.

Bredgaard, Thomas, Flemming Larsen, and Per Kongshøj Madsen. 2005. "The Flexible Danish Labour Market—A Review." *CARMA Research Papers* 1:2005.

Breen, Richard, ed. 2004. *Social Mobility in Europe*. Oxford: Oxford University Press.

Brighouse, Harry, and Adam Swift. 2014. *Family Values: The Ethics of Parent-Child Relationships*. Princeton, NJ: Princeton University Press.

Bronfenbrenner, Urie. 1974. "Developmental Research, Public Policy, and the Ecology of Childhood." *Child Development* 45 (1): 1–5.

———. 1977. "Lewinian Space and Ecological Substance." *Journal of Social Issues* 33 (4): 199–212.

———. 1979. *The Ecology of Human Development. Experiments by Nature and Design*. Cambridge, MA: Harvard University Press.

Brooks, David. 2017. "Giving Away Your Billion." *New York Times*, June 6, 2017.

Bukodi, Erzsébet, Marii Paskov, and Brian Nolan. 2020. "Intergenerational Class Mobility in Europe: A New Account." *Social Forces* 98 (3): 941–72.

Buolamwini, Joy. 2016. "How I'm Fighting Bias in Algorithms." *TEDxBeaconStreet*, November 2016.

Byler, David. 2020. "Public Opinion on Policing has Shifted. Here's How to Tell if the Changes will Stick." *Washington Post*, June 18, 2020.

Byun, Soo-yong, Kyung-keun Kim, and Hyunjoon Park. 2012. "School Choice and Educational Inequality in South Korea." *Journal of School Choice* 6 (2): 158–83.

California State Auditor. 2000. *Standardized Tests: Although Some Students May Receive Extra Time on Standardized Tests That Is Not Deserved, Others May Not Be Getting the Assistance They Need*. Technical Report 2000-108. Bureau of State Audits.

Camilli, Gregory, Sadako Vargas, Sharon Ryan, and W. Steven Barnett. 2010. "Meta-Analysis of the Effects of Early Education Interventions on Cognitive and Social Development." *Teachers College Record* 112 (3): 579–620.

Campbell, John L. 2002. "Ideas, Politics, and Public Policy." *Annual Review of Sociology* 28 (1): 21–38.

Cardiff, Christopher F., and Daniel B. Klein. 2005. "Faculty Partisan Affiliations in All Disciplines: A Voter-Registration Study." *Critical Review* 17 (3–4): 237–55.

Carneiro, Pedro, and James Heckman. 2003. "Human Capital Policy." NBER Working Paper Series 9495, National Bureau of Economic Research.

Carter, Prudence L., and Kevin G. Welner, eds. 2013. *Closing the Opportunity Gap: What America Must Do to Give Every Child an Even Chance*. New York: Oxford University Press.

Case, Anne, and Angus Deaton. 2020. *Deaths of Despair and the Future of Capitalism*. Princeton, NJ: Princeton University Press.

Castleman, Benjamin L., and Lindsay C. Page. 2014. *Summer Melt: Supporting Low-Income Students through the Transition to College*. Cambridge, MA: Harvard University Press.

———. 2015. "Summer Nudging: Can Personalized Text Messages and Peer Mentor Outreach Increase College Going among Low-Income High School Graduates?" *Journal of Economic Behavior and Organization* 115: 144–60.

Center on the Developing Child. 2007. *The Science of Early Childhood Development.* www.developingchild.harvard.edu.

Cherlin, Andrew J. 2009. *The Marriage-Go-Round.* New York: Random House.

———. 2010. "Demographic Trends in the United States: A Review of Research in the 2000s." *Journal of Marriage and the Family* 72 (3): 403–19.

Chetty, Raj, John N. Friedman, Emmanuel Saez, Nicholas Turner, and Danny Yagan. 2017. "Mobility Report Cards: The Role of Colleges in Intergenerational Mobility." NBER Working Paper Series 23618, National Bureau of Economic Research.

Chetty, Raj, David B. Grusky, Maximilian Hell, Nathaniel Hendren, Robert Manduca, and Jimmy Narang. 2017. "The Fading American Dream: Trends in Absolute Income Mobility since 1940." *Science* 356 (6336): 398–406.

Chetty, Raj, and Nathaniel Hendren. 2018. "The Impacts of Neighborhoods on Intergenerational Mobility II: County-Level Estimates." *The Quarterly Journal of Economics* 133 (3): 1163–1228.

Chetty, Raj, Nathaniel Hendren, Maggie R. Jones, and Sonya R. Porter. 2020. "Race and Economic Opportunity in the United States: An Intergenerational Perspective." *The Quarterly Journal of Economics* 135 (2): 711–83.

Chetty, Raj, Nathaniel Hendren, and Lawrence F. Katz. 2016. "The Effects of Exposure to Better Neighborhoods on Children: New Evidence from the Moving to Opportunity Experiment." *American Economic Review* 106 (4): 855–902.

Chetty, Raj, Nathaniel Hendren, Patrick Kline, Emmanuel Saez, and Nicholas Turner. 2014. "Is the United States Still a Land of Opportunity?" *American Economic Review* 104 (5): 141–47.

Chetty, Raj, Michael Stepner, Sarah Abraham, Shelby Lin, Benjamin Scuderi, Nicholas Turner, Augustin Bergeron, and David Cutler. 2016. "The Association between Income and Life Expectancy in the United States, 2001–2014." *JAMA* 315 (16): 1750–66.

Choi, Eleanor Jawon, Hyungsik Roger Moon, and Geert Ridder. 2019. "Within-District School Lotteries, District Selection, and the Average Partial Effects of School Inputs." *The Korean Economic Review* 35 (2): 275–306.

Churchwell, Sarah. 2018. *Behold, America: The Entangled History of 'America First' and 'the American Dream.'* New York: Basic Books.

Coates, Ta-Nehisi. 2014. "The Case for Reparations." *The Atlantic* 313 (5): 54–71.

Cohen, Joshua, and Charles Sabel. 2009. "Flexicurity." *Pathways* (Spring): 10–14.

Coleman, James S. 1987. "Families and Schools." *Educational Researcher* 16 (6): 32–38.

———. 1990. *Foundations of Social Theory.* Cambridge, MA: Harvard University Press.

———. 1993. "The Rational Reconstruction of Society: 1992 Presidential Address." *American Sociological Review* 58 (1): 1–15.

Coleman, James S., and Thomas Hoffer. 1987. *Public and Private High Schools: The Impact of Communities.* New York: Basic Books.

Coleman-Jensen, Alisha, Matthew P. Rabbitt, Christian A. Gregory, and Anita Singh. 2019. *Household Food Security in the United States in 2018.* ERR-270, U.S. Department of Agriculture, Economic Research Service.

Collins, Patricia Hill, and Sirma Bilge. 2016. *Intersectionality.* Cambridge: Polity.

Collins, Randall. 2004. *Interaction Ritual Chains.* Princeton, NJ: Princeton University Press.

Colodro-Conde, Lucia, Frühling Rijsdijk, María J. Tornero-Gómez, Juan F. Sánchez-Romera, and Juan R. Ordoñana. 2015. "Equality in Educational Policy and the Heritability of Educational Attainment." *PLoS ONE* 10: 11.

Congressional Budget Office. 2016. *The Distribution of Household Income and Federal Taxes, 2013.*

Conner, Alana, and Keith Epstein. 2007. "Harnessing Purity and Pragmatism." *Stanford Social Innovation Review* 5 (44): 61–65.

Consumer Federation of America. 2013. *Child Poverty, Unintentional Injuries and Foodborne Illness: Are Low-Income Children at Greater Risk?* https://consumerfed.org/pdfs/Child-Poverty-Report.pdf.

Corak, Miles. 2013. "Inequality from Generation to Generation: The United States in Comparison." In *The Economics of Inequality, Poverty, and Discrimination in the 21st Century,* edited by Robert Rycroft. Santa Barbara, CA: ABC-CLIO.

Correll, Joshua, Bernadette Park, Charles M. Judd, and Bernd Wittenbrink. 2002. "The Police Officer's Dilemma: Using Ethnicity to Disambiguate Potentially Threatening Individuals." *Journal of Personality and Social Psychology* 83 (6): 1314–29.

Correll, Shelley. 2017. "Reducing Gender Biases in Modern Workplaces: A Small Wins Approach to Organizational Change." *Gender and Society* 31 (6): 725–50.

Coser, Lewis A. 1974. *Greedy Institutions: Patterns of Undivided Commitment.* New York: Free Press.

Council of Economic Advisers. 2018. "The Opportunity Costs of Socialism." https://www.whitehouse.gov/wp-content/uploads/2018/10/The-Opportunity-Costs-of-Socialism.pdf.

Cowan, Benjamin, and Nathan Tefft. 2012. "Education, Maternal Smoking, and the Earned Income Tax Credit." *The B.E. Journal of Economic Analysis & Policy* 12 (1): 1–39.

Crawford, Margaret. 1995. *Building the Workingman's Paradise: The Design of American Company Towns.* New York: Verso.

Crenshaw, Kimberlé. 1989. "Demarginalizing the Intersection of Race and Sex: A Black Feminist Critique of Antidiscrimination Doctrine, Feminist Theory and Antiracist Politics." *University of Chicago Legal Forum* 1 (8): 139–67.

Crosnoe, Robert, Kate Chambers Prickett, Chelsea Smith, and Shannon Cavanagh. 2014. "Changes in Young Children's Family Structures and Child Care Arrangements." *Demography* 51 (2): 459–83.

Cunha, Flavio, and James Heckman. 2007. "The Technology of Skill Formation." *American Economic Review* 97 (2): 31–47.

Cunha, Flavio, James J. Heckman, Lance Lochner, and Dimitriy V. Masterov. 2006. "Interpreting the Evidence on Life Cycle Skill Formation." *Handbook of the Economics of Education* 1: 697–812.

Currie, Janet. 2009. "Healthy, Wealthy, and Wise: Socioeconomic Status, Poor Health in Childhood, and Human Capital Development." *Journal of Economic Literature* 47 (1): 87–122.

Currie, Janet, and Douglas Almond. 2011. "Human Capital Development before Age Five." *Handbook of Labor Economics* 4: 1315–1486.

Currie, Janet, and Duncan Thomas. 1995. "Does Head Start Make a Difference?" *American Economic Review* 85 (3): 341–64.

———. 2000. "School Quality and the Longer-Term Effects of Head Start." *The Journal of Human Resources* 35 (4): 755–74.

Dahrendorf, Ralf. 1987. "Max Weber and Modern Social Science." In *Max Weber and His Contemporaries*, edited by Wolfgang J. Mommsen and Jürgen Osterhammel. London: Allen and Unwin.

Darity, William A., Jr., and A. Kirsten Mullen. 2020. *From Here to Equality: Reparations for Black Americans in the Twenty-First Century*. Chapel Hill: University of North Carolina Press.

Davies, Christie. 1989. "Goffman's Concept of the Total Institution: Criticisms and Revisions." *Human Studies* 12 (1): 77–95.

Davis, Angela Y. 2003. *Are Prisons Obsolete?* New York: Seven Stories Press.

Davis, Jonathan, and Bhash Mazumder. 2017. "The Decline in Intergenerational Mobility after 1980." Chicago Fed Working Papers 2017-05.

De Simone, Lisa, Rebecca Lester, and Kevin Markle. 2020. "Transparency and Tax Evasion: Evidence from the Foreign Account Tax Compliance Act (FATCA)." *Journal of Accounting Research* 58 (1): 105–153.

Deary, Ian J., Martha C. Whiteman, John M. Starr, Lawrence J. Whalley, and Helen C. Fox. 2004. "The Impact of Childhood Intelligence on Later Life: Following Up the Scottish Mental Surveys of 1932 and 1947." *Journal of Personality and Social Psychology* 86 (1): 130–47.

Declercq, Eugene R., Carol Sakala, Maureen P. Corry, Sandra Applebaum, and Ariel Herrlich. 2013. *Listening to Mothers III: Pregnancy and Birth*. New York: Childbirth Connection.

DeLuca, Stefanie, Susan Clampet-Lundquist, and Kathryn Edin. 2016. *Coming of Age in the Other America*. New York: Russell Sage Foundation.

Deming, David J. 2017. "The Growing Importance of Social Skills in the Labor Market." *The Quarterly Journal of Economics* 132 (4): 1593–1640.

Desmond, Matthew. 2016. *Evicted: Poverty and Profit in the American City*. New York: Crown.

Dickens, William T., and James R. Flynn. 2001. "Heritability Estimates versus Large Environmental Effects: The IQ Paradox Resolved." *Psychological Review* 108 (2): 346–69.

Diffenbaugh, Noah S., and Marshall Burke. 2019. "Global Warming Has Increased Global Economic Inequality." *Proceedings of the National Academy of Sciences* 116 (20): 9808–13.

Dinius, Oliver J., and Angela Vergara, eds. 2011. *Company Towns in the Americas: Landscape, Power, and Working-Class Communities*. Athens: University of Georgia Press.

DiPrete, Thomas A., and Gregory M. Eirich. 2006. "Cumulative Advantage as a Mechanism for Inequality: A Review of Theoretical and Empirical Developments." *Annual Review of Sociology* 32 (1): 271–97.

DiPrete, Thomas A., Gregory M. Eirich, and Matthew Pittinsky. 2010. "Compensation Benchmarking, Leapfrogs, and the Surge in Executive Pay." *American Journal of Sociology* 115 (6): 1671–712.

Dobbin, Frank. 2009. *Inventing Equal Opportunity*. Princeton, NJ: Princeton University Press.

Doyle, Orla, Colm P. Harmon, James J. Heckman, and Richard E. Tremblay. 2009. "Investing in Early Human Development: Timing and Economic Efficiency." *Economics and Human Biology* 7 (1): 1–6.

Duflo, Esther. 2017. "Richard T. Ely Lecture: The Economist as Plumber." *American Economic Review* 107 (5): 1–26.

Duflo, Esther, and Abhijit Banerjee. 2019. "If We're Serious about Changing the World, We Need a Better Kind of Economics to Do It." *The Guardian*, October 30, 2019.

Duncan, Greg J., and Katherine A. Magnuson. 2005. "Can Family Socioeconomic Resources Account for Racial and Ethnic Test Score Gaps?" *The Future of Children* 15 (1): 35–54.

Durkheim, Emile. (1893) 2014. *The Division of Labor in Society*. New York: Simon and Schuster.

———. (1908) 1982. *The Rules of Sociological Method*. New York: Free Press.

Dynarski, Susan, and Mark Wiederspan. 2012. "Student Aid Simplification: Looking Back and Looking Ahead." *National Tax Journal* 65 (1): 211–34.

Easterlin, Richard A. 2017. "Economic Growth Increases People's Well-Being." In *Economic Ideas You Should Forget*, edited by Bruno S. Frey and David Iselin. Basel, Switzerland: Springer Nature.

Eberhardt, Jennifer L., Paul G. Davies, Valerie J. Purdie-Vaughns, and Sheri Lynn Johnson. 2006. "Looking Deathworthy: Perceived Stereotypicality of Black Defendants Predicts Capital-Sentencing Outcomes." *Psychological Science* 17 (5): 383–86.

Edin, Kathryn, and Maria Kefalas. 2005. *Promises I Can Keep: Why Poor Women Put Motherhood before Marriage.* Berkeley: University of California Press.

Edin, Kathryn, and Laura Lein. 1997. *Making Ends Meet: How Single Mothers Survive Welfare and Low-Wage Work.* New York: Russell Sage Foundation.

Edin, Kathryn J., and H. Luke Shaefer. 2015. *$2.00 a Day: Living on Almost Nothing in America.* New York: Houghton Mifflin Harcourt.

Edwards, John, Marion Crain, and Arne L. Kalleberg, eds. 2007. *Ending Poverty in America: How to Restore the American Dream.* New York: New Press.

Eisenberg, Nancy. 1986. *Altruistic Emotion, Cognition, and Behavior.* Hillsdale, NJ: Lawrence Erlbaum Associates.

Eisenberg, Nancy, Ivanna K. Guthrie, Amanda Cumberland, Bridget C. Murphy, Stephanie A. Shepard, Qing Zhou, and Gustavo Carlo. 2002. "Prosocial Development in Early Adulthood: A Longitudinal Study." *Journal of Personality and Social Psychology* 82 (6): 993–1006.

Eisenstadt, S. N. 1964. "Social Change, Differentiation and Evolution." *American Sociological Review* 29 (3): 375–86.

Elam-Evans, Laurie D., David Yankey, James A. Singleton, and Maureen Kolasa. 2014. "National, State, and Selected Local Area Vaccination Coverage among Children Aged 19–35 Months—United States, 2013." *Morbidity and Mortality Weekly Report* 63 (34): 741–48.

Ellis, Dean S. 1967. "Speech and Social Status in America." *Social Forces* 45 (3): 431–37.

Ellis, George, and Joe Silk. 2014. "Scientific Method: Defend the Integrity of Physics." *Nature* 516: 321–23.

Epp, Charles R., Steven Maynard-Moody, and Donald P. Haider-Markel. 2014. *Pulled Over: How Police Stops Define Race and Citizenship.* Chicago: University of Chicago Press.

Eppard, Lawrence M., Mark Robert Rank, and Heather E. Bullock. 2020. *Rugged Individualism and the Misunderstanding of American Inequality.* Lanham, MD: Lehigh University Press.

Eubanks, Virginia. 2018. *Automating Inequality: How High-Tech Tools Profile, Police, and Punish the Poor.* New York: St. Martin's Press.

European Commission. 2007. "Towards Common Principles of Flexicurity: More and Better Jobs through Flexibility and Security." Office for Official Publications of the European Communities.

Evans, William N., and Craig L Garthwaite. 2014. "Giving Mom a Break: The Impact of Higher EITC Payments on Maternal Health." *American Economic Journal: Economic Policy* 6 (2): 258–90.

Feinberg, Matthew, and Robb Willer. 2015. "From Gulf to Bridge: When Do Moral Arguments Facilitate Political Influence?" *Personality and Social Psychology Bulletin* 41 (12): 1665–81.

Fields, Karen E., and Barbara J. Fields. 2012. *Racecraft. The Soul of Inequality in American Life*. New York: Verso.

Figlio, David N. 2015. "Experimental Evidence of the Effects of the Communities in Schools of Chicago Partnership Program on Student Achievement." https://www.cisofchicago.org/wp-content/uploads/2016/08/CIS-of-Chicago-Evaluation_Full.pdf.

Figlio, David N., Jeremy Freese, Krzysztof Karbownik, and Jeffrey Roth. 2017. "Socioeconomic Status and Genetic Influences on Cognitive Development." *Proceedings of the National Academy of Sciences* 114 (51): 13441–46.

Financial Times Editorial Board. 2020. "Virus Lays Bare the Frailty of the Social Contract." *Financial Times*, April 3, 2020.

Fiscella, Kevin, Peter Franks, Marthe R. Gold, and Carolyn M. Clancy. 2000. "Inequality in Quality: Addressing Socioeconomic, Racial, and Ethnic Disparities in Health Care." *JAMA* 283 (19): 2579–84.

Fiscella, Kevin, and Harriet Kitzman. 2009. "Disparities in Academic Achievement and Health: The Intersection of Child Education and Health Policy." *Pediatrics* 123 (3): 1073–80.

Fischer, Claude S., Michael Hout, Martín Sánchez Jankowski, Samuel R. Lucas, Ann Swidler, and Kim Voss. 1996. *Inequality by Design: Cracking the Bell Curve Myth*. Princeton, NJ: Princeton University Press.

Fishkin, James S. 1983. *Justice, Equal Opportunity, and the Family*. New Haven, CT: Yale University Press.

Fiske, Susan T., and Hazel Rose Markus, eds. 2012. *Facing Social Class: How Societal Rank Influences Interaction*. New York: Russell Sage Foundation.

Flores, Jerry. 2016. *Caught Up: Girls, Surveillance, and Wraparound Incarceration*. Oakland, CA: University of California Press.

Forget, Evelyn L. 2011. "The Town with No Poverty: The Health Effects of a Canadian Guaranteed Annual Income Field Experiment." *Canadian Public Policy/Analyse de Politiques* 37 (3): 283–305.

Fourcade, Marion. 2010. *Economists and Societies: Discipline and Profession in the United States, Britain, and France, 1890s to 1990s*. Princeton, NJ: Princeton University Press.

———. 2012. "The Socialization of Capitalism or the Neoliberalization of Socialism?" *Socio-Economic Review* 10 (2): 369–74.

Freeman, Jo. 1975. *The Politics of Women's Liberation: A Case Study of an Emerging Social Movement and Its Relation to the Policy Process*. New York: David McKay Company.

Freese, Jeremy. 2008. "Genetics and the Social Science Explanation of Individual Outcomes." *American Journal of Sociology* 114: S1–S35.

Freese, Jeremy, and Molly M. King. 2018. "Institutionalizing Transparency." *Socius* 4:1–7..

Friedman, Milton, and Rose Friedman. 1990. *Free to Choose: A Personal Statement*. New York: Houghton Mifflin Harcourt.

Frisvold, David E. 2015. "Nutrition and Cognitive Achievement: An Evaluation of the School Breakfast Program." *Journal of Public Economics* 124: 91–104.

Fryer, Roland G., Jr. 2013. "Information and Student Achievement: Evidence from a Cellular Phone Experiment." NBER Working Paper Series 19113, National Bureau of Economic Research.

Fuest, Clemens. 2017. "Inequality Reduces Growth." In *Economic Ideas You Should Forget*, edited by Bruno S. Frey and David Iselin. Basel, Switzerland: Springer Nature.

Furstenberg, Frank F. 2008. "The Intersections of Social Class and the Transition to Adulthood." *New Directions for Child and Adolescent Development* 119: 1–10.

Furuta, Jared. 2017. "Rationalization and Student/School Personhood in U.S. College Admissions: The Rise of Test-Optional Policies, 1987 to 2015." *Sociology of Education* 90 (3): 236–54.

Galster, George, and Patrick Sharkey. 2017. "Spatial Foundations of Inequality: A Conceptual Model and Empirical Overview." *RSF: The Russell Sage Foundation Journal of the Social Sciences* 3 (2): 1–33.

Garces, Eliana, Duncan Thomas, and Janet Currie. 2002. "Longer-Term Effects of Head Start." *American Economic Review* 92 (4): 999–1012.

García, Jorge Luis, James J. Heckman, Duncan Ermini Leaf, and María José Prados. 2016. "The Life-Cycle Benefits of an Influential Early Childhood Program." NBER Working Paper Series 22993, National Bureau of Economic Research.

Gelman, Andrew. 2018. "How to Think Scientifically about Scientists' Proposals for Fixing Science." *Socius* 4: 1–2.

Gerber, Theodore P., and Michael Hout. 2004. "Tightening Up: Declining Class Mobility during Russia's Market Transition." *American Sociological Review* 69 (5): 677–703.

Gershgorn, Dave. 2017. "Crash Course: Google Explains How Artificial Intelligence Becomes Biased against Women and Minorities." *Quartz*, August 28, 2017.

Gibson, John E., William T. Scherer, and William F. Gibson. 2007. *How to Do Systems Analysis*. Hoboken, NJ: John Wiley.

Goel, Sharad, Justin M. Rao, and Ravi Shroff. 2016. "Precinct or Prejudice? Understanding Racial Disparities in New York City's Stop and Frisk Policy." *Annals of Applied Statistics* 10 (1): 365–94.

Goff, Phillip Atiba, Tracey Lloyd, Amanda Geller, Steven Raphael, and Jack Glaser. 2016. *The Science of Justice: Race, Arrests, and Police Use of Force*. Center for Policing Equity.

Goffman, Erving. 1961. *Asylums: Essays on the Social Situation of Mental Patients and Other Inmates*. Garden City, NY: Anchor Books.

Goldin, Claudia, and Lawrence F. Katz. 2008. *The Race between Education and Technology*. Cambridge, MA: Harvard University Press.

Goldrick-Rab, Sara, Robert Kelchen, Douglas N. Harris, and James Benson. 2016. "Reducing Income Inequality in Educational Attainment: Experimental Evidence on the Impact of Financial Aid on College Completion." *American Journal of Sociology* 121 (6): 1762–1817.

Goldstein, Dana, and Jugal K. Patel. 2019. "Need Extra Time on Tests? It Helps to Have Cash." *New York Times*, July 30, 2019.

Gordon, Robert J. 2016. *The Rise and Fall of American Growth: The U.S. Standard of Living since the Civil War.* Princeton, NJ: Princeton University Press.

Gordon, Roger, and Gordon B. Dahl. 2013. "Views among Economists: Professional Consensus or Point-Counterpoint?" *American Economic Review* 103 (3): 629–35.

Gorsky, Martin. 2008. "The British National Health Service 1948–2008: A Review of the Historiography." *Social History of Medicine* 21 (3): 437–60.

Granovetter, Mark. 1973. "The Strength of Weak Ties." *American Journal of Sociology* 78 (6): 1360–80.

———. 1974. *Getting a Job: A Study of Contacts and Careers.* Chicago: University of Chicago Press.

———. 1979. "The Idea of 'Advancement' in Theories of Social Evolution and Development." *American Journal of Sociology* 85 (3): 489–515.

———. 1983. "The Strength of Weak Ties: A Network Theory Revisited." *Sociological Theory* 1: 201–33.

———. 1985. "Economic Action and Social Structure: The Problem of Embeddedness." *American Journal of Sociology* 91 (3): 481–510.

———. 2017. *Society and Economy: Framework and Principles.* Cambridge, MA: Harvard University Press.

Green, Donald, Bradley Palmquist, and Eric Schickler. 2002. *Partisan Hearts and Minds: Political Parties and the Social Identities of Voters.* New Haven, CT: Yale University Press.

Green, Hardy. 2010. *The Company Town: The Industrial Edens and Satanic Mills that Shaped the American Economy.* New York: Basic Books.

Grodsky, Eric, and Melanie T. Jones. 2007. "Real and Imagined Barriers to College Entry: Perceptions of Cost." *Social Science Research* 36 (2): 745–66.

Gross, Neil. 2013. *Why Are Professors Liberal and Why Do Conservatives Care?* Cambridge, MA: Harvard University Press.

Gross, Neil, and Solon Simmons, eds. 2014. *Professors and Their Politics.* Baltimore: Johns Hopkins University Press.

Grusky, David B. 2012. "What to Do about Inequality." *Boston Review*, March 1, 2012.

Grusky, David B., Peter A. Hall, and Hazel Rose Markus. 2019. "The Rise of Opportunity Markets: How Did It Happen and What Can We Do?" *Dædalus* 148 (3): 19–45.

Grusky, David B., and Jasmine Hill. 2017. "Poverty and Inequality in the 21st Century." In *Inequality in the 21st Century*, edited by David B. Grusky and Jasmine Hill. New York: Perseus Books.

Grusky, David B., and Alair MacLean. 2016. "The Social Fallout of a High-Inequality Regime." *Annals of the American Academy of Political and Social Science* 663 (1): 33–52.

Guryan, Jonathan, Erik Hurst, and Melissa Kearney. 2008. "Parental Education and Parental Time with Children." *Journal of Economic Perspectives* 22 (3): 23–46.

Hagmann, David, Emily H. Ho, and George Loewenstein. 2019. "Nudging Out Support for a Carbon Tax." *Nature Climate Change* 9 (6): 484–89.

Haines, Herbert H. 1984. "Black Radicalization and the Funding of Civil Rights: 1957–1970." *Social Problems* 32 (1): 31–43.

Hair, Nicole L., Jamie L. Hanson, Barbara L. Wolfe, and Seth D. Pollak. 2015. "Association of Child Poverty, Brain Development, and Academic Achievement." *Journal of the American Medical Association: Pediatrics* 169 (9): 822–29.

Hamilton, Darrick, William Darity, Jr., Anne E. Price, Vishnu Sridharan, and Rebecca Tippett. 2015. *Umbrellas Don't Make It Rain: Why Studying and Working Hard Isn't Enough for Black Americans*. New York: The New School.

Hamilton, Darrick, Mark Paul, and William Darity, Jr. 2018. "An Economic Bill of Rights for the 21st Century." *American Prospect*, March 5, 2018.

Haney, Lynne. 2018. "Incarcerated Fatherhood: The Entanglements of Child Support Debt and Mass Imprisonment." *American Journal of Sociology* 124 (1): 1–48.

Hanley, Eric, and Matthew McKeever. 1997. "The Persistence of Educational Inequalities in State-Socialist Hungary: Trajectory-Maintenance versus Counterselection." *Sociology of Education* 70 (1): 1–18.

Hannah-Jones, Nikole. 2019. "Our Democracy's Founding Ideals Were False When They Were Written. Black Americans Have Fought to Make Them True." *New York Times Magazine*, The 1619 Project, August 14, 2019.

Hanson, Danielle. 2013. *Assessing the Harlem Children's Zone*. Heritage Foundation, Center for Policy Innovation.

Hare, Lynne B. 2015. "EVOP: An Underused Method." *Quality Progress* 48 (1): 52.

Härkönen, Juho, Hande Kaymakçalan, Pirjo Mäki, and Anja Taanila. 2012. "Prenatal Health, Educational Attainment, and Intergenerational Inequality: The Northern Finland Birth Cohort 1966 Study." *Demography* 49 (2): 525–52.

Harlem Children's Zone. 2009. *Whatever It Takes. A White Paper on the Harlem Children's Zone*. https://hcz.org/wp-content/uploads/2014/04/HCZ-White-Paper.pdf.

———. 2010. *The Cradle through College Pipeline: Supporting Children's Development through Evidence-Based Practices: A Document from the Harlem Children's Zone*. https://www.bpichicago.org/wp-content/uploads/2014/07/The-Cradle-through-College-Pipeline.pdf

Haskins, Anna R. 2014. "Unintended Consequences: Effects of Paternal Incarceration on Child School Readiness and Later Special Education Placement." *Sociological Science* 1: 141–158.

———. 2017. "Paternal Incarceration and Children's Schooling Contexts: Intersecting Inequalities of Educational Opportunity." *Annals of the American Academy of Political and Social Science* 674 (1): 134–62.

Hausman, Daniel, Michael McPherson, and Debra Satz. 2016. *Economic Analysis, Moral Philosophy, and Public Policy*. New York: Cambridge University Press.

Heckman, James J. 2006. "Skill Formation and the Economics of Investing in Disadvantaged Children." *Science* 312 (5782): 1900–02.

———. 2007. "The Economics, Technology, and Neuroscience of Human Capability Formation." *Proceedings of the National Academy of Sciences* 104 (33): 13250–55.

———. 2008. "Schools, Skills, and Synapses." *Economic Inquiry* 46 (3): 289–324.

———. 2014. "Professor Heckman on the State of the Union Address." *The Heckman Equation*. https://heckmanequation.org/resource/professor-heckman-on-the-state-of-the-union-address/.

———. 2017. Statement on Duncan et al. Paper [*sic*]. February 24, 2017. https://heckman equation .org/resource/statement-on-duncan-et-al-paper/.

Heckman, James J., and Sidharth Moktan. 2020. "Publishing and Promotion in Economics: The Tyranny of the Top Five." *Journal of Economic Literature* 58 (2): 419–70.

Heckman, James J., Seong Hyeok Moon, Rodrigo Pinto, Peter A. Savelyev, and Adam Yavitz. 2010. "The Rate of Return to the High Scope Perry Preschool Program." *Journal of Public Economics* 94 (1): 114–28.

Helliwell, John F., Richard Layard, Jeffrey D. Sachs , and J.-E. De Neve, eds. 2020. *World Happiness Report 2020*. New York: Sustainable Development Solutions Network.

Hempel, Carl G. 1965. *Aspects of Scientific Explanation: And Other Essays in the Philosophy of Science*. New York: Free Press.

Herd, Pamela, and Donald P. Moynihan. 2018. *Administrative Burden: Policymaking by Other Means*. New York: Russell Sage Foundation.

———. 2020. "The Coronavirus Stimulus Is Playing Hard to Get." *New York Times*, April 13, 2020.

Herzer, Dierk, and Sebastian Vollmer. 2013. "Rising Top Incomes Do Not Raise the Tide." *Journal of Policy Modeling* 35 (4): 504–19.

Hochschild, Arlie R. 2016. *Strangers in Their Own Land: Anger and Mourning on the American Right*. New York: New Press.

Hochschild, Jennifer L. 1996. *Facing Up to the American Dream: Race, Class, and the Soul of the Nation*. Princeton, NJ: Princeton University Press.

Hodgson, Geoffrey M. 2006. "What are Institutions?" *Journal of Economic Issues* 40 (1): 1–25.

Hofstadter, Richard. 1955. *The Age of Reform: From Bryan to FDR*. New York: Vintage.

Hoos, Ida R. 1972. *Systems Analysis in Public Policy: A Critique*. Berkeley: University of California Press.

Horowitz, Mark, Anthony Haynor, and Kenneth Kickham. 2018. "Sociology's Sacred Victims and the Politics of Knowledge: Moral Foundations Theory and Disciplinary Controversies." *American Sociologist* 49 (4): 459–95.

Hoynes, Hilary W. 2017. *The Success of the Earned Income Tax Credit*. http://econofact .org/the-success-of-the-earned-income-tax-credit.

Hoynes, Hilary W., and Ankur J. Patel. 2018. "Effective Policy for Reducing Inequality? The Earned Income Tax Credit and the Distribution of Income." *Journal of Human Resources* 53 (4): 859–90.

Huber, Gregory A., and Neil Malhotra. 2017. "Political Homophily in Social Relationships: Evidence from Online Dating Behavior." *Journal of Politics* 79 (1): 269–83.

Hutson, Matthew. 2017. "Even Artificial Intelligence Can Acquire Biases against Race and Gender." *Science* magazine, April 13, 2017.

Institute for Global Prosperity. 2017. *Social Prosperity for the Future: A Proposal for Universal Basic Services.* Institute for Global Prosperity/University College London.

Ioannidis, John P. A. 2005. "Why Most Published Research Findings Are False." *PLoS Medicine* 2 (8): 696–701.

Iyengar, Shanto, and Sean J. Westwood. 2015. "Fear and Loathing across Party Lines: New Evidence on Group Polarization." *American Journal of Political Science* 59 (3): 690–707.

Jackson, C. Kirabo, Rucker C. Johnson, and Claudia Persico. 2016. "The Effects of School Spending on Educational and Economic Outcomes: Evidence from School Finance Reforms." *The Quarterly Journal of Economics* 131 (1): 157–218.

Jackson, Michelle, ed. 2013. *Determined to Succeed? Performance versus Choice in Educational Attainment.* Stanford, CA: Stanford University Press.

Jackson, Michelle, and Elizabeth Buckner. 2016. "Opportunity without Equity: Educational Inequality and Constitutional Protections in Egypt." *Sociological Science* 3: 730–56.

Jackson, Michelle, and David R. Cox. 2013. "The Principles of Experimental Design and Their Application in Sociology." *Annual Review of Sociology* 39 (1): 27–49.

Jackson, Michelle, and Geoffrey Evans. 2017. "Rebuilding Walls: Market Transition and Social Mobility in the Post-socialist Societies of Europe." *Sociological Science* 4: 54–79.

Jackson, Michelle, John H. Goldthorpe, and Colin Mills. 2005. "Education, Employers, and Class Mobility." *Research in Social Stratification and Mobility* 23: 3–34.

Jackson, Michelle, and David B. Grusky. 2017. "A Post-Liberal Theory of Stratification." *British Journal of Sociology* 69 (4): 1096–1133.

Jackson, Michelle, and Brian Holzman. 2020. "A Century of Educational Inequality in the United States." *Proceedings of the National Academy of Sciences.* Forthcoming.

Jelveh, Zubin, Bruce Kogut, and Suresh Naidu. 2018. "Political Language in Economics." *Columbia Business School Research Paper,* 14–57.

Jencks, Christopher. 1980. "Heredity, Environment, and Public Policy Reconsidered." *American Sociological Review* 45 (5): 723–36.

Jerrim, John, and Lindsey Macmillan. 2015. "Income Inequality, Intergenerational Mobility, and the Great Gatsby Curve: Is Education the Key?" *Social Forces* 94 (2): 505–33.

Jiang, Yang, Maribel R. Granja, and Heather Koball. 2017. "Basic Facts about Low-Income Children: Children 6 through 11 Years, 2015." New York: National Center for Children in Poverty (NCCP), Mailman School of Public Health, Columbia University.

Johnson, Rucker C., and C. Kirabo Jackson. 2019. "Reducing Inequality through Dynamic Complementarity: Evidence from Head Start and Public School Spending." *American Economic Journal: Economic Policy* 11 (4): 310–49.

Jonsson, Jan O., David B. Grusky, Matthew Di Carlo, and Reinhard Pollak. 2017. "It's a Decent Bet that Our Children Will Be Professors Too." In *Inequality in the 21st Century*, edited by David B. Grusky and Jasmine Hill. New York: Perseus Books.

Kalil, Ariel, Rebecca Ryan, and Michael Corey. 2012. "Diverging Destinies: Maternal Education and the Developmental Gradient in Time with Children." *Demography* 49 (4): 1361–83.

Kalleberg, Arne L. 2011. *Good Jobs, Bad Jobs: The Rise of Polarized and Precarious Employment Systems in the United States, 1970s to 2000s.* New York: Russell Sage Foundation.

Kanbur, Ravi, and Adam Wagstaff. 2014. "How Useful Is Inequality of Opportunity as a Policy Construct?" Policy Research Working Paper 6980, World Bank.

Kao, Grace, and Jennifer S. Thompson. 2003. "Racial and Ethnic Stratification in Educational Achievement and Attainment." *Annual Review of Sociology* 29 (1): 417–42.

Katz, Lawrence F., and Alan B. Krueger. 2019. "The Rise and Nature of Alternative Work Arrangements in the United States, 1995–2015." *ILR Review* 72 (2): 382–416.

Katznelson, Ira. 2005. *When Affirmative Action Was White: An Untold History of Racial Inequality in Twentieth-Century America.* New York: W. W. Norton.

Keers, Robert, and Michael Pluess. 2017. "Childhood Quality Influences Genetic Sensitivity to Environmental Influences across Adulthood: A Life-Course Gene x Environment Interaction Study." *Development and Psychopathology* 29 (5): 1921–33.

Kenworthy, Lane. 2014. *Social Democratic America.* Oxford: Oxford University Press.

———. 2016. "Is Income Inequality Harmful?" https://lanekenworthy.net/.

———. 2019. *Social Democratic Capitalism.* Oxford: Oxford University Press.

Kim, Sunwoong, and Ju-Ho Lee. 2003. "The Secondary School Equalization Policy in South Korea." Unpublished paper, University of Wisconsin-Milwaukee.

King, Marissa D., Jennifer Jennings, and Jason M. Fletcher. 2014. "Medical Adaptation to Academic Pressure: Schooling, Stimulant Use, and Socioeconomic Status." *American Sociological Review* 79 (6): 1039–66.

King, Martin Luther, Jr. 1967. "Beyond Vietnam." Speech at Riverside Church, New York, NY, April 4, 1967.

Kirst, Michael W., and Mitchell L. Stevens, eds. 2015. *Remaking College: The Changing Ecology of Higher Education.* Stanford, CA: Stanford University Press.

Klinenberg, Eric. 2018. *Palaces for the People: How Social Infrastructure Can Help Fight Inequality, Polarization, and the Decline of Civic Life*. New York: Crown.

Knorr-Cetina, Karin D. 1981. *The Manufacture of Knowledge: An Essay on the Constructivist and Contextual Nature of Science*. New York: Pergamon Press.

Kornrich, Sabino, and Frank Furstenberg. 2013. "Investing in Children: Changes in Parental Spending on Children, 1972–2007." *Demography* 50 (1): 1–23.

Kraus, Michael W., and Wendy B. Mendes. 2014. "Sartorial Symbols of Social Class Elicit Class-Consistent Behavioral and Physiological Responses: A Dyadic Approach." *Journal of Experimental Psychology: General* 143 (6): 2330–40.

Kraus, Michael W., Jun Won Park, and Jacinth J. X. Tan. 2017. "Signs of Social Class: The Experience of Economic Inequality in Everyday Life." *Perspectives on Psychological Science* 12 (3): 422–35.

Krieger, Nancy, Jarvis T. Chen, Pamela D.Waterman, David H. Rehkopf, and S. V. Subramanian. 2005. "Painting a Truer Picture of US Socioeconomic and Racial/Ethnic Health Inequalities: The Public Health Disparities Geocoding Project. *American Journal of Public Health* 95 (2): 312–23.

Krueger, Alan B. 2012. "The Rise and Consequences of Inequality in the United States." Speech at the Center for American Progress, January 12, 2012.

Krugman, Paul. 2016. "101 Boosterism." *New York Times*, April 20, 2016.

Kuran, Timur, and Cass R. Sunstein. 1999. "Availability Cascades and Risk Regulation." *Stanford Law Review* 51: 683–768.

LaLonde, Robert J. 2003. "Employment and Training Programs." In *Means-Tested Transfer Programs in the United States*, edited by Robert A. Moffitt. Chicago: University of Chicago Press.

Lamont, Michèle. 2012. "Toward a Comparative Sociology of Valuation and Evaluation." *Annual Review of Sociology* 38 (1): 201–21.

———. 2018. "Addressing Recognition Gaps: Destigmatization and the Reduction of Inequality." *American Sociological Review* 83 (3): 419–44.

———. 2019. "From 'Having' to 'Being': Self-worth and the Current Crisis of American Society." *British Journal of Sociology* 70 (3): 660–707.

Landersø, Rasmus, and James J. Heckman. 2017. "The Scandinavian Fantasy: The Sources of Intergenerational Mobility in Denmark and the US." *Scandinavian Journal of Economics* 119 (1): 178–230.

Lareau, Annette. 2011. *Unequal Childhoods: Class, Race, and Family Life*. Berkeley: University of California Press.

Larson, Charles P. 2007. "Poverty during Pregnancy: Its Effects on Child Health Outcomes." *Paediatrics and Child Health* 12 (8): 673–77.

Lee, Dohoon, and Sara McLanahan. 2015. "Family Structure Transitions and Child Development: Instability, Selection, and Population Heterogeneity." *American Sociological Review* 80 (4): 738–63.

Lehman, Joseph G. 2010. *An Introduction to the Overton Window of Political Possibility.* Mackinac Center for Public Policy. https://www.mackinac.org/12481.

Leiserowitz, Anthony, Edward Maibach, Seth Rosenthal, John Kotcher, Parrish Bergquist, Matthew Ballew, Matthew Goldberg, Abel Gustafson and Xinran Wang. 2020. *Climate Change in the American Mind: April 2020.* New Haven, CT: Yale Program on Climate Change Communication.

Levien, Roger E. 2000. "RAND, IIASA, and the Conduct of Systems Analysis." In *Systems, Experts, and Computers: The Systems Approach in Management and Engineering, World War II and After,* edited by Agatha C. Hughes and Thomas P. Hughes. Cambridge, MA: MIT Press.

Levine, Adam Seth. 2015. *American Insecurity: Why Our Economic Fears Lead to Political Inaction.* Princeton, NJ: Princeton University Press.

Lewin, Kurt. 1935. *A Dynamic Theory of Personality. Selected Papers.* Translated by Donald K. Adams and Karl E Zener. New York: McGraw-Hill.

———. 1936. *Principles of Topological Psychology.* Translated by Fritz Heider and Grace Moore Heider. New York: McGraw-Hill.

Li, Bobai, and Andrew G. Walder. 2001. "Career Advancement as Party Patronage: Sponsored Mobility into the Chinese Administrative Elite, 1949–1996." *American Journal of Sociology* 106 (5): 1371–408.

Lin, Nan. 2001. *Social Capital: A Theory of Social Structure and Action.* Cambridge, UK: Cambridge University Press.

Linden, Sander van der, Anthony Leiserowitz, and Edward Maibach. 2018. "Scientific Agreement Can Neutralize Politicization of Facts." *Nature Human Behaviour* 2: 2–3.

Lindsey, Almont. 1962. *Socialized Medicine in England and Wales: The National Health Service, 1948–1961.* Chapel Hill: University of North Carolina Press.

Lochner, Lance, and Alexander Monge-Naranjo. 2012. "Credit Constraints in Education." *Annual Review of Economics* 4 (1): 225–56.

Lockwood, David. 1964. "Social Integration and System Integration." In *Explorations in Social Change,* edited by G. K. Zollschan and W. Hirsch. Boston: Houghton Mifflin.

Lupton, Ruth, John Hills, Kitty Stewart, and Polly Vizard. 2013. *Labour's Social Policy Record: Policy, Spending, and Outcomes, 1997–2010.* Social Policy in a Cold Climate, Research Report (SPCCRR01). Centre for Analysis of Social Exclusion, London School of Economics and Political Science, London, UK.

Magnuson, Katherine, and Lawrence M. Berger. 2009. "Family Structure States and Transitions: Associations with Children's Wellbeing during Middle Childhood." *Journal of Marriage and Family* 71 (3): 575–91.

Magnuson, Katherine, and Greg J. Duncan. 2016. "Can Early Childhood Interventions Decrease Inequality of Economic Opportunity?" *RSF: The Russell Sage Foundation Journal of the Social Sciences* 2 (2): 123–41.

Mani, Anandi, Sendhil Mullainathan, Eldar Shafir, and Jiaying Zhao. 2013. "Poverty Impedes Cognitive Function." *Science* 341 (6149): 976–80.

Manoli, Day, and Nicholas Turner. 2018. "Cash-on-Hand and College Enrollment: Evidence from Population Tax Data and the Earned Income Tax Credit." *American Economic Journal: Economic Policy* 10 (2): 242–71.

Marinescu, Ioana. 2018. "No Strings Attached: The Behavioral Effects of U.S. Unconditional Cash Transfer Programs." NBER Working Paper Series 24337, National Bureau of Economic Research.

Markus, Anne Rossier, Ellie Andres, Kristina D. West, Nicole Garro, and Cynthia Pellegrini. 2013. "Medicaid Covered Births, 2008 through 2010, in the Context of the Implementation of Health Reform." *Womens Health Issues* 23 (5): e273–e280.

Marwell, Nicole P., and Michael McQuarrie. 2013. "People, Place, and System: Organizations and the Renewal of Urban Social Theory." *Annals of the American Academy of Political and Social Science* 647 (1): 126–43.

Marx, Karl. (1843) 1970. *A Contribution to the Critique of Hegel's Philosophy of Right.* Translated by Annette Jolin and Joseph O'Malley. Cambridge, UK: Cambridge University Press.

Massey, Douglas S., Jonathan Rothwell, and Thurston Domina. 2009. "The Changing Bases of Segregation in the United States." *Annals of the American Academy of Political and Social Science* 626 (1): 74–90.

Maynard, Rebecca A., and Richard J. Murnane. 1979. "The Effects of a Negative Income Tax on School Performance: Results of an Experiment." *The Journal of Human Resources* 14 (4): 463–76.

McCall, Leslie. 2013. *The Undeserving Rich: American Beliefs about Inequality, Opportunity, and Redistribution.* New York: Cambridge University Press.

McCall, Leslie, Derek Burk, Marie Laperrière, and Jennifer A. Richeson. 2017. "Exposure to Rising Inequality Shapes Americans' Opportunity Beliefs and Policy Support." *Proceedings of the National Academy of Sciences* 114 (36): 9593–98.

McClay, Wilfred M. 1994. *The Masterless: Self and Society in Modern America.* Chapel Hill: University of North Carolina Press.

McLanahan, Sara, and Christine Percheski. 2008. "Family Structure and the Reproduction of Inequalities." *Annual Review of Sociology* 34 (1): 257–76.

Merton, Robert K. 1968. "The Matthew Effect in Science: The Reward and Communication Systems of Science Are Considered." *Science* 159 (3810): 56–63.

Milanovic, Branko. 2019. *Capitalism, Alone: The Future of the System That Rules the World.* Cambridge, MA: Harvard University Press.

Mitnik, Pablo A., Erin Cumberworth, and David B. Grusky. 2016. "Social Mobility in a High-Inequality Regime." *Annals of the American Academy of Political and Social Science* 663 (1): 140–84.

Moller, Stephanie, Joya Misra, and Eiko Strader. 2013. "A Cross-National Look at How Welfare States Reduce Inequality." *Sociology Compass* 7 (2): 135–46.

Morgan, Kenneth O. 2001. *Britain since 1945: The People's Peace*. Oxford: Oxford University Press.

Mullainathan, Sendhil, and Eldar Shafir. 2013. *Scarcity: Why Having Too Little Means So Much*. New York: Time Books, Henry Holt.

Munoz-Dardé, Véronique. 1998. "Rawls, Justice in the Family and Justice of the Family." *The Philosophical Quarterly* 48 (192): 335–52.

———. 1999. "Is the Family to be Abolished Then?" *Proceedings of the Aristotelian Society* 99 (1): 37–56.

Murnane, Richard J., and Sean F. Reardon. 2018. "Long-Term Trends in Private School Enrollments by Family Income." *AERA Open*, 4 (1).

Murray, Charles. 2016. "A Guaranteed Income for Every American." *Wall Street Journal*, June 3, 2016.

Nagahawatte, N. Tanya, and Robert L. Goldenberg. 2008. "Poverty, Maternal Health, and Adverse Pregnancy Outcomes." *Annals of the New York Academy of Sciences* 1136 (1):80–85.

Neckerman, Kathryn M., and Florencia Torche. 2007. "Inequality: Causes and Consequences." *Annual Review of Sociology* 33 (1): 335–57.

Newport, Frank. 2015. "Americans Continue to Say U.S. Wealth Distribution Is Unfair." *Gallup News*, May 4, 2015.

———. 2016. "Americans' Satisfaction with Ability to Get Ahead Edges Up. *Gallup News*, January 21, 2016.

———. 2017. "In U.S., Support for Government-Run Health System Edges Up." *Gallup News*, December 1, 2017.

NICHD Early Child Care Research Network. 2002. "The Interaction of Child Care and Family Risk in Relation to Child Development at 24 and 36 Months." *Applied Developmental Science* 6 (3): 144–56.

Nichols, Austin, and Jesse Rothstein. 2015. "The Earned Income Tax Credit." In *Economics of Means-Tested Transfer Programs in the United States*, edited by Robert A. Moffitt. Chicago: University of Chicago Press.

Nussbaum, Martha. 2003. "Capabilities as Fundamental Entitlements: Sen and Social Justice." *Feminist Economics* 9 (2–3): 33–59.

———. 2007. Foreword to "Constitutions and Capabilities: 'Perception' against Lofty Formalism." *Harvard Law Review* 121: 4–97.

———. 2011. *Creating Capabilities: The Human Development Approach*. Cambridge, MA: Harvard University Press.

Obama, President Barack. 2014a. Remarks at the College Opportunity Summit, Ronald Reagan Building, Washington, DC, December 4, 2014.

———. 2014b. State of the Union Address. White House Office of the Press Secretary. https://obamawhitehouse.archives.gov/the-press-office/2014/01/28/president-barack-obamas-state-union-address.

Okbay, Aysu, et al. 2016. "Genome-Wide Association Study Identifies 74 Loci Associated with Educational Attainment." *Nature* 533: 539–42.

Okun, Arthur M. (1975) 2015. *Equality and Efficiency: The Big Tradeoff.* Washington, DC: Brookings Institution Press.

Ordabayeva, Nailya, and Daniel Fernandes. 2017. "Similarity Focus and Support for Redistribution." *Journal of Experimental Social Psychology* 72: 67–74.

Ostry, Jonathan D., Andrew Berg, and Charalambos G. Tsangarides. 2014. "Redistribution, Inequality, and Growth." IMF Staff Discussion Note SDN/14/02.

Page, Benjamin I., and Robert Y. Shapiro. 1992. *The Rational Public: Fifty Years of Trends in Americans' Policy Preferences.* Chicago: University of Chicago Press.

Page, Emily E., and Alayna M. Stone. 2010. *From Harlem Children's Zone to Promise Neighborhoods: Creating the Tipping Point for Success.* Georgetown Public Policy Institute.

Pager, Devah, and Hana Shepherd. 2008. "The Sociology of Discrimination: Racial Discrimination in Employment, Housing, Credit, and Consumer Markets." *Annual Review of Sociology* 34 (1): 181–209.

Pager, Devah, Bruce Western, and Bart Bonikowski. 2009. "Discrimination in a Low-Wage Labor Market: A Field Experiment." *American Sociological Review* 74 (5): 777–99.

Parsons, Talcott. 1937. *The Structure of Social Action.* New York: McGraw-Hill.

———. 1964. *The Social System.* New York: Free Press/Macmillan.

Pattillo-McCoy, Mary. 1999. *Black Picket Fences: Privilege and Peril among the Black Middle Class.* Chicago: University of Chicago Press.

Perrin, Guy. 1992. "The Beveridge Plan: The Main Principles." *International Social Security Review* 45 (1–2): 39–52.

Persico, Claudia, David Figlio, and Jeffrey Roth. 2016. "Inequality before Birth: The Developmental Consequences of Environmental Toxicants." NBER Working Paper Series 22263, National Bureau of Economic Research.

Persson, Torsten, and Guido Tabellini. 1994. "Is Inequality Harmful for Growth?" *American Economic Review* 84 (3): 600–21.

Peterson, David. 2016. "The Baby Factory: Difficult Research Objects, Disciplinary Standards, and the Production of Statistical Significance." *Socius* 2: 1–10.

Pew Research Center. 2017. *Support for Same-Sex Marriage Grows, Even among Groups that Had Been Skeptical.* Washington, DC: Pew Research Center.

Pew Research Center. 2011. "The Elusive 90% Solution." *Pew Research Center,* March 11, 2011.

Phillips, Deborah. 2013. "Child Care as Risk or Protection in the Context of Welfare Reform." In *From Welfare to Childcare: What Happens to Young Children When Mothers Exchange Welfare for Work?*, edited by Natasha Cabrera, Robert Hutchens, and H. Elizabeth Peters. Mahwah, NJ: Lawrence Erlbaum Associates.

Piketty, Thomas. 2013. *Capital in the Twenty-first Century.* Translated by Arthur Goldhammer. Cambridge, MA: Harvard University Press.

Piketty, Thomas, and Emmanuel Saez. 2003. "Income Inequality in the United States, 1913–1998." *The Quarterly Journal of Economics* 118 (1): 1–41.

Polsky, Daniel, Michael Richards, Simon Basseyn, Douglas Wissoker, Genevieve M. Kenney, Stephen Zuckerman, and Karin V. Rhodes. 2015. "Appointment Availability after Increases in Medicaid Payments for Primary Care." *New England Journal of Medicine* 372 (6): 537–45.

Porter, Eduardo. 2020. *American Poison: How Racial Hostility Destroyed Our Promise.* New York: Alfred A. Knopf.

Puma, Michael, Stephen Bell, Ronna Cook, Camilla Heid, Pam Broene, Frank Jenkins, Andrew Mashburn, and Jason Downer. 2012. "Third Grade Follow-up to the Head Start Impact Study: Final Report." OPRE Report 2012-45. *Administration for Children and Families.*

Quade, E. S. 1972. *Systems Analysis: A Tool for Choice.* Santa Monica, CA: RAND Corporation. https://www.rand.org/pubs/papers/P4860.html.

Quillian, Lincoln, Devah Pager, Ole Hexel, and Arnfinn H. Midtbøen. 2017. "Meta-analysis of Field Experiments Shows No Change in Racial Discrimination in Hiring over Time." *Proceedings of the National Academy of Sciences* 114 (41): 10870–75.

Ramey, Craig T., David MacPhee, and Keith O. Yeates. 1982. "Preventing Developmental Retardation: A General Systems Model." In *Facilitating Infant and Early Childhood Development,* edited by J. M. Joffee and L. A. Bond. Hanover, NH: University Press of New England.

Ramey, Garey, and Valerie A. Ramey. 2010. "The Rug Rat Race." *Brookings Papers on Economic Activity* 41 (1): 129–99.

Rawls, John. 1971. *A Theory of Justice.* Cambridge, MA: Harvard University Press.

———. 1993. *Political Liberalism.* New York: Columbia University Press.

Ray, Victor. 2019. "A Theory of Racialized Organizations." *American Sociological Review* 84 (1): 26–53.

Reardon, Sean F., Ericka S. Weathers, Erin M. Fahle, Heewon Jang, and Demetra Kalogrides. 2019. "Is Separate Still Unequal? New Evidence on School Segregation and Racial Academic Achievement Gaps." https://cepa.stanford.edu/sites/default/files/wp19-06-v092019.pdf.

Reay, Michael J. 2012. "The Flexible Unity of Economics." *American Journal of Sociology* 118 (1): 45–87.

Reed, Howard, and Stewart Lansley. 2016. *Universal Basic Income: An Idea Whose Time Has Come.* Compass: https://www.compassonline.org.uk/wp-content/uploads/2016/05/UniversalBasicIncomeByCompass-Spreads.pdf.

Reese, Hope. 2016. "Why Microsoft's 'Tay' AI bot Went Wrong." *Tech Republic,* March 24, 2016.

Reeves, Richard V. 2017. *Dream Hoarders: How the American Upper Middle Class Is Leaving Everyone Else in the Dust, Why That Is a Problem, and What to Do about It.* Washington, DC: Brookings Institution Press.

Reich, Rob. 2016. "Repugnant to the Whole Idea of Democracy? On the Role of Foundations in Democratic Societies." *PS: Political Science and Politics* 49 (3): 466–72.

Renter, Elizabeth. 2015. "You've Got Medicaid—Why Can't You See the Doctor?" *U.S. News and World Report,* May 26, 2016.

Reskin, Barbara. 2012. "The Race Discrimination System." *Annual Review of Sociology* 38 (1): 17–35.

Reynolds, Arthur J., Arthur J. Rolnick, Michelle M. Englund, and Judy A. Temple, eds. 2010. *Childhood Programs and Practices in the First Decade of Life.* New York: Cambridge University Press.

Richburg-Hayes, Lashawn, Caitlin Anzelone, Nadine Dechausay, and Patrick Landers. 2017. "Nudging Change in Human Services: Final Report of the Behavioral Interventions to Advance Self-Sufficiency (BIAS) Project." OPRE Report 2017-23.

Ridgeway, Cecilia L. 2014. "Why Status Matters for Inequality." *American Sociological Review* 79 (1): 1–16.

———. 2019. *Status. Why Is It Everywhere? Why Does It Matter?* New York: Russell Sage Foundation.

Ripple, William J., Christopher Wolf, Thomas M. Newsome, Phoebe Barnard, and William R. Moomaw. 2020. "World Scientists' Warning of a Climate Emergency." *BioScience* 70 (1): 8–12.

Rivera, Lauren A. 2015. *Pedigree: How Elite Students Get Elite Jobs.* Princeton, NJ: Princeton University Press.

Rivera, Lauren A., and András Tilcsik. 2016. "Class Advantage, Commitment Penalty: The Gendered Effect of Social Class Signals in an Elite Labor Market." *American Sociological Review* 81 (6): 1097–1131.

Roberts, David. 2017. "The McKibben Effect: A Case Study in How Radical Environmentalism Can Work." *Vox,* November 17, 2017.

Rogers, Brishen. 2017. "Forum: Basic Income in a Just Society." *Boston Review,* May 15, 2017.

Rogoff, Kenneth. 2012. "Rethinking the Growth Imperative." *Project Syndicate,* January 2, 2012.

Rönnlund, Michael, Anna Sundström, and Lars-Göran Nilsson. 2015. "Interindividual Differences in General Cognitive Ability from Age 18 to Age 65 Years Are Extremely

Stable and Strongly Associated with Working Memory Capacity." *Intelligence* 53: 59–64.

Rosenfeld, Michael J. 2017. "Moving a Mountain: The Extraordinary Trajectory of Same-Sex Marriage Approval in the United States." *Socius* 3: 1–22.

Roth, Alvin E. 2002. "The Economist as Engineer: Game Theory, Experimentation, and Computation as Tools for Design Economics." *Econometrica* 70 (4): 1341–78.

Rothstein, Richard. 2017. *The Color of Law: A Forgotten History of How Our Government Segregated America*. New York: Liveright.

Saez, Emmanuel, and Gabriel Zucman. 2019. *The Triumph of Injustice: How the Rich Dodge Taxes and How to Make Them Pay*. New York: W. W. Norton.

Salesses, Philip, Katja Schechtner, and César A. Hidalgo. 2013. "The Collaborative Image of the City: Mapping the Inequality of Urban Perception." *PLoS ONE* 8 (7): e68400.

Sammartino, Frank, and Norton Francis. 2016. *Federal-State Income Tax Progressivity*. Washington, DC: Urban Institute and Brookings Institution, Tax Policy Center.

Sampson, Robert J. 2012. *Great American City: Chicago and the Enduring Neighborhood Effect*. Chicago: University of Chicago Press.

Sánchez-Jankowski, Martín. 2008. *Cracks in the Pavement: Social Change and Resilience in Poor Neighborhoods*. Berkeley: University of California Press.

Sanders, Bernie. 2020. "Bernie Sanders: The Foundations of American Society Are Failing Us." *New York Times*, April 19, 2020.

Scheidel, Walter. 2017. *The Great Leveler: Violence and the History of Inequality from the Stone Age to the Twenty-first Century*. Princeton, NJ: Princeton University Press.

———. 2020. "Why the Wealthy Fear Pandemics." *New York Times*, April 9, 2020.

Scheve, Kenneth, and David Stasavage. 2010. "The Conscription of Wealth: Mass Warfare and the Demand for Progressive Taxation." *International Organization* 64 (4): 529–61.

Schifeling, Todd, and Andrew J. Hoffman. 2019. "Bill McKibben's Influence on U.S. Climate Change Discourse: Shifting Field-Level Debates through Radical Flank Effects." *Organization and Environment* 32 (3): 213–33.

Schneider, Daniel, Orestes P. Hastings, and Joe LaBriola. 2018. "Income Inequality and Class Divides in Parental Investments." *American Sociological Review* 83 (3): 475–507.

Schweinhart, Lawrence J., Jeanne Montie, Zongping Xiang, W. Steven Barnett, Clive R. Belfield, and Milagros Nores. 2005. *Lifetime Effects: The High/Scope Perry Preschool Study through Age 40*. Ypsilanti, MI: High/Scope Press.

Scott-Clayton, Judith. 2012. "Information Constraints and Financial Aid Policy." NBER Working Paper Series 17811, National Bureau of Economic Research.

Selzam, S., E. Krapohl, S. von Stumm, P. F. O'Reilly, K. Rimfeld, Y. Kovas, P. S. Dale, J. J. Lee, and R. Plomin. 2017. "Predicting Educational Achievement from DNA." *Molecular Psychiatry* 22: 267–72.

Semega, Jessica, Melissa Kollar, John Creamer, and Abinash Mohanty. 2019. "Income and Poverty in the United States: 2018." *Current Population Reports* P60-266.

Semuels, Alana. 2016. "Good School, Rich School; Bad School, Poor School: The Inequality at the Heart of America's Education System." *The Atlantic*, August 25, 2016.

Sen, Amartya. 1999. *Development as Freedom*. New York: Anchor.

Shah, Anuj K., Sendhil Mullainathan, and Eldar Shafir. 2012. "Some Consequences of Having Too Little." *Science* 338 (6107): 682–85.

Sharkey, Patrick. 2010. "The Acute Effect of Local Homicides on Children's Cognitive Performance." *Proceedings of the National Academy of Sciences* 107 (26): 11733–38.

———. 2013. *Stuck in Place: Urban Neighborhoods and the End of Progress toward Racial Inequality*. Chicago: University of Chicago Press.

———. 2018. "The Long Reach of Violence: A Broader Perspective on Data, Theory, and Evidence on the Prevalence and Consequences of Exposure to Violence." *Annual Review of Criminology* 1 (1): 85–102.

Sharkey, Patrick, and Robert J. Sampson. 2015. "Violence, Cognition, and Neighborhood Inequality in America." In *Social Neuroscience: Brain, Mind, and Society*, edited by Russell K. Schutt, Larry J. Seidman, and Matcheri S. Keshavan. Cambridge, MA: Harvard University. Press.

Sharkey, Patrick, Amy Ellen Schwartz, Ingrid Gould Ellen, and Johanna Lacoe. 2014. "High Stakes in the Classroom, High Stakes on the Street: The Effects of Community Violence on Students' Standardized Test Performance." *Sociological Science* 1: 199–220.

Shavers, Vickie L., Pebbles Fagan, Dionne Jones, William M. P. Klein, Josephine Boyington, Carmen Moten, and Edward Rorie. 2012. "The State of Research on Racial/Ethnic Discrimination in the Receipt of Health Care." *American Journal of Public Health* 102 (5): 953–66.

Shavit, Yossi, Richard Arum, and Adam Gamoran. 2007. *Stratification in Higher Education: A Comparative Study*. Stanford, CA: Stanford University Press.

Shedd, Carla. 2015. *Unequal City: Race, Schools, and Perceptions of Injustice*. New York: Russell Sage Foundation.

Shelby, Tommie. 2016. *Dark Ghettos: Injustice, Dissent, and Reform*. Cambridge, MA: Harvard University Press.

Sherman, Rachel. 2017. *Uneasy Street: The Anxieties of Affluence*. Princeton, NJ: Princeton University Press.

Shipler, David K. 2011. "Connecting the Dots." In *Ending Poverty in America: How to Restore the American Dream*, edited by John Edwards, Marion Crain, and Arne Kalleberg. New York: New Press.

Shonkoff, Jack P., and Deborah A. Phillips. 2000. *From Neurons to Neighborhoods: The Science of Early Childhood Development*. Washington, DC: National Academies Press.

Simon, Herbert A. 1996. *The Sciences of the Artificial.* 3rd ed. Cambridge, MA: MIT Press.

Simpson, Brent, and Robb Willer. 2015. "Beyond Altruism: Sociological Foundations of Cooperation and Prosocial Behavior." *Annual Review of Sociology* 41 (1): 43–63.

Sireci, Stephen G., Stanley E. Scarpati, and Shuhong Li. 2005. "Test Accommodations for Students with Disabilities: An Analysis of the Interaction Hypothesis." *Review of Educational Research* 75 (4): 457–90.

Small, Mario Luis. 2006. "Neighborhood Institutions as Resource Brokers: Childcare Centers, Interorganizational Ties, and Resource Access among the Poor." *Social Problems* 53 (2): 274–92.

———. 2009. *Unanticipated Gains: Origins of Network Inequality in Everyday Life.* Oxford: Oxford University Press.

Smith, Carly P., and Jennifer J. Freyd. 2014. "Institutional Betrayal." *American Psychologist* 69 (6): 575–87.

Soss, Joe, and Vesla Weaver. 2017. "Police Are Our Government: Politics, Political Science, and the Policing of Race–Class Subjugated Communities." *Annual Review of Political Science* 20 (1): 565–91.

Standing, Guy. 2017. *Basic Income. And How We Can Make It Happen.* London: Penguin.

Stevens, Mitchell L. 2014. "College for Grown-Ups." *New York Times,* December 11, 2014.

Sumner, William Graham, and Albert Galloway Keller. 1927. *The Science of Society.* New Haven, CT: Yale University Press.

Sunstein, Cass R. 1996. "Social Norms and Social Roles." *Columbia Law Review* 96 (4): 903–68.

———. 2017. *Misconceptions about Nudges.* https://ssrn.com/abstract=3033101.

Swift, Adam. 2004. "Would Perfect Mobility Be Perfect?" *European Sociological Review* 20 (1): 1–11.

Szelényi, Szonja. 1998. *Equality by Design: The Grand Experiment in Destratification in Socialist Hungary.* Stanford, CA: Stanford University Press.

Tankersley, Jim, and Ben Casselman. 2020. "The Liberal Economists Behind the Wealth Tax Debate." *New York Times,* February 21, 2020.

Taubman, Paul. 1976. "The Determinants of Earnings: Genetics, Family, and Other Environments: A Study of White Male Twins." *American Economic Review* 66 (5): 858–70.

Thaler, Richard H., and Cass R. Sunstein. 2008. *Nudge: Improving Decisions about Health, Wealth, and Happiness.* New York: Penguin.

Tharps, Lori L. 2014. "The Case for Black With a Capital B." *New York Times,* November 18, 2014.

Thomas, Catherine, David Kalkstein, and Gregory Walton. 2020. "How the Coronavirus Crisis Is Opening the Door to Universal Social Policies in the U.S." *Time Magazine,* June 17 2020.

Thorpe, Andrew. 1997. *A History of the British Labour Party*. British Studies Series. London: Palgrave.

Throsby, David. 2017. "A Rising Tide Raises All Boats." In *Economic Ideas You Should Forget*, edited by Bruno S Frey and David Iselin. Basel, Switzerland: Springer Nature.

Tierney, Joseph P., Jean Baldwin Grossman, and Nancy L. Resch. 1995. *Making a Difference: An Impact Study of Big Brothers Big Sisters*. Philadelphia: Public/Private Ventures.

Tocqueville, Alexis de. (1835) 2010. *Democracy in America*. Edited by E. Nolla. Translated by J. T. Schleifer. Indianapolis: Liberty Fund.

Tönnies, Ferdinand. (1887) 2001. *Community and Civil Society*. Translated by Jose Harris and Margaret Hollis. Cambridge, UK: Cambridge University Press.

Torche, Florencia. 2011. "The Effect of Maternal Stress on Birth Outcomes: Exploiting a Natural Experiment." *Demography* 48 (4): 1473–91.

Torche, Florencia, and Catherine Sirois. 2019. "Restrictive Immigration Law and Birth Outcomes of Immigrant Women." *American Journal of Epidemiology* 188 (1): 24–33.

Tough, Paul. 2008. *Whatever It Takes: Geoffrey Canada's Quest to Change Harlem and America*. New York: Houghton Mifflin.

Turner, Jonathan. 1997. *The Institutional Order*. New York: Longman.

Underwood, Bill, and Bert Moore. 1982. "Perspective-Taking and Altruism." *Psychological Bulletin* 91 (1): 143–73.

UNICEF. 2004. *Vitamin and Mineral Deficiency: A Global Progress Report*. Ottawa: Micronutrient Initiative and UNICEF.

Urban Institute. 2011. *State and Local Backgrounders*. https://www.urban.org/policy-centers/cross-center-initiatives/state-local-finance-initiative/state-and-local-backgrounders.

U.S. Department of Education. 2013. *For Each and Every Child: A Strategy for Education Equity and Excellence*. Washington, DC.

Van Der Maas, Han L. J., Conor V. Dolan, Raoul P. P. P. Grasman, Jelte M. Wicherts, Hilde M. Huizenga, and Maartje E. J. Raijmakers. 2006. "A Dynamical Model of General Intelligence: The Positive Manifold of Intelligence by Mutualism." *Psychological Review* 113 (4): 842–61.

Varner, Charles, Marybeth Mattingly, and David B. Grusky. 2017. "The Facts behind the Visions." *Pathways* (Spring): 3–8.

Verba, Sidney, and Norman H. Nie. 1972. *Participation in America: Political Democracy and Social Equality*. Chicago: University of Chicago Press.

Vericker, Tracy, Julia Isaacs, Heather Hahn, Katherine Toran, and Stephanie Rennane. 2012. *How Targeted Are Federal Expenditures on Children? A Kids' Share Analysis of Expenditures by Income in 2009*. Washington, DC: Urban Institute and the Brookings Institution.

Voigt, Rob, Nicholas P. Camp, Vinodkumar Prabhakaran, William L. Hamilton, Rebecca C. Hetey, Camilla M. Griffiths, David Jurgens, Dan Jurafsky, and Jennifer L.
Eberhardt. 2017. "Language from Police Body Camera Footage Shows Racial Disparities in Officer Respect." *Proceedings of the National Academy of Sciences* 114 (25):
6521–26.

Waal, Frans B. M. de. 2008. "Putting the Altruism Back into Altruism: The Evolution of
Empathy." *Annual Review of Psychology* 59 (1): 279–300.

Waldfogel, Jane. 2010. *Britain's War on Poverty.* New York: Russell Sage Foundation.

Watamura, Sarah Enos, Deborah A. Phillips, Taryn W. Morrissey, Kathleen McCartney,
and Kristen Bub. 2011. "Double Jeopardy: Poorer Social-Emotional Outcomes for
Children in the NICHD SECCYD Experiencing Home and Child-Care Environments that Confer Risk." *Child Development* 82 (1): 48–65.

Weber, Max. (1922) 1978. *Economy and Society. An Outline of Interpretive Sociology.* Edited by Guenther Roth and Claus Wittich. Berkeley: University of California Press.

Weick, Karl E. 1976. "Educational Organizations as Loosely Coupled Systems." *Administrative Science Quarterly* 21 (1): 1–19.

Whitmore, Diane. 2002. *What Are Food Stamps Worth?* Working Papers 847, Industrial
Relations Section, Princeton University.

Whitney, Bridget M., Christina Mainero, Elizabeth Humes, Sharon Hurd, Linda Nicco-
lai, and James L. Hadler. 2015. "Socioeconomic Status and Foodborne Pathogens in
Connecticut, USA, 2000–2011." *Emerging Infectious Diseases* 21 (9): 1617–24.

Williams, David R., Jourdyn A. Lawrence, and Brigette A. Davis. 2019. "Racism and
Health: Evidence and Needed Research." *Annual Review of Public Health* 40 (1):
105–25.

Williams, David R., and Selina A. Mohammed. 2009. "Discrimination and Racial Disparities in Health: Evidence and Needed Research." *Journal of Behavioral Medicine*
32 (1): 20–47.

Wilson, William Julius. (1987) 2012. *The Truly Disadvantaged: The Inner City, the Under-
class, and Public Policy.* Chicago: University of Chicago Press.

World Economic Forum. 2015. *Outlook on the Global Agenda 2015.* https://reports
.weforum.org/outlook-global-agenda-2015/.

———. 2019. *The Global Risks Report 2019.* https://www.weforum.org/reports/the
-global-risks-report-2019.

World Health Organization. 2010. *Childhood Lead Poisoning.* World Health Organization report. http://www.who.int/ceh/publications/leadguidance.pdf.

Wright, Erik Olin. 2010. *Envisioning Real Utopias.* London: Verso.

Wuebbles, Donald J., David W. Fahey, and Kathy A. Hibbard. 2017. *Climate Science
Special Report: Fourth National Climate Assessment.* Vol. 1. Washington, DC: U.S.
Global Change Research Program.

York, Benjamin N., Susanna Loeb, and Christopher Doss. 2019. "One Step at a Time: The Effects of an Early Literacy Text-Messaging Program for Parents of Preschoolers." *The Journal of Human Resources* 54 (3): 537–66.

Young, Cristobal. 2017. *The Myth of Millionaire Tax Flight: How Place Still Matters for the Rich*. Stanford: Stanford University Press.

———. 2018. "Model Uncertainty and the Crisis in Science." *Socius* 4: 1–7.

INDEX

Page numbers in italic indicate material in figures.

INEQUALITIES

A forum for authoritative and innovative social science scholarship on inequality, offering cutting-edge research and novel arguments about the most consequential social trend of our time

David Grusky and Paula England, series editors

Editorial Board
Mario Luis Small, Elizabeth A. Armstrong, Florencia Torche, Kim Weeden, Emmanuel Saez, and Shelley Correll

—

Michelle Jackson, *Manifesto for a Dream: Inequality, Constraint, and Radical Reform* 2020

CPSIA information can be obtained
at www.ICGtesting.com
Printed in the USA
LVHW101518290323
742924LV00003B/378

9 781503 614154